Preserving Historic New England

Preserving Historic New England

Preservation, Progressivism,
and the Remaking of Memory

JAMES M. LINDGREN

New York   Oxford
Oxford University Press
1995

To
Mary Ann, Brian, and Charlie

Oxford University Press

Oxford   New York
Athens   Auckland   Bangkok   Bombay
Calcutta   Cape Town   Dar es Salaam   Delhi
Florence   Hong Kong   Istanbul   Karachi
Kuala Lumpur   Madras   Madrid   Melbourne
Mexico City   Nairobi   Paris   Singapore
Taipei   Tokyo   Toronto

and associated companies in
Berlin   Ibadan

Published by Oxford University Press, Inc.
198 Madison Avenue, New York, New York 10016

Oxford is a registered trademark of Oxford University Press

Library of Congress Cataloging-in-Publication Data
Lindgren, James Michael, 1950–
Preserving historic New England : preservation, progressivism,
and the remaking of memory / James M. Lindgren.
p. cm.   Includes bibliographical references and index.
ISBN 0-19-509363-1
1. Historic preservation—New England—History.   2. Society for
the Preservation of New England Antiquities—History.   I. Title.
F5.L73   1996
363.6′9—dc20   95-10368

1 3 5 7 9 8 6 4 2

Printed in the United States of America
on acid-free paper

ACKNOWLEDGMENTS

Preserving Historic New England has been many years in the making. It is only natural, particularly in a book about the preservation of traditions, to acknowledge those who helped in one way or another. Ever since primary school, I have been intrigued by history and read it like nothing else. Buildings have also fascinated me, whether the Art Deco motels of Miami Beach, the skyscrapers of my native Chicago, or the discarded (and seemingly) haunted houses of Victorian America. Little did I know that these interests would eventually establish my scholarly niche. My parents deserve my gratitude, at the very least for putting up with, if not fostering, those childhood obsessions, but more generally for helping to provide an education that strengthened those interests. I earned a Bachelor's and Master's degree in History and special thanks go out to Professor Edwin King of the University of Dayton for his assurance that there was a future in the past. In the depressed economy of 1978, I began to study architectural history, and things started to click. Thanks to the CETA program, I found work as a field surveyor for a historic preservation project. Through the help of Norman H. Pollock, I then secured a temporary appointment teaching history at Old Dominion University.

Before matriculating in a doctoral program in 1979, I asked prospective schools about the possibility of combining history and historic preservation in a dissertation. No school gave me a better answer than the College of William and Mary and its always affable Edward P. Crapol, Director of the Graduate Program in History. Williamsburg was the natural place for such a project, and interdisciplinary studies were long overdue. The dissertation was a comparative analysis of two historic preservation organizations that were founded during the progressive era and still serve as mainstays in the field: the Association for the Preservation of Virginia Antiquities (APVA) and the Society for the Preservation of New England Antiquities (SPNEA). Richard B. Sherman directed the project, and was assisted by Thad W. Tate, Edward Crapol, M. Boyd Coyner, and Shomer Zwelling. Many other scholars at William and Mary, including James Axtell, George Rudé, and William Appleman Williams, helped me to understand the intricate workings of culture. James P. Whittenburg, then Director of the Graduate Program, aided my search for funding to undertake the first steps of this study. My thanks come late, but with enthusiasm. Some later research was funded by a small grant from the New York State/United University Professions PDQWL program. A sabbatical from SUNY at Plattsburgh gave me a semester to sketch the first of many drafts. Hearty thanks go out as well to Mary

McGee and Tom Schiavone for putting their North End roof over my head and meals on the table while I worked on different occasions at the archives in Boston.

Many scholars read the dissertation and its offshoots as I revised the project for publication. My appreciation goes out (in the order of reading) to Michael Kammen, Charles B. Hosmer, Jr., Alan Trachtenberg, Cary Carson, Jackson Lears, Michael Wallace, David Hall, Abbott Lowell Cummings, Gary Kulik, Richard Candee, Harvey Green, and Richard Peet. Abbott Cummings and the late Charles Hosmer were generous enough to read the manuscript on more than one occasion. As is so typical, the advice they gave often went in different directions. My task of making the bended arrow straight was not easy, but I was forced to write what I hope is a more instructive and compelling narrative. What merit the reader finds in my work is to the credit of their suggestions; the faults are of my own making.

The comparative history of the APVA and SPNEA that formed my doctoral thesis had insurmountable limits for a more extensive study. Each organization had its own rationale; each defined preservation differently; each voiced its own gospel of preservation. Those contrasts pushed me away from comparative history and into a study of each in its own context. As a result, I wrote *Preserving the Old Dominion: Historic Preservation and Virginia Traditionalism* (Charlottesville and London: University Press of Virginia, 1993), while keeping my eye and keyboard on *Preserving Historic New England*. A few readers suggested that I focus this study as a biography of SPNEA's founder William Sumner Appleton, Jr., but that idea simply proved untenable. Many of his personal papers were destroyed after his death in 1947, and I concluded that his importance derived not only from his interactions with fellow preservationists but from their common reaction to changes in New England's society and culture during the progressive era. Most readers recognized those facts and encouraged me to explore more deeply the complex dimensions of Yankee culture that Appleton and SPNEA revealed. *Preserving Historic New England* examines, therefore, the preservation movement formed by Appleton and SPNEA in the first three decades of the twentieth century.

This book would have been impossible had not SPNEA (pronounced *spin-ee-uh*) shown its interest, facilitated my research, and extended me every possible courtesy. Abbott Cummings and Ellie Reichlin, respectively former executive director of SPNEA and former director of its archives, most deserve my appreciation. More recently, their successors, Jane C. Nylander and Lorna Condon, helped me to finish the project. For diverse bits of information that I received from other sources I also wish to thank staff members of the American Antiquarian Society, the Ancient Monuments Society (England), the Boston Athenaeum, the Boston Landmarks Commission, the Boston Public Library, the Boston Society of Architects, the Bostonian Society, the Brookline Preservation Commission, Cary Memorial Library (Lexington, Mass.), the Peabody Essex Museum, Harvard

University Archives, the Lexington Historical Society, the Massachusetts Historical Society, the Massachusetts State Library, the Mount Vernon Ladies' Association, Old Sturbridge Village, Simmons College Archives, and the Virginia Historic Landmarks Commission. Over the years, various questions have also been answered by Charles Brownell, Frederic C. Detwiller, and Dell Upton. Access to distant materials was never easy, but the interlibrary loan department of SUNY at Plattsburgh helped whenever possible. Excerpts of this study have appeared in *The New England Quarterly* (December 1991), and I wish to thank its editor, William Fowler, Jr., for permission to reproduce those materials. I am also grateful to my editor at Oxford University Press, Joyce Berry, and her assistant Scott Epstein for helping this project along the path to publication.

Last, but not least, I owe more than a nice line of thanks to my own family. Brian and Charlie, whose interests are typical for an eleven and seven year old respectively, had to bear with my academic idiosyncrasies while we motored about on summer vacations and perambulated through the historic countryside. My spouse, Mary Ann Weiglhofer, helped by urging me to think about the many corners that always seem to round out life. There's a little bit of Brian, Charlie, and Mary Ann tucked into each of the many seams of this book.

CONTENTS

ILLUSTRATIONS

Preserving Historic New England

PROLOGUE

Year by year as the nineteenth century waned, the North End house in which Paul Revere had lived and from which he went on his fateful midnight ride seemed more threatened by adjacent tenements. By 1900 the compact neighborhood had the dubious distinction of being "the most crowded one hundred acres of land on earth." The locale had once been Boston's finest, but a diverse population of destitute immigrants now lived there. By sheer numbers alone, they seemed destined to alter the city's Yankee identity. Samuel Adams Drake, a popular antiquary, voiced nothing but disdain when he found the air around the house "thick with the vile odors of garlic and onions—of maccaroni and lazzaroni," while the adjacent "dirty tenements swarm[ed] with greasy voluble Italians."[1] Yankee social workers, meanwhile, were warning that degeneracy and crime were on the rise.

If the fate of Revere's house resembled that of Boston's other seventeenth-century dwellings, its days were numbered. Yet, when threatened with demolition, the landmark was saved by a select band of Yankees in 1905. The state's most prominent dignitaries headed the list of supporters, including the governor, lieutenant governor, and mayor, but the drive was actually designed by a neophyte preservationist, William Sumner Appleton, Jr. A descendant of the Puritans and grandson of one of New England's major industrialists, Appleton melded the cultural and economic concerns of his forebears as he laid out the campaign. Accommodating the city's commerce, he wanted the house remade into a museum "which would draw visitors from all parts." Hoping also to Americanize the newcomers by revitalizing Revere's memory, he wanted it to be "a constant incentive to patriotic citizenship and the study of our national institutions."[2]

Appleton's campaign succeeded, and, with the house safely in their hands, preservationists restored the dwelling to old-time appearances. That restoration, however, revealed another angle in the remaking of history. Architect Joseph Everett Chandler demolished the third story that Revere had known, while others who thought the original house had been one story also wanted the second removed. Chandler and Appleton felt otherwise, and most appreciated the dwelling's remade medieval features, principally its second-story overhang with pendants, timbered framing, and casement windows.[3] They reinvented the house, both literally and figuratively. With almost all new materials, it was born anew to foster patriotism, Anglo-Saxonism, and acceptable Yankee values. So began Appleton's forty-year career as a preservationist.

3

Shortly after, at the age of thirty-five, he founded the Society for the Preservation of New England Antiquities (SPNEA). In 1910 it was the first regional historic preservation organization in the United States. Until the day he died in 1947, he devoted himself to SPNEA and remaking the preservation movement. Later colleagues and scholars have acknowledged his formative hand. In 1933 Leicester B. Holland of the Historic American Buildings Survey gave SPNEA "priority in the work of preservation of historic spots" in the country, as did historian Charles B. Hosmer, Jr., thirty years later.[4]

More recently, W. Brown Morton, while writing for the International Council on Monuments and Sites, declared that "a new day had dawned" with Appleton. William O. Murtagh credited SPNEA with "almost single-handedly" reorienting the field from a preoccupation with romanticized history to one stressing architectural aesthetics, scientific method, and historical scholarship. According to Murtagh, "today's broadly accepted standards of professionalism on how one treats buildings in the restoration process owe their basis to Appleton." SPNEA developed "the philosophical dictates which still guide the conscientious professional today."[5]

At present, there are thousands of preservationists, curators, and public historians in the United States who have been taught that Appleton and such colleagues at SPNEA as Norman M. Isham and George F. Dow were trailblazers in their profession. SPNEA's story has become the model of how to treat artifacts as historical documents, protect them through a scientific regimen, and present them to the public through period houses, folk museums, preservation archives, and living-history programs.[6]

Too few scholars have examined the roots of the profession, however, and instead have focused on its evolution. Their analyses have been written largely from the perspective of Appleton and his interest in scientific method, organized activity, and aesthetics. Convinced that preservation represents a sacred trust, they have pictured the movement as altruistic and enlightened. Much can be said along those lines, but the movement's record is not so easily cut and dry. Few museums or preservation societies are packrats that squirrel away all things. Their curators endlessly make decisions not only about preserving a building or an artifact but displaying and interpreting it to the public.[7]

Accordingly, *Preserving Historic New England* is a study of what Morton called "the watershed" in the history of American preservation.[8] This book examines the rationale for preservation, the influence of progressivism and the Colonial Revival, and the cultural politics of remaking the New England memory in the first three decades of the twentieth century. Epitomized by SPNEA, the virtues of today's movement, as well as its failings, can be found taking root in those transitional years. Appleton and SPNEA did slowly transform the field and break loose from earlier work, which was ad hoc in planning, unscientific in method, and romantic in its reading of history. They advocated instead corporate organization, meritocratic control, scientific method, and business-minded principles, and these features were adopted by later organizations such as the National Park Service and the Colonial Williamsburg Foundation. In so doing, SPNEA spurred the creation of a profession that still serves as custodians of this material culture.

Historic preservation in New England during the progressive era represented much more than protecting landmarks and building a profession. It embodied a contest, sometimes of crisis proportions, over the definition of past, present, and future. Fundamentally it concerned what Michel Foucault called the "relations of power." It involved the deliberate use of preserved symbols, their display in appealing settings, and the attempt to make them relevant. Historic preservation was anything but a retreat by a dispossessed elite from the chaos of the fin de siècle, as some have charged. "The cult of the antique in furniture and decoration," Lewis Mumford thought, was a distraction from the upheavals of industrialism and urbanism. "The attempt to take over the time-bound vestiges of other periods," he wrote in 1938, represented "concrete utopias of escape: the desire to establish little dream islands in the steely sea of reality."[9]

Historian Richard Hofstadter went a step further. The ancestral, patriotic, and historical societies of the late nineteenth and early twentieth centuries were founded by white Anglo-Saxon Protestants, he said, as bulwarks against the rise of parvenus and the challenges of immigrants. Placing these societies within a "status revolution," he suggested that "many old-family Americans, who were losing status in the present, may have found satisfying compensation in turning to family glories of the past." Arthur Mann similarly claimed that this elite formed clubs not simply to study "their English forebears and merchant grandfathers" but to exclude "the new arrivals."[10] Genteel antiquaries, reformers, and patriots, according to these interpreters, were isolated and resentful, and, like an ostrich with its head in the sand, escaped to the comforts of their proud past.

What these critics failed to address, however, was Yankee progressivism and its remaking of memory. Much like an umbrella whose ribs meet at a central shaft, the era's cultural politics were framed by themes well studied by subsequent scholars. John Higham has probed the nativism of anxious Yankees, E. Digby Baltzell their elite institutions, Jackson Lears their antimodernism, and Eileen Boris their interest in the arts and crafts. John Bodnar has recently studied the era's remaking of ethnic memory, David Glassberg its pageantry, and David Lowenthal and Michael Kammen its concern for cultural preservation.[11] These students largely examine the forces that bolstered the preservation movement. Yet the landmarks that were preserved as "history" became weights in the cultural battles of the progressive era. Thus, *Preserving Historic New England* will assess the threats that preservationists perceived and the ways in which they remade history and bequeathed it to the future through restored buildings.

SPNEA's crusade reflected the era's dominant currents of progressivism, the Colonial Revival, and professionalism. Contrary to the myth of progressivism as a democratic movement, and without citing the endless debate among historians about its contradictions, the progressive era in New England was mostly one of conservative reform. Mugwump reformers initiated the drive purportedly to purify a political system tainted by immigrants, instill proper Yankee values in a heterogeneous population, and boost prosperity in the depressed 1890s.[12]

Progressives inherited those aspirations, but increasingly founded voluntary organizations, such as SPNEA, to study society's problems, popularize their agenda, and shape culture. In varying degree, those groups emulated the progressive canon: They were modeled along corporate lines, scientific in method, and focused on the particular task of a newly emerging profession. The profile of progressives was largely one of educated Protestants who had old American roots, held property, lived comfortably in the suburbs, small towns, or stable neighborhoods, and voiced a commitment to a variety of reforms that allegedly would improve their communities. Those characteristics obviously applied to a minority of Americans; the era's truly democratic reformers represented more directly the perspectives of workers and farmers, as well as women, immigrants, and African-Americans. All the while, progressives invoked heartfelt yearnings for the past's imagined order, focused on economic development, and strove to regenerate older values for a newer age.[13]

The campaigns of progressives were often ad hoc and loose. As a result, each reform, including preservation, requires careful scrutiny to determine not only if its advocates subscribed to the consensual beliefs in progress and capitalism but if it was able to draw support from "non-progressive" constituencies. The preservation movement, for one, was able to enlist the aid of Yankees who differed politically—from reactionary conservatives to relatively liberal settlement workers—but they shared a common belief in the importance of landmark conservation for setting the future tone of society. It is important to remember that preservation and progressivism were not synonymous. Like two overlapping circles, they had substantial common ground, but also idiosyncratic elements.

Running concurrent with progressivism was the Colonial Revival. Nowadays, it is customary to trace its origins to those quiet, seaside villages of New England where tourists or summer residents during the 1870s and 1880s escaped the hurly-burly city and savored a taste of an old-time world. As it swept New England, the Colonial Revival mixed those older surroundings and newer wealth, along with the myth of history and the reality of those landscapes, in a reassuring, but intoxicating, brew. Although distinct in different regions, the Colonial Revival encompassed sentiments that shaped art and architecture, as well as more basic cultural values. At heart, it represented a longing for stability and roots. So tied to the class and cultural values of old-family Americans who could afford the embellishments that created the milieu, the Colonial Revival became a counterweight against the unwelcome, but seemingly inevitable, present. Just as its proponents would refashion their homes and furniture to reflect a colonial ambience, so, too, did they remake their customs. They commonly covered their day with a colonial veneer.[14]

If anything, the Colonial Revival's intellectual roots had been planted well before the Civil War in an attempt to harness industrialism through traditionalism. As a loosely defined, but deeply held belief system, traditionalism had shifted in meaning with the changing economy and society. In the seventeenth century, that adaptation was subtle, but as industrial capitalism took hold in the nineteenth century, the pace of change escalated.[15] Tradition-minded Yankees tried to protect the many customs that defined an individual's place and behavior in society, but it became a fool's errand as the values of home and workplace were increasingly bifurcated. Darwinism and the boom-and-bust economy spurred aspiring Yankees to emphasize change, growth, and progress during the Gilded Age.

Tradition-minded Yankees were increasingly abandoning what others called traditionalism. For example, Thomas Gold Appleton, uncle of SPNEA's founder, rebelled when he thought that philistinism had taken over Boston. The affluent often built ostentatious homes, abandoned public service, and ignored the needy. In fact, rich Yankees had been doing that for over a century, but a wave of centennial celebrations after 1876 and the ascent of the Colonial Revival further brought the meaning of America into question. As the nation's workers demanded another revolution to attain the liberties never won, and as the virtuous republic of 1776 paled before the materialistic empire of the fin de siècle, the region's elite became more pretentious, self-serving, and trapped in what Thorstein Veblen called conspicuous consumption. In turn, many tradition-minded Yankees rationalized their abandonment of noblesse oblige, the simple life, or community leadership by supporting other traditions, such as endowing a trust for their college, joining a historical society, or building a Colonial Revival home.[16]

Like most mythological systems, the ingredients of traditionalism during the Colonial Revival were open to interpretation. It included a comfortable picture of the region that had been created by numerous painters, preachers, and professors—one of a pastoral countryside with small villages where a homogeneous, peaceful people lived in sturdy two-story, white-painted dwellings nestled around a common and meeting house. Not only did that picture diverge significantly from the reality of the seventeenth and most of the eighteenth centuries, it contrasted starkly with the present. Even in 1860, New England stood out as the one region that was the most industrialized, most populated by immigrants and Catholics, and most rapidly changing in the nation.[17] Later Yankees continued to revise the image of the past, recodify earlier values, and invent a history to fit their present needs.

Traditionalism, it was said, grew out of that imagined landscape. Its value system included a belief in local government, respect for private property, and an acceptance of laissez-faire capitalism. Aesthetically, traditionalists could embrace not only the Colonial Revival but more generally the artistic legacy of Europe. As a result, some chose the sensibilities of the Gothic, others the embellishments of the Renaissance. Those traditionalists who shaped SPNEA, on the other hand, most closely identified with the preindustrial, medieval world. On a personal level, traditionalists valued individual honor, family togetherness, the work ethic, love of country, and female domesticity, all of which, incidentally, had been refashioned for the industrial, market society of the nineteenth century. Tradition-minded Yankees accepted progress, saw its negative side, but varied widely in response.

Traditionalists also differed over the meaning of their ancestors' material legacy. Most tradition-minded Bostonians regarded the likes of Faneuil Hall and Old North Church as important but, as with the Old South Meeting House and the Old State House, only a vocal minority bucked progress to prevent their demolition. The example of the Old South in 1876 was important in that a preservation coalition, bankrolled and led by affluent women, declared that old, respected buildings represented a public trust. Those buildings had an ideological use, especially as Boston's political economy and social fabric were so traumatically changing.[18] Most cared little, however, for the humble buildings of the seventeenth century that would draw SPNEA's attention.

The ranks of traditionalism were anything but static or limited to those with Puritan roots. As in the case of industrialist Nathan Appleton, the dominant culture of New England had expanded by absorbing new families, traditions, and economic systems. Historian Samuel Eliot Morison acknowledged that Boston's upper class, the Brahmins, grew year by year. "The way to get in," he said, was to live in the right neighborhood, send your children to the right schools, and prove "a certain minimum of breeding and manners."[19] While control of the region's economy shifted from the landed gentry to merchants to industrialists, the Brahmins were losing ground in the national economy to New York tycoons. All the while, the immigrants were gaining politically, especially by the early 1900s. The Brahmins strove to reassert their grip over the regional economy and culture. With their extended families, Brahmins defined the economic and social elite and its institutions. As of the 1890s, over half of Boston's millionaires were listed in the tradition-minded *Social Register*.[20]

As ones who customarily relished public service, Brahmins tried to shape the emerging order, but had been stymied by privatism in the Gilded Age. With the coming of progressivism they staffed numerous volunteer organizations, involving campaigns to reform politics, Americanize immigrants, or preserve an old building. The role of SPNEA comes into sharper perspective here. Although it was one of many Brahmin-created organizations, it was a private society with a public mission. Just as the Association for the Preservation of Virginia Antiquities (APVA) had been founded in 1889 by old-stock elite who nourished respect for their heritage, so, too, did SPNEA. It cultivated within the ranks of both established and rising elite an appreciation of the material culture of early Yankees.

Traditionalism still evolved and maintained its continuity to an appreciable degree. As a Brahmin who lent his hand to SPNEA, Morison compared this culture to a mother-wine. "The wine of New England is not a series of successive vintages, each distinct from the other, like the wines of France," he thought; "it is more like the mother-wine in those great casks of port and sherry that one sees in the *bodegas* of Portugal and Spain, from which a certain amount is drawn off every year, and replaced by an equal volume of the new. Thus the change is gradual, and the mother-wine of 1656 still gives bouquet and flavor to what is drawn in 1956." The growers and vintners were a "hierarchy of parsons, professionals, and artists." Their lineage did not necessarily stem from the Puritans, but they aided the dominant culture and countered the political ascendancy of newcomers.[21]

Appleton and SPNEA thought that the preservation of early Yankee materials would flavor the mother-wine. Brahmins commonly found these "old Colonial forms" worthy of protection. They were "so agreeable," said Henry Cabot Lodge, because they represented Yankee creativity based on English customs. Yet preservationists worried that New England's culture was adrift. As in the era's eclectic architecture, it was obvious that Boston had become a motley tribute to mammon. "Our streets are rapidly becoming a compendium of all known architectural styles," Chandler regretted. Like his contemporary Emile Durkheim, he believed that a culture could not survive without preserving those reminders of its origins and character.[22]

SPNEA joined a cluster of institutions, including the Massachusetts Historical Society (MHS, 1791), Boston Athenaeum (1807), and New England Historic Genealogical Society (NEHGS, 1845), which had been created largely by Harvard men to forge an upper-class solidarity. Such an intimate network, especially while Boston's society and politics changed so immeasurably, enabled them to preserve class authority and such Brahmin values as gentility, aesthetics, and respect for tradition. These private clubs and societies absorbed worthy parvenus and made their adoption of respectable values more certain.[23] SPNEA actually represented a newer phase of this Brahmin institution building. Earlier groups had a very select membership, as did the ancestral societies. SPNEA, on the other hand, opened its doors to all who would protect the heritage that Appleton, Isham, Dow, and their colleagues defined for New England.

That heritage included old buildings. Unlike ancient writings set in difficult prose, buildings were visible, practical, and open vessels to which an interpretation could be added. One visitor to an old home might see the discarded material of a primitive era. Other visitors might think differently had they been told in the church, newspaper, and schoolroom that the same home was a symbol of a hearty, brave people who had lived in small villages.[24] Those buildings stood mute before the uninformed sightseer, but preservationists thought that their weather-beaten boards and timbered frames quietly condemned the cultural drift of modern America. So typical for the Colonial Revival, they longed for the security of an older world, which they pictured much like an old house built on a foundation of traditional values, and whose timbers were joined through a mortise and tenon of deferential democracy and select leadership.

Such a view, of course, had no place for the untidy episodes that did not fit this picture. Whether the case involved SPNEA, the Concord Woman's Club, or so many other private societies, tradition-minded Yankees wanted a past that was usable. In the footsteps of those nineteenth-century writers and painters who literally reinvented their region's history and landscape, preservationists protected materials that made those myths concrete. Preserved buildings, in the end, helped universalize the myths that had been spoken from the pulpit and podium, read in verse and prose, and accepted as the New England that once was.[25]

Although historic preservation was part of the Colonial Revival movement, preservationists often found fault with its machine-made, mass-marketed imitations. They accepted those facsimiles, such as reproduced hardware or even an entire village, if the original had been lost or a greater goal was served. The authentic material culture of the colonial and Federal periods, on the other hand, became the idealized symbol and tangible representation of the past. Those in the arts-and-crafts movement admired the craftsmanship as well as the artisan's ethic and community within the medieval guild. Ancestral societies equated these materials with their forebears and the claim to priority that passed through later generations. Patriotic societies saw these relics as manifestations of earlier men and (infrequently) women who showed the strength and courage necessary in the here and now. Turn-of-the-century Yankees who prized tradition also valued the look of antiquity in their landscape. At the same time as cities swelled, factories boomed, and modern supplanted old, however, New England's ancient houses were being toppled or modernized at an alarming rate. Like worn-out garments, Yankees discarded old buildings in search of the newest fashion, including the bogus Colonial Revival.

The preservation movement actually went to the heart of the most contentious issue in the early twentieth century: Whose culture would prevail as the nation went through the throes of immigration, industrialization, and modernization? Although George Orwell would claim that one "who controls the present controls the past," these tradition-minded elite also believed that one who controls the present shapes the future.[26] Much in the vein of the Mount Vernon Ladies' Association (MVLA), which sheltered the home of Washington, or the APVA, which saved Jamestown and Williamsburg, Appleton and SPNEA preached a gospel of preservation, a message that the future prosperity and stability of their land rested on the willingness of the present to respect the inheritance of the past. Committed to an imagined past and shocked by recent changes in their land, they feared a loss of influence, social breakdown, and cultural amnesia.

SPNEA's gospel reflected a belief that old ways should shape the new, but ironically the European peasants who flooded New England fundamentally held the same notion. In this contest of cultures, what counted was political, economic, and cultural weight. SPNEA was not founded by any John Doe off Main Street, but by a descendant of one of the region's most influential families. Just as Henry Francis du Pont could devote his life and wealth to a museum in Delaware, so, too, did Appleton make SPNEA his life's benefaction. He wrapped SPNEA around the strings of his Beacon Hill upbringing and perspective. Gleaned from the classrooms of Harvard, the drawing rooms of elite clubs, and the committee rooms of professional organizations, Appleton distilled his experiences in SPNEA. Over the years his preservation society would acquire a long list of properties, groom the region's movement in its image, and develop a philosophy that, like a jigsaw puzzle, Appleton pieced together. It not only had the markings of Yankees such as Charles Eliot Norton but interlocked with the contours of Brahmin organizations.

While Appleton's father had been an antiquary, what made SPNEA's founder different was not only what he learned from his coworkers but the imprint of progressivism. His adoption of scientific method, corporate structure, and business-minded planning—features that were virtual hallmarks of the era—made SPNEA the first corporation in the business of preservation.[27] SPNEA introduced new financial tools (such as matching grants, revolving funds, and life tenancy) to make its business more efficient.

As Appleton reoriented preservation to the professional disciplines of archaeology, architecture, and history, SPNEA launched a wave of interdisciplinary research that was so much a part of the Colonial Revival. At the time, few historians considered the documentary worth of material culture. Relying in great part on written records and focusing on great men, those historians also largely ignored the vernacular. Meanwhile, American archaeologists mostly devoted their labors to Old World civilizations, while architects copied the latest European fashion. In effect, American historians, architects, and archaeologists were ignoring much of their own past. Appleton and SPNEA not only pushed them to study their own roots but tried to inspire the public by recreating an old-time environment through historic showhouses, period rooms, and folk parks.

Another tenet of SPNEA's professionalism was the call for modern management of the preservation movement. Prior to that time, preservation work had been idiosyncratic, haphazard, and technically weak. Unlike the APVA or New England's historical and patriotic groups, Appleton wanted preservation to be undertaken by societies that would focus their efforts full-time on architecture. That move was closely tied to the managerial style of progressivism and ultimately led to the founding of such organizations as the National Trust for Historic Preservation (1949) and state preservation offices. This brand of preservation would also be governed by business-minded planning. Knowing the commercial bent of his Yankee peers, and foreseeing the movement of the late twentieth century, Appleton wanted preservation to fit capitalist economies. Historic buildings could enhance tourism, be adapted for commercial ventures, or add to the net worth of a neighborhood.

Appleton's professionalism and aestheticism were actually new forms of elitism that reflected the male worlds of architecture and archaeology. This reorientation subsequently pushed more of the populace, most noticeably women, toward the margins and less involvement in their own history. As those who had first shaped the movement at Mount Vernon and the Old South Meeting House, women generally defined a building's worth by a sense of personalism. Common during the Victorian period among men and women, personalism was a belief that human sentiments were intangibly linked to a building's earthen materials. Just as a roof and four walls sheltered a family, so, too, did humans form a social bond through architecture. With its focus on the interconnectedness of spirit, flesh, and nature, personalism placed importance on a building's ties to such values as love of family, respect for community, personal intimacy, and humility before God. Put simply, personalism stressed the material and immaterial bonds that made people human. Its emphasis on those less tangible qualities was often described as sentimentalism and romanticism; its accent on the home found an outlet in campaigns to Americanize immigrants, reform the school curriculum, and restore old-time values.[28]

The preservation movement instead fell under the impress of architectural aesthetics and corporate models, all of which were male in orientation and became the makings of professionalism. As a result, older fashioned men and women were relegated to the field's sidelines, not simply in its leading organizations but in the very definition of what deserved protection. At the same time, SPNEA's precepts excluded other interpreters of New England's history who did not meet its measure, whether Irish-American admirers of the 1776 Revolution, such as John Fitzgerald, or amateurish Yankees, such as Wallace Nutting.

Just as this professionalism was exclusionary, so, too, was the stereotypical picture of that old-time Yankee. In reality, seventeenth-century New England had been populated not only by diverse (and culturally distinct) English settlers, but Native Americans, Africans, and others. The preserved past instead pictured a homogenized Yankee. People of color, as well as most women, entered this preserved past largely as characters on the periphery or ones without a past. The trend continues until today.[29]

As SPNEA helped to redefine the past, it was at first one star in a constellation of elite organizations. Yankee preservationists cast their light on neglected buildings, however, and extended the definition of not only heritage but the Colonial Revival. Tradition-minded Yankees had regarded historic landmarks as part of their legacy, but the more simple constructs of clapboard and stone would now be considered as well. SPNEA acquired over two-dozen buildings in its first two decades (Appendix A), and almost fifty before Appleton's death but, unlike Colonial Williamsburg or Greenfield Village, it did not rely on the bottomless coffers of an industrial baron. Yankee elite sanctioned SPNEA as their means of preserving historic New England.

1

"It Belongs to Men Like You"

William Sumner Appleton and the Makings of a Preservationist

SPNEA bore the distinct stamp of its founder William Sumner Appleton, Jr. (1874–1947). Born into the Brahmin caste and reared in the traditions of Beacon Hill, Harvard University, and Boston's elite institutions, Appleton made preservation his life's work and benefaction. SPNEA enlisted the help of many prominent Yankees, but none surpassed that of Appleton. His lifelong career was rooted within his own history. Undoubtedly one of the most prominent families in New England, the Appletons traced their lineage to Samuel Appleton, a settler of Ipswich, Massachusetts, in 1636. The founder of SPNEA was born at 39 Beacon Street, one of Boston's finest bow-fronted houses (Fig. 1-1). Designed by Alexander Parris in a restrained Greek Revival style, the house was built for Nathan Appleton in 1818–19.[1] Nathan's life, first as a farm boy, then as a merchant and industrialist, and finally as a public servant, molded the family. He founded one of the nation's first integrated textile mills in 1828, but feared that an industrial economy would replicate the class conflict and degradation of Europe's factories.

Subsequently, Appleton became an apostle of a new order, one in which culture would both continue the customs of his Puritan forebears and civilize industrial capitalism. As moralists preached an individualistic reform in the heat of the Second Great Awakening, he suggested a practical use of culture—as a control mechanism on the lower classes. An example himself of America's social mobility, he asked his workers living in those burgeoning, unfamiliar mill towns to emulate the attributes he pictured as bringing his own success—self-discipline, abstemiousness, hard work, and prudence.[2]

Appleton also believed that money-making was an honorable profession. In the 1830s and 1840s he was the largest stockholder in American cotton manufacturing enterprises, a system whose exploitation of labor in North and South was patently clear. He used his wealth not only to join the tight-knit Brahmin caste but to win seats in both chambers of the Massachusetts General Court and in the U.S. House of Representatives. Revealing the ties that interwove commerce and culture, he developed,

Fig. 1-1   Appleton-Parker Houses, 39 and 40 Beacon Street, Boston, c. 1886
(Courtesy, Society for the Preservation of New England Antiquities)

but only later in his life, a keen interest in genealogy and heraldry that
led to his election to the MHS, the NEHGS, and the American Antiquarian Society (AAS). Appleton represented the traditions of economic opportunity, individual achievement, and the Protestant work ethic. Indicative of his stature, the memorial service at King's Chapel for this parvenu
millionaire drew the likes of Oliver Wendell Holmes and James Russell
Lowell.[3]

Appleton's defense of family interests prompted him, like so many
Brahmins, to place his wealth (almost two million dollars) in a trust. This
fund enabled his heirs to kindle an appreciation of culture, and its annuities tried to protect spendthrifts from their own worst faults. Trusts
also discouraged them from pursuing business ventures that required a
mass of capital.[4] The careers of two of his four sons reveal the outcome.

Thomas Gold Appleton became the dean of Boston's literary society.
So different from his business-minded father, he believed that New England's social mobility and commerce had introduced "philistine" values.
Criticizing the society that had created his father's success, he said: "There
is a recognized evil in democracy—the want of that fixedness which the
human spirit craves. . . . Flux and movement are everywhere. Professions,
residences, beliefs are changeable and changed, and everyone is at a loss
to recognize his accepted value." The frantic quest for newness and money

destroyed America's stability, order, and customs. He befriended like-minded Charles Eliot Norton and idealized old Boston where "foreigners were comparatively unknown."[5] He imagined an earlier age with its spiritualism, hierarchy, and happy and honorable souls. The real new stood so apart from the mythical old.

His half-brother William Sumner Appleton, father of SPNEA's founder, carried on Nathan's interest in genealogy and heraldry. While Tom complained about Boston's philistines, his half-brother scrutinized gravestones in ancient cemeteries, collected antiques, coins, and curios, and patronized the elite societies that defined Brahminism. "The Massachusetts Historical Society, the Boston Museum of Fine Arts, the Athenaeum and the Bostonian Society," claimed one biographer, "could hardly have gotten along without William Sumner Appleton." He took pride in his caste identity. As a "thorough, exact, and methodical" genealogist, he investigated the ancestral claims of suspect Yankees "and he remorsely pricked many bubble reputations."[6] His expertise in heraldry led him to edit the *Heraldric Journal* and design a suitable arms and seal for Harvard College. In 1871 he married his cousin, Edith Stuart Appleton of Baltimore. Like so many Brahmins, he purchased a pew at King's Chapel (Unitarian in theology) and raised his three daughters and one son in Boston's elite traditions.

Thirty-nine Beacon Street provided an aristocratic setting around which William Sumner Appleton, Jr. (Sumner as he was known) developed his sense of Brahmin ancestry and gentility. There on the second floor his aunt Fanny had married Henry Wadsworth Longfellow in 1843. Even Edgar Allan Poe had attended a soiree, but was told to leave when his behavior did not match the family's measure. Reacting to censure by those who lived adjacent to the Common and Frog Pond, Poe called his native town "Frogpondium."[7]

In the following years Sumner spent much time at his aunt Harriot's nearby house at 28 Mount Vernon. Henry James called it "the happiest street-scene the country could show," and that was precisely what the young Appleton wanted. Like his uncle Tom who had rebelled against paternal authority, Sumner gradually became estranged from his father. His aunt and his uncle Greeley S. Curtis, an architect and engineer by training, took him in for long periods. Sumner readily attached himself to their family of ten children. The Curtis's summer home in Manchester, Massachusetts, even contained salvaged details from the demolished John Hancock house on Beacon Hill. "Not only the balustrade, newell, hand rail and steps, but the wainscoting on the wall" were there, and he remembered going up and down Hancock's staircase "ten thousand times."[8] That staircase, the Mount Vernon streetscape, and 39 Beacon Street all instilled an architectural memory that taught him lessons in aesthetics and traditionalism.

During his youth, Beacon Hill was the citadel of Boston's aristocracy. There lived Francis Parkman, George Bancroft, Harriet Beecher Stowe,

Louisa May Alcott, and many others who had crafted a mythical picture
of the past. The exclusivity of the neighborhood stemmed from roots in
family, caste, and local history. Beacon Hill had slowly declined after
1875, however. As neighborhoods in the North, South, and West Ends
swarmed with immigrants, wealthy Yankees left the Hill for newer homes
built in the outer suburbs or townhouses in the Back Bay. With this loss
of status, some streets became rows of rooming houses for transients,
while others opened up to stores, clubs, and apartments. Beacon Hill, as
a result, was losing its symbolic significance as the heart and soul of Brahminism. Beacon Street suffered the most as taller buildings and shops
crept in.[9]

Appleton's father sold the house, and moved the entire family to Europe in 1887 for over a year. Upon his return, Sumner attended St. Paul's
in Concord, New Hampshire, the first of the Brahmin-created boarding
schools and one particularly committed to the traditions of the British
gentry. Within the male world of St. Paul's, he mixed with the children
of Brahmins and New York and Philadelphia industrialists. Stricken by
diptheria, he took his college entrance examinations in a wheelchair and
matriculated at Harvard University in 1892.[10]

While the nation suffered through a ruinous depression, Appleton attended college from 1892–96 and immersed himself in Harvard's gentlemanly environment. Under its president Charles W. Eliot, Harvard became even more the lynchpin in the network of Brahminism.[11] Its
education imparted an ideological system that stressed a student's obligation to community through mugwump politics, upper-class institutions,
and conservative economics. Elitism permeated its instruction, and students learned that democracy produced chaos, New England's heritage
deserved respect, and stability offered future certainty. Appleton absorbed
its spirit as he emerged from his less-than-congenial family life and its
accompanying ill health.

The finest scholars of the day reinforced his traditionalism and class
identity. In 1893–94 he studied English under Barrett Wendell, with
whom he maintained an association many years later. At that time in the
1890s, the mugwump professor incessantly voiced his hostility to democracy, his fears about immigration, and his contempt for mass society. A
lover of New England, but mostly old England, he stressed ancestry, upbringing, and tradition as the Brahmin's only hope. His despair often got
the best of him. In 1893 he felt that "we Yankees are as much things of
the past as any race can be. America has swept from our grasp. The future
is beyond us. And we have not the great background of European tradition to console ourselves with. Our best memories are that we have tried
to fix ideals for other folks to live by." Wendell's chauvinism and cynicism
led Eliot to fear that "many people" would "underestimate his judgment
and good sense."[12]

Trying to cure the angst that so commonly afflicted traditionalists,
Wendell later immersed himself in his family home and its six generations

of memorabilia. "In New England the old order passes so swiftly," he mourned, "that I know hardly any other place so wholly of the olden time" than the Jacob Wendell house in Portsmouth. As was so often the case with antimodernism, he reinvented the olden time by removing the house's Victorian features and adding colonial ones, including a "Chinese puzzle" garden outside.[13] Wendell similarly told his students to pass on their traditions, and his wife Edith Greenough Wendell would frequently aid SPNEA.

Appleton heard a similar message from philosopher George Santayana. America's mentality, he said, was divided between a lust for invention and a respect for tradition. He rejoiced that "the hereditary spirit" still prevailed in the intellectual sphere, but feared it was rapidly losing its priority to "aggressive enterprise."[14] Philosopher William James taught Appleton to question traditionalism, however. A psychologist and an exponent of pragmatism, James stressed that humans were morally free agents who could determine their fate and alter inhibiting traditions. Influenced by Darwin's concept of evolution, James taught that change was the essence of life and urged his students to see ideas not as static entities, but historically and pragmatically as part of their experience in time and place.

Historian Edward Channing instructed him in four courses on Tudor-Stuart England, medieval-modern history, and colonial- and revolutionary-era America. One of his generation's great historians and son of Transcendentalist William Ellery Channing, he encouraged his students, including Morison, to view history as a process where individuals acknowledge their heritage, but adapt in their time and environment. Both Channings surely added their own invention to New England history as they helped rehabilitate the Puritan's image as a foil to criticize their own society.[15]

Channing's colleague Albert Bushnell Hart taught Appleton U.S. history, 1783–1865. As one of Harvard's best classroom speakers, Hart similarly stressed that New England developed through a blend of cultural adaptation and preservation. He embodied the new professionalism, the scientific pursuit of historical evidence that purportedly treated source materials objectively and accurately. Bedrock assumptions still guided his studies. He believed that Anglo-Saxons had created democracy, governments gelled around local identities, institutions evolved out of environmental necessity, and everyday common life provided a basis for understanding history. Appleton enrolled in his History 10 in 1894–95 and learned to see history as a daily attempt by people to solve real problems. In his day, Hart witnessed formidable threats and endorsed immigration restriction, mugwump politics, and turn-of-the-century antiimperialism.[16]

Considering his later career, Appleton most fell under the impress of Charles Eliot Norton, perhaps the foremost arbiter of aesthetics in the nation. Harvard's elective system, Norton's provocative teaching, and the broad appeal of Fine Arts 3 and 4 enabled Appleton to enter a world little known to him. The young student admitted, for example, that his "ignorance of old New England architecture was as great as anyone's very well could be." Although Norton's coursework focused on art and architecture from the Greeks through the medieval period, it provided a foundation for Appleton's later work. A close friend of English critic John Ruskin, Norton shared his philosophy of art and his belief that the environment shaped morality. As Norton told his students, the fine arts represented "the most unimpeachable evidence of the mental and moral condition of a race at the time of their production." Even the old meeting house at Hingham, his ancestral town, told a tale about the days of its erection in 1681. It was "grave, sombre, austere," and "the expression of the moral convictions and material conditions of the men who built it."[17]

He told Harvard's young men that civilization owed a great debt to the past, and the legacy embodied in the Pantheon, the cathedral at Chartres, and the meeting house at Hingham deserved study and protection. Whether it was the Athenian citizen or medieval artisan, Norton said that they had practiced self-control, temperate living, and a moral idealism that translated into works of beauty, energy, and morality. To be sure, his picture reflected more of his admiration for their aesthetics than an actual understanding of their history. He lamented that America had lost contact with those civilizations, and encouraged preservation and archaeology, serving as the first president of the Archaeological Institute of America.[18]

Norton's lectures included wide-ranging ruminations on politics and culture. "From first to last," said a chronicler of Harvard, he "emphasized the ethical and social implications of the fine arts." Colleagues such as Hart and Denman Ross reiterated his philosophy of art and culture. A convinced mugwump, Norton often condemned the privatism of America's elite. As in Greece's decline or the corruption of Renaissance Italy, unhindered individualism had created selfish citizens, a lowered sense of character, and an enervating materialism. Civilization represented a trust, therefore, that one generation was duty bound to preserve and enhance. "It belongs to you," he lectured, "and to men like you who have the advantage of learning the true signs of the highest life of a nation, and the ways in which that life is best prompted."[19]

Though pessimistic, Norton told his students to see the humanities, including the homes of old American families, as one of the "strongest forces in the never-ending contest against the degrading influences of the spirit of materialism." Voicing a gospel of preservation, he mourned that his contemporaries were discarding "the inheritance of memories and associations which dignify and exalt life, which connect it by visible monuments with the past and the future."[20]

The buildings of the colonial and revolutionary eras were repositories of those memories, but they were quickly falling as a result of population mobility, "the spirit of equality," and "the diffusion of wealth and material comfort." In the late nineteenth century, a record number of Amer-

icans deserted their family or ancestral homes while fleeing from the newcomers or searching for distant prosperity. In Boston, for example, an
estimated 650,000 people left the town during the 1880s, while some
800,000 immigrants arrived.[21] Yankees abandoned ancient or once-fash-
ionable structures, while boomers razed old buildings and erected apartments to house the desperate throng. Norton told Appleton that those
hereditary homes represented the foundation of a stable community by
anchoring Yankees to a bedrock of landscape and heritage.

At root, Norton kindled a sense of personalism; he believed that past
and present were linked through material things that encapsulated the
spirit of their forebears and rekindled their memory. He warned Americans:

> No human life is complete in itself; it is but a link, however individual in
> its form, however different from every other, in a chain reaching back in-
> definitely into the past, reaching forward indefinitely into the future. . . .
> To maintain in full vigor the sense of the dependence of the individual life
> upon the past, more is needed than a mere intellectual recognition of the
> fact. Such is the frailty of our nature that our principles require to be sup-
> ported by sentiment, and our sentiments draw nourishment from material
> things, from visible memorials, from familiar objects to which affection may
> cling. And it is this nourishment that the true home supplies.

Norton told his students that any assault on these homes was pernicious,
but his lament was colored by not only the rapidity of Gilded Age change
but myth. That mobility and demolition had been typical, even in the
early settlements where sons and grandsons left the family home for
greener pastures.[22]

Norton publicized his vision of work, home, and tradition in an influential essay "The Lack of Old Homes in America" (1889). His notion of
the future challenged an even more popular image of Boston drawn by
utopian socialist Edward Bellamy in *Looking Backward, 2000–1887*
(1888). Both regretted the degradation of work and worker, the anomie
of modern man, and the wretchedness of urban civilization. Their con-
trasting visions tell much about Boston's sense of the future, and the
accommodation eventually reached by the preservation movement. Bellamy found hope not in Norton's mythical village, but in a technological
paradise without the class and ethnic divisions of the Gilded Age. Most
tellingly, Bellamy envisaged none of Norton's old buildings. His protagonist Justin West, a wealthy Bostonian, had no wish to stay in the family
home, "a large, ancient wooden mansion, very elegant in an old-fashioned
way within, but situated in a quarter that had long since become unde-
sirable for residence, from its invasion by tenement houses and manufac-
tories."[23]

Like Rip Van Winkle, West falls asleep in 1887, but awakens in 2000.
Astonished, he walks around Boston, but it had undergone "a complete

metamorphosis," much along the proposed lines of the city-beautiful movement and progressivism. Gone were its "ancient landmarks" and narrow lanes. Instead, he saw "a great city" with "miles of broad streets, shaded by trees and lined with fine buildings." Modern Bostonians, moreover, cared little for antique furniture, silver, or hand-me-downs from earlier times. Evidently, Bellamy and Norton both believed that the Industrial Revolution had destroyed the bonds of mankind and recognized that society needed a unifying ethos. They found it in opposing worlds.[24] One preached a push-button progress, the other preindustrial tradition.

Norton's aestheticism was imported from England, but changed remarkably in the American context. He admired William Morris, the socialist who had founded an arts-and-crafts movement to promote aesthetics and reform. So unlike his American followers, however, Morris hoped that his movement would nurture an alternative economy. He pictured it best in *News from Nowhere* (1891)—rebuffing the vision of Bellamy and Norton—in which he described a socialist utopia that had repudiated industrialism, reinstituted handicrafts, and returned to the pre-Renaissance architectural tradition.[25] Yankee preservationists borrowed Morris's notions of aesthetics, arts and crafts, and simple living but, fearing his socialism, gradually added their own traditionalism.

Norton was repulsed by the cultural chaos around him. In 1893 he traveled to Chicago for the Columbian Exposition, for example, and saw the ostentatious Court of Honor with its Beaux Arts edifices, as well as the pandemonious Midway Plaisance with "its immense 'border' of vulgarities." The fair thoroughly displayed the bizarre, gilded tastes of American culture. Appleton also attended the fair and saw his beloved Hancock house, remodeled as the Massachusetts State building, juxtaposed with South Sea island huts, Chinese pagodas, and Arab mosques. If architecture expressed the nation's *Zeitgeist*, as Norton believed, America had lost its defining spirit.[26]

Inspired by Morris, Norton promoted the arts-and-crafts movement to rekindle respect for family homes and earlier traditions. Believing that "the hand was the instrument of the soul," he decried the proliferation of machine-made goods, their uniformity and lack of beauty, and the barbarizing consequences of their manufacture. Like Appleton, Isham, and many other Yankees who would soon coalesce through SPNEA, Norton prized the craftsmanship of medieval artisans and idealized their society for its religious faith, communal pride, and simple living. Accordingly, he helped form the Boston Society of Arts and Crafts (BSAC) in 1897 and predicted that it would kindle attitudes that would improve "the character of the workman no less than of his work." But, as it turned out, the BSAC fell into the hands of those who craved beauty more than labor reform. Handicrafts became saleable commodities in a market economy, and consumption defined their importance.[27]

As is so often the case in a college education, the spirit of Norton, Hart, and their colleagues only slowly took material form in Appleton's life. He graduated in 1896 but, with his poor eyesight, had to rely on friends to help him prepare for exams. Thereupon, Sumner made the grand tour of Europe with his tutor to polish his gentlemanly manners. He returned to Boston, and in subsequent years spent much time in the sheltered drawing rooms of its elite clubs. He socialized at the Union and Harvard clubs, pursued a genealogical bent at the NEHGS, volunteered at the MHS, and became active in the Sons of the Revolution (SR). As in earlier days when Harvard provided the forces to keep the working-class populace in order, he even joined the First Corps Cadets, Massachusetts Volunteer Militia. Largely led by Brahmins, these clubs reinforced upper-class solidarity.[28]

After his father's death in 1903, Appleton lived comfortably, but not ostentatiously, on an annuity of approximately $6,000 from his grandfather's estate (Fig.1-2). A later associate had Veblen's critique of unproductive aristocrats in mind when he accused him of belonging to the "leisure class." Sumner complained, however, that this stipend kept him from amassing enough capital to enter business. He did try to sell real estate, but suffered a "nervous breakdown." He attributed the collapse to an astigmatism, as did Norton many years earlier when he suffered similar ill health.[29]

Such "nervousness" commonly afflicted the gentry in the Victorian era. Eye strain did burden Appleton, but environmental pressures also brought on the anxiety and enervation. Descended from old and distinguished New England families, both Appleton and Norton felt their father's pressure, went into business, but failed to find the expected success. What apparently cured their neurasthenia was a therapy of antimodernism and historical study. Both immersed themselves in work that consumed their energy, fascinated their interest, and offered personal meaning. Norton studied Ruskin and Dante, while Appleton joined the patriotic movement. Appleton's neurasthenia stemmed from as much anomie as astigmatism.[30]

Meanwhile, Appleton's three sisters had married and moved away; he gave up the family house at Holbrook and the pew at King's Chapel; and he made the seasonal rounds, as he would for many years, between southern Maine, Squam Lake in New Hampshire, and Cape Cod. His taste for the colonial was enhanced by visits to coastal villages where Yankees lived in that reassuring haze of the Colonial Revival. He became a "frequent guest" of John Templeman Coolidge, for example, at Little Harbor in Portsmouth. All the while, he was active, but frustrated, courting young ladies, and he remained a bachelor like his uncles Tom and Nathan.[31]

His recuperation was slow, and he considered selling real estate again, but instead chose to attend graduate school at Harvard's Bussey Institution and enrolled in three mining courses. Some members of the Appleton family operated a mine in the West, and he even traveled to Nevada to visit the camps in the prospect of joining their venture. He stopped in San Francisco to see what survived the earthquake and fire of 1906, but his walks about the ruined city aggravated his depression.[32]

FIG. 1-2   William Sumner Appleton, Jr., 1917 or before (Photograph by T. C. Marceau, Courtesy, Society for the Preservation of New England Antiquities)

By chance he enrolled in a fourth course in the 1906–7 term. He never did attend the mining courses, but fell in love with Denman Ross's course in the school of architecture, "Theory of Pure Design." A student of Norton, Ross also showed Ruskin's belief that artistic taste and individual character were inseparable, but added his own theory to evaluate the harmony, balance, and rhythm of art, architecture, and antiques. He taught that art and society could not be separated. "Art is the experience of life," he said, and "nothing else, indeed [was] of any consequence." True to traditionalism, he rebuked the legacy of the French Revolution and its "ills of Equality, Fraternity and Liberty." He asked: "Shall we be led by these ideals or shall we be led by the contrary ideals of Superiority, of Exclusive Devotions and Self-Sacrifice."[33]

Active in the BSAC, Ross tried to bring his principles not only to its craftsmen but to Boston's children through programs in the public schools. Later called "the greatest collector America has produced," he introduced to his students a wide range of objects from manuscripts to textiles to sculpture. He collected on all continents, the least of which North America. Appleton would be one to correct his neglect. His preoccupation with Ross's class in 1907 led him to walk the old streets of Cambridge, Salem, and Newburyport. He never did well academically, however, and was "killed" by one examination and did "very poorly" on another.[34] In what was an amazing turn for Appleton, however, the course gelled his earlier training under Norton, his work in real estate, and his commitment to Brahmin society. Together with his ongoing work for the SR, this set him on his lifelong career.

2

"A Constant Incentive to Patriotic Citizenship"

Progressivism and the Remaking of Memory

Appleton emerged from Harvard while New England was facing the throes of industrialization, urbanization, and modernization. In the late nineteenth century the region's physical and human landscape was dramatically changing. A floodtide of immigrants was hitting the coast and reshaping the political system, but their "ancestral lines," he said while reiterating the myth of a single forebear, "failed to run back through our own Puritan stock." When foreigners moved in, Yankees moved out and the very definition of New England as the land of John Winthrop, Paul Revere, and Daniel Webster seemed in doubt. At the same time, the region's landmarks were falling, and he lamented that too many Yankees showed only "casualness" toward this "marvelous heritage from the past."[1] As in a continuous loop, therefore, the meaning of historic preservation would revolve around a track of immigration, ethnic politics, and economic development, as much as progressivism and the Colonial Revival.

These heated battles over landscape and culture found their outlet in the progressive movement. As in much of the nation, progressives worked to reorder society according to more customary lines and values. Reflecting diverse sentiments and goals, progressivism was an eclectic reform whose adherents, at the very least, seemed determined to heal a fractured society, boom a troubled economy, or incorporate scientific, business-style management into the mainstream of society. In general, progressives believed in Protestantism, individualism, and capitalism. Despite their criticism of recent economic trends, and separating their kind from more radical or reactionary types, they believed that industrial capitalism had created social and economic progress. They were generally native-born, middle- or upper-class professionals who were disturbed by the many signs of disorder. Like Charles Knowles Bolton, president of SPNEA through the 1910s and 1920s, they held a nostalgic view of the past, but invoked a "progressive spirit" to "bind together" their fractured society.[2]

Like an umbrella, progressivism could cover those who were conservative, liberal, and much in between. The nation embraced progressivism in the early twentieth century, but there were those who did not, whether they were reactionary conservatives, radical socialists, or machine politicians. Yet lines did blur between some of them. As Richard McCormick conceded, "No historian has yet solved the riddle of what personal, social, or psychological factors distinguished Progressives from conservatives."[3]

If nothing else, progressivism was paradoxical and ambiguous. Unsettled by industrialization, immigration, and modernization, but holding tight to the anchors of their religion and culture, progressives protected their mythical image of an earlier society and economy, as well as it values, but their ideology often kept them from facing its inherent and quite substantive modern contradictions. One only needs to think of the changing notions of work, opportunity, and freedom to see how the image and reality of New England were inconsistent. Progressives had a penchant for what historian Robert Crunden called "innovative nostalgia," and that remaking of history surely surfaced in the preservation movement.[4]

Typical for the movement, Massachusetts progressives believed that they had an obligation to restrain the era's insurgents—the immigrant politicians, socialists, and labor unionists who challenged the customary division of wealth and power. They worked to reform society along hierarchical lines and redefined their traditions to accommodate not only the needs of corporate industry, as in the rapid mechanization of the factory and the tremendous growth of consumer goods, but the professionalism of science.[5]

Usually descended from older Yankee families, Massachusetts progressives derived directly from the mugwumps. Well educated and socially prominent, mugwumps preached a conservative philosophy based on enlightened rule and individualistic values. Considering themselves outnumbered by the popular classes, they bemoaned the decline of social standards and the rise of big money and machine politics. With a deep strain of elitism and antimodernism, they strove to regenerate older traditions. The floodtide of new immigrants stressed them even more, particularly when compounded by the well-known fact that the Yankee's own birthrate was half that of the foreigners. Tradition-minded New Englanders differed, however, in their reaction to the newcomers. Some demanded immigration restriction, as did Thomas Bailey Aldrich. Believing that democracy and "new immigrants" could not mix, he asked if it was wise "to leave the gates unguarded" to those "who waste the gifts of freedom."[6] As they upheld tradition, mugwumps prized their memory, sweetened by myth and wishful thinking, of an earlier unvarying harmony in New England. Though it was an invention, it would ultimately be enshrined through preserved landmarks.

Like so many mugwumps of the Gilded Age, progressives valued the serene life of small towns. Norton, for one, felt a world of difference between the Boston of 1800 and 1888. "The air then had something of morning freshness and sweetness, compared with its present noonday heat and dust," he waxed.

The community was more homogeneous and its members were better acquainted. The habits of life were simpler; the interests of men were less
mixed and varied; there were more common sympathies, more common
and controlling traditions and associations. . . . It was a cheerful time,—a
time of exhilarating hope, of large promise, of legitimate confidence. Sel-
dom has there been a society in which the moral atmosphere was clearer
or more wholesome.

As a result, many tradition-minded urbanites cared little for city life, other
than the amenities of upper-crust living. As with Appleton and Bolton
who eventually recovered their hereditary country home, they voiced
pride in the rural life of their forebears. Like the yeoman farmer and
Transcendentalist, they valued the natural order, but hated the urban
disorder.[7]

Oddly enough, Yankees themselves kept open the region's doors to the
immigrants. Facing southern competitors and radical unions, tradition-
minded Yankees typically welcomed the newcomers as cheap laborers,
but soon clashed over work and pay. Those immigrants from Eastern and
Southern Europe proved dramatically different from the farm girls of Nathan Appleton's mill at Lowell. Culturally alien to Yankee notions of
work, deference, and individualism, they commonly sought strength from
ethnic associations or labor unions.[8]

Massachusetts progressives accepted the right of workers to organize,
but feared their combined power. They most feared radical unions such
as the Industrial Workers of the World. Unlike Boston's conservative
unions that accepted the capitalist system, appealed to skilled workers,
and numbered almost 100,000 members, the IWW preached its radicalism to the most oppressed, semi- or unskilled workers. After the Lawrence
textile strike of 1912, the IWW sparked a wave of labor activism throughout New England. Before assemblies numbering 25,000, the IWW openly
denounced New England's historic order of Protestant individualism and
deferential democracy. Tradition-minded Yankees of Bolton's stripe worried about the repercussions of their "ruthless battle against society." He
called Wobbly founder William "Big Bill" Haywood a "murderous
leader."[9]

Progressives easily borrowed from more reactionary Yankees as they
criticized these unions. For one, Wallace Nutting could hardly be called
progressive, but his image of the lost society was one that buttressed the
elitism of progressives. Reinforcing the notions of hierarchy and deference, he used the example of a medieval cathedral to glorify the common
workers who had "put their shoulders to the ropes and marched with
joyous songs to draw together the great stones that in their harmonized
unity, under the hand of an inspired artist, became an embodiment of
their loftiest imaginings, rising over their cottages."[10] Disillusioned by the
new order, Nutting turned to a full- time promotion of the arts and crafts.

So, too, did Ralph Adams Cram promote craftsmanship as a brake against unionization. He would address SPNEA's annual meeting in 1914 and "plead for hand work in old buildings." A reactionary who bashed unions at any opportunity, Cram mixed antimodernism, antiradicalism, and traditionalism. Unlike the spirit that animated the English crafts movement, he deplored the power of unions and told SPNEA that the arts-and-crafts movement and historic preservation would help counter "the crushing & leveling influence of trades-unionism." Accustomed to the work ethic and class authority that their forebears had instilled in earlier Yankees, preservationists faulted trade unions for upsetting New England's historic balance. Too many workers, said Bolton, held to "the crude theory that the less hours each man works the more work there will be for all."[11]

Even more, changes in Boston's landscape worried progressives (Fig. 2-1). During the nineteenth century, old-time Boston had metamorphosed from a small, packed seaport to a pandemonious city of factories, high-rise tenements, and exuberant enterprise. The great fire of 1872 had scorched sixty-five acres in the memory of old-timers. As one chronicler described the fire, "Little cared the monster for the revered localities where Benjamin Franklin was born, where Edward Everett once lived, or where Daniel Webster's family gathered about his fireplace." In the zeal to rebuild, town fathers erased more of old Boston's look by banning wooden roofs, revising sinuous and narrow streets, and enacting more demanding building codes.[12]

At the same time, Boston's population leaped. In 1870 it numbered 250,526; by 1905 it had more than doubled to 595,380. By 1910 it was the fifth largest city in the United States with a population of 670,585. At the turn of the century not only did the metropolis have over one million people and account for forty percent of the state's population but over three-quarters of the state's residents lived in cities. Old-time Massachusetts was indeed a thing of the past. By 1915 foreigners (first-generation and foreign-born stock) composed more than seventy percent of Boston's population. As a whole, more than sixty percent of New England's populace was foreign.[13]

The construction of modern transportation systems fostered an urban sprawl that covered a ten-mile radius. Most of Boston's neighboring towns changed almost overnight. Commuters inundated one-time country villages, or immigrants sought their old housing stock. From 1870 to 1905, for example, Brookline jumped from 6,650 to 23,436, and Cambridge from 36,934 to 97,434.[14] As Boston took on more complex urban forms, the wealthier classes moved to choice neighborhoods, such as the Back Bay or near the Fens. Even more left for the outer suburbs where new homes often emulated Colonial Revival designs and, unlike the older city, included larger yards and grid streets without alleys. Those affluent Yankees still owned substantial holdings in the city, leaving most Bostonians as renters.[15]

Within such dichotomies between tenement neighborhood and Colo-

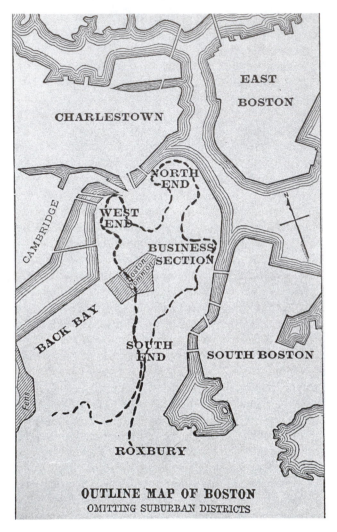

EAST
BOSTON

CHARLESTOWN

NORTH END

CAMBRIDGE

WEST END

BUSINESS SECTION

Boston Common

BACK BAY

SOUTH END

SOUTH BOSTON

Fens

ROXBURY

OUTLINE MAP OF BOSTON
OMITTING SUBURBAN DISTRICTS

FIG. 2-1 Outline map of Boston, showing seventeenth- and twentieth-century boundaries (Wolfe, *Lodging House Problem*)

nial Revival suburb, immigrant and Yankee, and peasant and patrician, Boston society seemed ever more fragmented. The city had long been divided by class and, to a lesser extent, ethnicity, but Appleton feared that the region was so fractured "on lines of race and religion" that disorder would prevail. The widening chasm was easily visible in the city's landscape. The old and sometimes historic dwellings of Boston, if they survived fire or demolition, housed the newcomers. For example, the mansions of the South End largely became lodging houses. According to one writer who joined Appleton in the "Boston-1915" movement, the hallmark of its progressivism, "many of the fine old streets turned squalid, others turned shabby" and the whole represented "a bleak waste of fine old houses fallen on poorer days." Almost every house held lodgers, and the "Rooms to Let" signs marked the neighborhood's decline. Some unscrupulous realtors bought out whole houses, stripped them of anything valuable, and forced the exodus of the last old families.[16]

The once-dignified West End suffered even more. By the turn of the century, said that writer, it resembled "a thickly populated rabbit hutch where few but the politicians and a scattering of social workers feel certain of what they are dealing with, or how the dealing is to be done." The district was overwhelmingly populated by immigrants—Irish, Jews, Italians, Poles, and Ukranians—and African-Americans who, Benjamin Flower warned in the social gospel of 1893, "are bravely battling for life's barest necessities, while year by year the conditions are becoming more hopeless, the struggle for bread fiercer, the outlook more dismal."[17] Appleton saw that firsthand in the late 1890s as he daily canvassed Cambridge Street house by house for a local realtor. He became quite familiar with the hallmark of the West End's old order, the first Harrison Gray Otis house. Around it were tenements and lodging houses, but SPNEA would choose it as its headquarters in 1916.[18] Meanwhile, the West End's chaos was spreading and threatening Beacon Hill.

As the number of foreigners skyrocketed, traditional Yankees feared, as did Henry James, the loss of their region's Anglo-Saxon identity. Upon his return to Boston after a quarter-century stay in Europe, he observed the immigrants one Sunday afternoon in 1906 on Boston Common, the once holy meeting ground of his Puritan forebears and whose Beacon Hill site was but a short distance from the West End. "No note of any shade of American speech struck my ear," he wrote.

> The types and faces bore them out; the people before me were gross aliens to a man, and they were in serene and triumphant procession. . . . Therefore had I the vision, as filling the sky, no longer of the great Puritan "whip," the whip for the conscience and the nerves, of the local legend, but that of a huge applied sponge saturated with the foreign mixture and passed over almost everything I remembered and might still have recovered.[19]

Thereafter, James joined the battle to recover the landmarks defining that old character. In this contest over the city's identity, an increasing (but never large) number of Yankees argued that their collective memory should include prominent buildings. Samuel Adams Drake, whose books represent milestones in remaking the Yankee memory and linking it to buildings, thought that those sites would "arouse the imagination, as nothing else can." In *Old Landmarks and Historic Personages of Boston* (1900), he begged Bostonians "not to remain indifferent to the threatened spoliation of what we lay claim to as our inalienable inheritance, our birthright."[20]

As Boston boomed, however, Drake's appeal was drowned out in the roar of construction. James walked about the Capitol in 1906, but discovered in horror that the wrecking ball was quickly taking its toll. Speaking the mind of old Boston, he voiced sentiments that preservationists have uttered ever since. He looked for a familiar "pair of ancient houses" on Ashburton Place, a tiny street on which stood the NEHGS and where Appleton lived, and found

> but a gaping void, the brutal effacement, at a stroke, of every related object, of the whole precious past. . . . The act of obliteration had been breathlessly swift, and if I had often seen how fast history could be made I had doubtless never so felt that it could be unmade still faster. It was as if the bottom had fallen out of one's own biography, and one plunged backward into space without meeting anything.[21]

James walked to Park Street, adjacent to the Common, and admired the street's "old distinction." He found it "incontestable" that "on the whole continent" there did not exist "an equal animated space more exempt from the vulgarity" than the row that ended with the church built in 1809. The Park Street Church "holds the note," he said, "the note of the old felicity, and remains by so doing a precious public servant." He was dismayed that it had been recently threatened by developers who wanted to erect a tall office building. The congregation had faced hard times after many had moved to more secluded and up-scale areas. It approved the sale, but only after female pewholders were barred from voting. A preservation campaign garnered impressive support, yet Bostonians split on the issue. The building was unexpectedly saved when the syndicate's deal fell through. The episode showed, he said, "the impudence of private greed" and raised "the question of what the old New England spirit may have still, intellectually, aesthetically, or for that matter even morally, to give." That boom from 1898–1908 revealed "the heedless rush of modern civilization," said a later SPNEA supporter, as the city's skyline became "a distorted mass" of smokestacks, high-rises, and warehouses.[22]

That memory of old-time Boston, romanticized by Drake and James, was challenged on different fronts by those Bostonians who wanted either to uplift the newcomer or boom development. Robert A. Woods, a progressive social worker, believed that this memory impeded urgently needed action. "The indifference of the so-called good citizen" to the hovels of the immigrants, he claimed, "is largely because his best effort to produce a mental picture of his city in its essential human aspects results in something vague, scattered, out-of-date." Ironically, that sentiment was also voiced by Woods's adversary, John Fitzgerald. "In too many instances," the mayor said, "old Boston sits at the tomb of its ancestors and fingers the withered leaves of laurel they won in bygone days. Old Boston is cold and proud, wrapped in the mantle of Puritanism, not progressive enough." George French of the Chamber of Commerce called that memory an "affectation and fraud." Those who ignored the city's slums and high-rises, as well as the pressing need of development, should be "convicted of ignorance and slap-dash judgments."[23]

More significantly, ethnic insurgents at the polling place challenged the memory and power of Yankees. By the 1880s the Irish in Boston already outnumbered Yankees and had enough clout by 1892 to close the Public Library for Saint Patrick's Day. Aldrich warned that Saint Patrick was "in full defiant possession now, his colors waving everywhere" above the American flag. The Boston mayoral election of 1905 revealed the outcome. The Democratic Party candidate, John Fitzgerald, claimed that "New England is more Irish today than any part of the world outside Ireland"; he startled Yankees by telling them that "Boston is an Irish city."[24]

Recognizing the necessity of united opposition, Boston's Yankee lawyers, merchants, and traditionalists, together with social workers such as Woods, had formed the Good Government Association in 1903. Much like the ensuing "Boston-1915" movement, the GGA was a standard-bearer for Yankee progressivism. Fighting the Irish Democracy, which itself was noticeably fractured, the GGA upheld policies dear to Brahmin and businessman alike. The Goo-Goos, as they were unflatteringly called, endorsed the candidacy of Republican Louis Frothingham, former Speaker of the state's House of Representatives and later SPNEA supporter. The vicious contest of 1905 portended the more bitter battles to come.

Fitzgerald's triumph led the GGA's historian to conclude that "Old Boston . . . became a thing of the past." The Democratic Party was left deeply divided, however, and old Boston still had much clout. The GGA investigated Fitzgerald's city hall, found enough impropriety, and publicized that to deny him reelection in 1907. Yet he won again (by a razor's edge) in 1910. While the GGA candidate, millionaire banker James J. Storrow, equated "Fitzgeraldism" with corruption, "Honey Fitz" pictured it as a campaign of his honest principles against Yankee aristocrats and trusts.[25]

Fitzgerald called Brahmins the "scions of the blue-blooded aristocracy." Boston's descent into self-centered greed, he claimed, had begun with the "lords of the loom" and the "lords of the long wharf" of the mid-nineteenth century. Fewer than twenty-five families, including the Appletons, composed the oligarchy that "has been too long deaf to the aspirations of the young Irish, Italians, Jews, and Frenchmen in our midst." He jabbed at tight-fisted Brahmins who criticized his public works programs, and threatened their sense of domestic peace in the Back Bay by proposing construction of a row of houses along the Charles River. No one knew if he was serious when he also proposed building a new City Hall on the Public Garden, a site that separated the Back Bay from the city's sprawl and whose peaceful splendor kindled the Brahmins' love of nature. Those Yankees could not have imagined it getting worse, but his successor, James Michael Curley, proposed selling the garden the day after his inauguration and using half of the money to build a park more accessible to the people.[26]

Fitzgerald's cultural politics were as ominous as he meddled with Yankee history. Never forgetting that Ireland's demise had begun with Elizabethan colonization and culminated with the Puritan Conquest, he did his best to redefine the memory of New England. While in the Common Council, he shifted the focus from the Puritans to a non-English discoverer by introducing an order to make October 12 a local holiday to honor Columbus. His Italian constituents in the North End were delighted. As a state senator, he successfully promoted legislation in 1893 to change the Puritan's dour Fast Day into a state holiday for Patriot's Day on April 19. As a U. S. Congressman, "Honey Fitz" also led the campaign in 1897 to move the deteriorated frigate *Constitution* from Portsmouth to Boston and preserve it for posterity. Obviously willing to glorify the American Revolution, he hoped Eire would emulate it. As Boston's mayor, he staged "Old Home Week," a seven-day bash that celebrated the town's history and promoted its economy.[27] The GGA criticized him for spending too much money on the celebration.

His successor Curley antagonized the Brahmins to no end. While Fitzgerald had quietly reached an accommodation with Boston's businessmen, Curley ran as a populist, adopted an antibusiness stance, and spearheaded the enactment of an impressive list of reforms. Like no other politician in the city's history, he outlasted his critics. Even with his party divided, he served four terms in the U.S. House of Representatives, four as mayor, and one as governor. Curley made his first political marks by attacking Brahmins as "blue-nosed bigots." The son of an immigrant from County Galway, he was raised in a Roxbury tenement neighborhood of destitute immigrants and dirt streets. He doubted "whether the wealthy residents of Beacon Hill and the Back Bay ever realized how sordid conditions were in such districts of the city as Ward Seventeen." His father worked eleven hours a day for ten cents an hour as a hodcarrier.[28]

Curley was amazed by the sight of the "stately residences" in the Back Bay, "the most aristocratic rectangle in America." His mother worked there as a maidservant and, like all Irish, entered the palatial homes through the back door. "These mansions . . . seemed like castles," and he "learned that in them lived some of the feudal barons who exploited Irish labor." At times unscrupulous, Curley regarded himself as a protagonist in a grand struggle. His loyal followers derided the Yankees as bigots; their children chalked the sidewalks of Beacon Hill with scathing graffiti. He resigned from Congress in 1913, and won the mayoralty in a divisive contest. Bolton reacted quite typically for Yankees when he declared that only "a democracy run mad" could have produced such "surely ridiculous rulers" as Curley.[29]

Similarly, Woods and the GGA bitterly characterized Fitzgerald and

Curley as immigrant ward bosses "subversive of the American party system, not to speak of every holy tradition of our free Republic." Woods condemned those Yankees who left this cancer unchecked or benefited from the spoils. He warned that the Irish accounted for the vast majority of all the immigrants on the dole, and his colleague Frederic Bushee attributed it to their "social and moral degeneracy."[30] Since ward politics had brought the Irish to power, the GGA proposed introducing at-large elections for aldermen. Appleton went a step further and swung the GGA to promote a complex electoral revision—proportional representation—that would have given Yankees more clout, diluted the ethnic vote, and thereby replaced mayors of Curley's caliber with "a higher class of elected officials."[31] Nothing came of his plan.

No better case study of this clash could be found than the campaign Appleton launched in 1905 in the North End. The neighborhood had once been the home of Boston's finest families, as evidenced by the congregation that built Christ Church. The whims of fashion and modern conveniences lured them toward the West End and then Beacon Hill, however. As the North End became the immigrant quarter, the hand of progress largely passed it by, but it remained the most historic section of the city.

When the North End's population shifted, Boston quaked. By the 1880s the Irish had left it for South Boston, Roxbury, and other locales on the trolley lines. Soon after, more Italians than Irish lived there, as well as 6,000 Jews. Proper Bostonians feared the place, but they did create the Massachusetts Society for Promoting Good Citizenship, and adherents such as Edwin D. Mead, editor of *The New England Magazine*, labored in the 1880s to teach its youngsters about Yankee history, as did Edward G. Porter, author of *Rambles in Old Boston* (1887). In an appeal that influenced Appleton, Porter urged Bostonians to preserve the more humble edifices of older days: "Very little has ever been attempted in the case of private and ordinary dwellings, a few of which—and only a few—of the early time yet stand as instructive, though often modest, reminders of the past." Those houses could be found only in the North End, "a section rarely visited" by Anglo-Americans, despite the fact that "historically, it is by far the most interesting part of our metropolis."[32]

The narrow interest of Mead and Porter contrasted strangely with the social gospel of Benjamin Flower. In the tradition of William Morris, but so unlike later progressives, he castigated Boston's elite who owned such slums. "Surely Shylock ought soon to be able to buy a high place in public esteem on such a rich harvest of blood money," he protested, "and how munificent might be his gifts to churches, colleges, and libraries; while, if he owns several such buildings, he would still be able to live in sumptuous luxury." He visited a North End mission where children were asked to sing "My Country, 'Tis of Thee," and pained to think: "What grim satire was I hearing! Little dwarfed lives, starving in poverty and wretchedness, in the filth of the slums, singing, 'Sweet Land of Liberty!' I was glad that they did not comprehend the meaning of the song, for it would have made life more bitter." He angrily thought that while these denizens of the ghetto withered on life's vine, the residents of Beacon Hill rode in stately carriages, drank champagne, and protected their fine homes. Quoting Morris, and illustrating the gulf that would separate the English and American preservation movements, Flower begged Boston's affluent to "open wide the door" of opportunity to these newcomers.[33]

Unlike Flower's assaults on Boston's rich, the conservative philosophy of Woods would win the approval of its preservationists. As the best known of Boston's social workers and a chief philosopher of the settlement movement, Woods typified the ethnocentrism of Yankee progressivism. Middle-class in thought, suburban in origins, and educated at elite colleges, he was a stranger to the city. Shocked by what he perceived as the slum's deleterious morality, he battled against its saloons and dance halls. Like preservationists, he hoped to revive earlier traditions—beliefs in church and volunteer activity, and values such as thrift, individualism, and industry. Patronizing toward the newcomers, he joined those progressives who demanded the restriction of immigration and the implementation of social controls. Woods warned Bostonians that the immigrants' children were out of control, their political machines corrupt, and too few Brahmins did anything to cure these cancers. Knowing that these immigrants were determined to protect their traditions, he attacked their "ignorant conservatism" and warned in 1902 that "the newcomer remains an enemy to all that is best in American life." He knew that the question was: Whose traditions would prevail?[34]

Bolton endorsed the labors of Woods and his coworkers, and called them "earnest, sane people." Eventually, SPNEA's campaign to preserve Yankee culture would work hand-in-hand with the Americanization campaign of these social workers. Progressives such as Woods and Bolton commonly placed their hopes in the public school system. Symbolically, the city had named its schools in the North End after Revere, Hancock, and John Eliot. Patriotic Yankees, including Appleton representing the SR, in turn placed portraits of Washington in these schools. Success came only slowly, but it was sweet. Yankee social workers watched one child lead his class in a patriotic recital, for example. "To hold two hundred fellow pupils spellbound," they said, "while one thunders the speech of John Adams from the platform, with only a suggestion of Italy in one's accent, is perhaps as intoxicating as any success of after life."[35]

When Yankees approached the neighborhood's Old North Church or Revere's home, they invariably asked social workers about the acculturation of these newcomers. Many Yankees expressed their pessimism, and turned up the heat on the campaigns to preserve their culture and Americanize the aliens. Bushee observed in 1903, for example, that Italians "learn English slowly and are in general very ignorant." With ethnocentric eyes he saw "an increase in drunkenness and sexual depravity" in their lives, and concluded that they "show the beginning of a degenerate class." He must have pricked Yankee nerves and thrifty pocketbooks when he predicted that "the next generation will bring forth a large crop of dependants, delinquents, and defectives to fill up our public institutions."[36]

Within this context came Appleton's first step as a preservationist, and that involved the campaign to save Revere's home (c. 1680). Since his ownership (1770–1800), its sight stirred the hearts of patriots and antiquaries. In 1900 Boston had but four extant seventeenth-century wooden dwellings, but only the Revere house remains today to show the once-dominant styling. Drake complained, however, that "about every other house [nearby] was either a dram-shop or a brothel." Amidst the crowd, he moaned:

> Pure air is indeed a luxury. Pah! the atmosphere is actually thick with the vile odors of garlic and onions—of maccaroni and lazzaroni. The dirty tenements swarm with greasy voluble Italians. . . . One can scarce hear the sound of his own English mother-tongue from one end of the square to the other; and finally (can we believe the evidence of our own eyes?), here is good Father Taylor's old brick Bethel turned into a Catholic chapel! . . . Shade of Cotton Mather! has it come to this, that a mass-house should stand within the very pale of the thrice consecrated old Puritan sanctuary?[37]

Drake lamented that Boston's elite had discarded the Revere house like an "outworn garment." It resembled a "poor relation upon whom the rich man now turns his back." While an upper story was used as a cigar factory, and its first floor housed poor families, it occupied ground around which was being built more profitable multi-story apartments (Fig. 2-2). After it was threatened with demolition, old-time Yankees launched a preservation drive. A committee of distinguished citizens formed the Paul Revere Memorial Association (PRMA). Appleton, then historian for the SR, became secretary. As "the architect of the Association," he relied on the likes of GGA-figurehead Storrow to raise the funds.[38]

Writing in the Boston *Post*, Appleton called Revere "the most picturesque of national celebrities," and asked how long his house would stand. "When a similar question faced our fathers with reference to John Hancock's house," he wrote, "they stood aside and let the famous house be pulled down." He needed $30,000 for the house's purchase, restoration, and maintenance, but a "small number of persons" had already donated over $7,000. Appleton tried to persuade the public to fund what the Brahmins had begun. One day, for example, he signed over 600 circulars. Appealing to the city's economic boosters, he predicted that a museum "would draw visitors from all parts." The PRMA's charter reiterated a gospel of preservation for the Americanizers. So much a part of the Colonial Revival, its work would foster "patriotism, philanthropy, civic virtue, and pride" along the lines of Revere.[39]

The PRMA's president, Lieutenant Governor Curtis Guild, Jr., aptly

FIG. 2-2   Paul Revere House, Boston, before restoration, c. 1900–1906 (Photograph by Henry Peabody, Courtesy, Society for the Preservation of New England Antiquities)

beat the drum of tourism to harmonize with the hymn of the civil religion. He called the house a "Mecca" for "thousands of pilgrims from all over the country seeking the shrines of American history. Even if no reverence for the past and no patriotic sentiment existed, the preservation of such a memorial has a distinct money value." Past owner of the Boston *Commercial Bulletin*, Guild knew that sentiment and patriotism would not alone justify preservation. As the *Globe* wrote, the Revere home "is more potent than any other one landmark in drawing . . . many thousands of strangers . . . who spend a great deal of money here."[40]

Descended from a seventeenth-century Puritan, Guild showed that traditionalism could easily mix with boosterism and progressivism. Although he lived in the Back Bay, he praised Revere's house as an example of "this pure type of an old colonial home." Its humble, austere appearance would inspire the neighborhood's newcomers from Italy and other lands. Such inspiration, it was thought, was sorely needed. At the same time as Woods was warning that these Italians "showed a certain lack of self-reliance and 'push,'" and that violent crime, gambling, drinking, and licentiousness were on the rise, Guild pictured Revere (originally Rivoire) as an immigrant who learned Yankee traditions of initiative, work, and responsibility. "Situated as it is in the very heart of the North End and surrounded today by a foreign born population," his house, said Guild, "will serve as a daily lesson to the youth of that district in Massachusetts ideals of loyalty, simplicity and civic pride." Revere's self-sacrifice and legacy would remind "new citizens of the service due from them and from their children to the Commonwealth."[41]

Other Bostonians remembered Revere's legacy differently. Some prized his business skill, inventiveness, and "determination of purpose." Modern Bostonians could have emulated these traits, for example, at the Revere Copper Company the patriot had founded that was "rapidly falling into ruins" after being "absorbed by stronger elements in competition." Bostonians resented those robber barons of Gotham who manipulated the economy. If Revere was alive in 1906, said the *Herald*, "he might feel called upon to 'spread the alarm' that should wake the nation from its lethargy in regard to the trusts."[42]

The campaign to purchase the house easily met the $12,000 goal. Even Boston's youngsters gave their nickels and pennies, and showed a philanthropy proportionately more generous than that of many Brahmins. Some children also contributed to the purchase of commemorative reproductions linked to the drive, but controversy followed. The Irish-American who chaired Boston's school committee, for example, not only opposed Brahmins asking poor children to give their pennies for an ersatz Revere bowl but questioned the worthiness of Revere as a role model. "Paul's bowl was filled with rum, not pennies," he teased. "He should have been arrested for drunk driving when he warned that the British were coming."[43]

Such blasphemy prompted well-placed traditionalists to raise the ante. Nathaniel and Paula Revere Thayer, for instance, gave $2,000 to the drive, and she would be later rewarded by Governor Calvin Coolidge with an appointment as Director of Immigration and Americanization. Appleton used the sanctioned authority of the state as well to spur the drive. "To avoid taxation," he incorporated the PRMA as an educational institution that would promote civic virtue and patriotism.[44]

With the house purchased, the PRMA hired Chandler to begin the restoration. Informed opinion differed on his work and showed that some Yankees questioned just how Revere's memory should be remade (Fig. 2-3). The house's third floor was there in Revere's time, but it was removed. Another architect suggested further that an authentic restoration

FIG. 2-3   Paul Revere House, restored (Photograph by Samuel Chamberlain, in M. A. DeWolfe Howe, *Who Lived Here?* [New York, 1952], 130)

should have returned the building to its ostensibly original one-story height. Chandler and Appleton disagreed, and the former claimed that the house had been unique as "the only example in our cities" of a projecting second story in both its main house and ell. Any restoration that removed the overhang would have robbed Boston of its distinction. What Chandler specifically appreciated as reminders of the Anglo-Saxon past were the overhangs and timbered framing, and he added other medieval features such as casement windows and pendants.[45]

Chandler remade the house to reflect that medieval construction and incorporated almost all new materials. As a result, some commented that the house was "over restored outside and in"; if Revere was alive, he perhaps would not have recognized his own home. The timber-framed building looked especially awkward, said a later SPNEA member, "amidst uncouth surroundings" in that "Babel of nationalities." But such relics or symbols were precisely what Chandler, Appleton, and the PRMA wanted so as to inculcate patriotism, buttress Anglo-Saxonism, and remind the immigrants that Revere's simple life, work ethic, and willingness to Americanize were laudable virtues. So much a part of the civil religion's penchant for relics, it was later reported that "all the old wood taken from the house was preserved, and has since been made into small souvenirs, which are on sale at the house."[46]

Appleton's work with the Revere house revealed one side of the progressive coin. While many demanded immigration restriction, Appleton and Bolton instead lent their energies to the campaigns to Americanize the newcomers and protect Yankee culture. Thereafter, the North End kept their focus. Bolton continued to worry, for example, "how to best stir the immigrants' interest & pride in civic affairs." When those foreigners reverted to their native cultures, he, like many who attributed character to race, called it "a eugenic failure."[47]

Bolton recognized that few adult immigrants openly accepted Anglo-American culture. He knew Russian-born author Mary Antin, the epitome of the good immigrant, but realized that her optimistic story of willing assimilation and strident patriotism was "not typical in the least." All the while, he endorsed the efforts of social workers to discipline and uplift those newcomers. Brahmins often cited the maxim of Oliver Wendell Holmes that it took four or five generations to make a gentleman, and Bolton added that it required at least "two generations [for immigrants] to grow to our standards." Meanwhile, he worked to ensure that "our standards," embodied in this material culture, were preserved. Appleton similarly warned that such ethnic blocks had to be broken up to quicken "the Americanizing processes so very much needed among our new comers."[48]

Both would be involved in the preservation of Old North Church (Christ Church). Built in 1723 and appreciated for its aesthetics, Yankees remembered Old North mostly as a patriotic shrine where a signal—"One if by land, two if by sea"—was relayed to Revere on the night of 18 April 1775. Once a Yankee stronghold, Appleton regretted that it "gradually lost its constituency to suburban churches, while the old homes in the neighborhood were being taken by Jews and Italians." He praised those Yankees who took action to stem its decline. After the church's ownership had been left to eight pewholders, it was transferred to the Episcopal bishop who sold the remaining pews to tradition-minded Yankees and thereby raised funds for its preservation. Bolton served as a senior warden at the church from 1912 to 1936, and wrote a guidebook *Christ Church, 1723* (1913, rev. 1923) for the tourists whose donations provided its wherewithal. The restoration was aided by R. Clipston Sturgis, a well-known Brahmin architect in the BSAC, a denizen of the summer colony at Little Harbor, and owner of much of the trim from the Hancock house. After the remade church was separated from the surrounding hovel, the yard "which was formerly dirty and unsanitary," said Appleton, "is now a charming flower garden with brick walls and shrubbery."[49]

Despite the preservation of Old North and the Revere home, *la via vecchia* of Italy became the norm for the neighborhood. Multi-storied brick tenements crowded the church, and prompted Bolton's eye to focus on the few framed dwellings of earlier vintage. "A fine old wooden house facing the [Parkman] Place has just been sold to two Dagos," he lamented in 1914, and he drew in his notebook its fret, cornice, and shield for posterity. Those Yankees who dared approach were startled "to find Christ Church translated into *Chiesa del Cristo*," but sighed at least when they saw "an American flag flying at one end of the church."[50]

Italians, in turn, deplored the patronizing attitude of Yankees. Enrico

C. Sartorio, an Episcopal clergyman of the North End, realized that they were waging war on his culture and concluded that "the psychological motive which fosters social work in America is the spirit of standardizing." Those Yankees were trying to teach their middle-class values to a people whose proud traditions were so different. He saw the strong family life of Italians disintegrate as Yankee institutions such as the public school not only turned youth against their parents but stressed pecuniary gain and material advancement as the defining qualities of America. Many Italians resisted. Sartorio heard some say after briefly leaving the North End, for instance, "I have been down to America today."[51] Older Italians tried to preserve what Americanizers tried to change. Two preservation movements existed; the question was "Whose culture would be preserved?"

While leading the drive to preserve Revere's home, Appleton orchestrated a campaign to protect the Old State House of Massachusetts (Fig. 2-4). Built in 1712, but forlorn after the 1872 fire, it stood in the way of new office buildings on State Street. It had been scheduled for demolition in 1881, and Bostonians supported its preservation only after Chicagoans embarrassed them by offering to purchase and move the building. Spurred by the formation of the Bostonian Society, the Old State House was partially (and erroneously) restored in 1882, and the counterfeit created controversy thereafter.

FIG. 2-4 Old State House, Boston, c. 1904 (Photograph by Henry Peabody, Courtesy, Society for the Preservation of New England Antiquities)

Patriotic Yankees remembered it best as the backdrop for Revere's engraved print depicting the Boston Massacre. Yet Yankee progressives, more than antiquaries of the 1880s, were determined to find usable memories for the site. In 1887, for example, the MHS and NEHGS protested against a bill passed by the General Court that provided $10,000 for a monument to honor the men killed at the massacre. The MHS saw the paradox. Not only had those earlier victims included an Irishman and African-American, but in 1886 Chicago police had murdered protesting strikers at the Haymarket Massacre. Brahmins realized that any endorsement of the tactics used by Boston workers against an imperial monopoly in 1770 could implicitly sanction the actions of modern workers fighting corporate monopoly. The dress, language, and behavior of those Revolutionary-era martyrs, moreover, violated every standard of proper Victorian conduct. As a result, the MHS declared that the victims of 1770 had not been patriots, but "hoodlums, rioters, and ruffians."[52]

Influenced by the burgeoning civil religion of the progressive era, Appleton and the next generation of Brahmins, however, would deradicalize the building and use it as a monument to liberty and republican government. He turned his attention to the preservation of the Old State House in 1905. The owner, the Boston Transit Commission, already used a ground-floor room in the building as an engineer's office, but proposed using a major part for its subway. As historian for the SR, Appleton chaired an investigative committee. When transit officials proposed building ticket offices and a subway entrance, the SR protested, but sought a compromise whereby what Appleton called their "bad" changes would be redeemed by the creation of a museum in the building for the Bostonian Society. At the same time, however, he told other business groups that the conversion of the building for subway purposes was "a great mistake to be prevented at all costs."[53] The subway, symbolic of the progress that so many Bostonians desired, challenged a symbol of tradition.

The SR acknowledged Appleton's ongoing work on the Revere and Old State houses by elevating him to its vice-presidency. As in the Revere house campaign, Appleton became the workhorse in the drive to save the Old State House, while more prominent Brahmins headed the movement. General Hazard Stevens, a Civil War hero and well-known lawyer, became the front man to open the strategic doors. Preservationists intensified their campaign by accusing the transit company in public meetings before Mayor Fitzgerald of committing "vandalism." They compared the company's plan with Britain's "desecration" of the Old South Meeting House during the Revolution. Appleton told transit officials that "the presence of business" in the building had already revealed their lack of patriotism. His prominence was well noted; he received top billing in some of the newspapers, stood on center stage in meetings with the mayor and governor, and led the troops in the patriotic societies.[54] Governor Guild "strongly condemned" the transit plan. Appleton and Stevens met with the mayor, but after he "shuffled and equivocated" for a month,

Guild threatened to take the issue to the General Court. Fitzgerald relented.[55]

Preservationists turned up the heat on the transit company. On 8 March 1907, Stevens told a legislative committee that transit officials had "prostituted" the building, considerably altered its structure, and mocked its patriotic importance much like "Scipio Africanus, after his destruction of Carthage." After praising Appleton's work in the campaign, he appealed to them "in filial memory of the patriots," as well as "for the sake of young manhood and young womanhood growing up in an age of commercialism." Eben Francis Thompson, president of the Massachusetts Society of the SR, also condemned the "narrow and short-sighted policy" that had placed this building at risk. He urged its preservation because it would shape the "character and intelligence" of Bostonians, as well as "their skill and industry, their public spirit, [and] their just pride in her past."[56]

Women raised a dissenting voice. They had long spearheaded preservation, as in the case of the Old South Meeting House, but the state regent of the Daughters of the American Revolution (DAR) regretted that, as in the recent vote on the Park Street Church, "the august committee agrees with the Apostle Paul when he says, 'Oh, let the women keep silence all.'" Yet she spoke and even proposed that "a stay" be put on the subway's construction. If men were deluded by the cloud of commercialism, she thought, "the women must come to the rescue."[57] What is important to remember about this debate is not simply the split along gender lines but that Appleton and SPNEA would try to ameliorate, not alienate, the ambitions of the business elite.

Appleton continued to meet with Stevens, Guild, and city officials to administer the restoration of the Old State House, supervised again by Chandler. To this day, the first and second floors of the Old State House hold a museum leased to the Bostonian Society, but its street-level basement quarters the subway station. Most Bostonians accepted the compromise. As a later SPNEA member said, the building was "miraculously preserved and perfectly restored within," and amidst the high-rises it "stands as a mute reminder of the penalty prosperity exacts in loss of distinction."[58]

Another thread in Appleton's preservationist fabric was added by his work from 1906 to 1909 on the beautification of Boston, an important element in the city's progressive movement. In 1906 the Boston Society of Architects (BSA) invited proposals for a systematic examination of the city's needed improvements. Together with such organizations as the Chamber of Commerce and the Metropolitan Improvement League (1904), the BSA issued an illustrated pamphlet that touched on everything from traffic to parks to building codes. Much like *Looking Backward*, the BSA wanted to modernize "the Hub."[59] Appleton submitted in 1906 at least three versions of what he called his "metropolitan Back Bay Basin Scheme." What began the process was legislation passed by the state in

1903 authorizing the construction of a dam on the Charles River that would restrict the tides, keep out Boston's sewage, and thus make the Charles more scenic. The dam would also eliminate the mud flats and wharf rats that Beacon Street residents had always tried to ignore.[60]

Appleton's work fit neatly into larger plans instigated by progressives and civic-minded developers who wanted not only to assure the city's economic vitality but order and beautify the metropolis. For example, he found the ideas of Boston landscape architect Arthur Shurtleff "very Interesting." Involved in the same scheme to beautify the Charles, Shurtleff (later Shurcliff) was on his way to establishing a heady reputation. He would redesign Boston Common in 1918 and then construct gardens for Colonial Williamsburg and Sturbridge Village, as well as the Paul Revere Mall in the North End.[61]

The proposals of Boston's architects, together with those of Shurtleff and Appleton, became part of an ambitious program announced in 1909. Led by retailer and director of the Chamber of Commerce Edward A. Filene and lawyer Louis D. Brandeis, the "Boston-1915" movement called on the city's organizations and civic-minded elite to unite their disparate efforts, reorder their work in a more businesslike fashion, and prepare for a grand exposition in 1915 to celebrate a modernized Boston. Patriotism was not enough to improve the city, Filene warned. Echoing a principal tenet of progressivism, he wanted efficiency, order, and business methods to accomplish "the same thing [in Boston] that Hill and Harriman did for their railroad systems." Claiming that the city was trapped by smugness and inertia, "1915" leaders wanted the exposition to rejuvenate the city's economy and society.[62]

The "1915" movement encapsulated Boston progressivism. It captured the city's Puritan conscience when it proposed projects to ease the class conflict between manager and laborer, establish better public schools, and eradicate the slums. "Boston-1915" would showcase the city's efficiency, order, and progress through its strengthened child-labor restrictions, workers' compensation laws, and preventive clinics for the poor, as well as new parks, safe factories, and clean neighborhoods. Observers called it "a man's movement," moreover, and differentiated it from feminine social reform. It called for energetic public men to act forcefully and rebuild the city. It represented Filene's philosophy, as did ultimately SPNEA's membership, that "an ounce of public spirit in each of a thousand men can be made more useful than a pound in each of ten men." Filene wanted his progressivism to become hegemonic. Critics accused him of trying to establish "the Filennium."[63]

"Boston-1915" held a City Exposition in November 1909 at the Old Art Museum to illustrate the type of work that might be accomplished. Several hundred organizations contributed their ideas and proposals, and over 200,000 citizens viewed the display. Appleton exhibited his plans for the Charles River and Brookline parks.[64] "Boston-1915" expanded its leadership in 1910 by establishing study groups to examine the city's pressing issues and ensure "Boston's prosperity, its civic development, and its social regeneration." Nominated as a director of the Conference on Civic Organizations, Appleton joined the likes of pacifist Robert T. Paine and Americanizer D. Chauncey Brown on the committee. He was elected its chairman and became a member of the executive committee of "Boston-1915." Considering the committee "second to none in importance," he addressed issues of "Good Citizenship" relating to everything from parks to immigrants. His group even discussed his proposal to revise the city's electoral system.[65]

The progressivism of "Boston-1915" was keenly illustrated by proposals that received an airing before his committee. Not only was there a push to establish a Bureau of Municipal Research so as to study the city's needs scientifically, but a drive to limit fireworks to ensure a "Saner Fourth" of July celebration. Tradition-minded Americans had long thought that both immigrant and working-class native had turned Independence Day into an unruly frolic. Appleton's committee even heard proposals to restrict billboards on public roads, part of a nascent conservation movement.[66]

Appleton suddenly resigned from "Boston-1915" in November 1910. What partly prompted his resignation was an attempt by the executive committee to politicize his agenda. The movement claimed to be nonpartisan, but its leaders wanted to consolidate city departments and hit Fitzgerald's patronage. Appleton objected because he "never cared a thing about the subject of consolidation."[67] Most surprisingly, he created no place in his committee for preservation; most sentiment actually ran counter to the interest of antiquities. Endless suggestions were made to straighten out old streets, improve building standards (and remove old dwellings), and modernize the town. Indeed the promotional literature called on "progressive" Bostonians to imitate Rio de Janeiro. There a "pest hole" was transformed into "one of the finest cities in the world," partly by creating a broad avenue that required the demolition of over 1,100 homes. Just as conservatives had rebuilt Paris a half-century earlier to instill order among Parisian workers, and quickly crush revolts should they occur, so, too, did many Bostonians fear the old neighborhoods that seemed alien and out of control. A proposal to eliminate all wooden buildings in the North and West Ends subsequently recommended a "moving out process" so that numbers were "rapidly reduced."[68]

"Boston-1915" never succeeded in its goal of holding an exposition; the movement died in the legislature in 1912. It did spur the creation of a Boston planning board and the calling of a state constitutional convention, but it did not boost the cause of preservation. It must have been patently clear to SPNEA's founder that city leaders found antiquities useful only if they enriched their coffers.[69]

Appleton gave his time to groups other than "1915." Carrying on his father's interest, he helped the MHS with its coin collection. He served on the NEHGS council and chaired the Joint Committee on Cooperation in Patriotic Work, an attempt to unify the efforts of various societies in the state. He found that work "very interesting," and confided to the secrecy of his diary that some aspects were "almost exciting."[70] What ultimately shaped SPNEA were not only these contacts and experiences, but his third trip to Europe in 1909. Over a four-month span, he visited such places as the archaeological museum at Florence, the cathedrals of France, and London's public buildings. He was evidently impressed by the restoration work in France. He took note of the "many old timbered houses" in Bourges, called the seventeenth-century chateau of Verneuil "perfectly superb," observed the changes at Carcassonne since his visit in 1896 and found the walled city "glorious," and described the Pont du Sard at Nîmes as "certainly stupendous."[71]

What finally energized him to establish a preservation organization was his work in 1909 for the SR in Concord and Lexington. Traditionalists often commemorated Patriot's Day there because the landscape had the mythical ambience of a New England village. Appleton particularly kept a watchful eye on Lexington's "property of revolutionary value." When the Old Belfry blew down in a winter storm, he wanted it reerected on the site "it occupied on the day of the fight." With a concern bordering on the religious, he demanded that "every particle of the genuine old belfry still in existence should be preserved" and protected from "vandals and relic hunters." Appleton worried most about the apparently insensitive refurbishment of the obscure Jonathan Harrington house (Fig. 2-5). He brought in Chandler and Colonial Dames leader Edith Wendell to survey the damage.[72]

Believing that the Harrington house "should be saved as it is," and not refitted for modern comforts, Appleton claimed that the house symbolized the battle of April 19 in which Harrington, a Minuteman, received a mortal wound and died in his wife's arms. As "one of the most inspiring [episodes] in the history" of the Revolution, he wrote, "the existence of the unaltered Harrington House has been the strongest reminder of the owner's heroism, sacrifice, and devotion to duty." While the house was being remodeled, he warned that "the material alterations which the house is at this moment undergoing cannot fail to lessen the fact provided by a visit to the battle field, and the loss will be permanent in that no reconstruction is likely ever to give us back what we are losing."[73] Just as Norton had worried about the devaluation of symbols, so, too, did Appleton fear that a renovation would sully its ability to foster patriotism and community service.

The case of Harrington and his home offers some insight into the connections between the civil religion, preservation, and the remaking of memory. Before Appleton's time, much had been written about the battle at which Harrington died, but the reasons for his resistance to those British troops went unrecorded. Shortly after his death, his family disap-

FIG. 2-5 Jonathan Harrington House, Lexington, Mass. (Photograph by The Halliday Historic Photograph Co., Courtesy, Society for the Preservation of New England Antiquities)

peared from the record. Such a tale, and the equally important gaps in the documents, lent themselves to later myth-makers. Part of that revision can be seen in the changing iconographical picture of the battle. The skirmish was first pictured in 1775 as an insignificant encounter in which the chaotic, and apparently reluctant, colonials were bested by British troops. Over the years the battle's depiction slowly shifted to the point where a mural commissioned in 1886 for the Lexington town hall showed the courageous patriots resisting the enemy in an ordered unwavering fashion.[74]

Along those same lines, zealous patriots later elevated Harrington from anonymity to icon when they appropriated his legacy, honored his sacrifice, and remade the Minutemen as defenders of their notions of liberty, property, and nation, or what the American Legion would call 100-percent Americanism. The story was enhanced by the fact that another Jonathan Harrington, who had also fought that day in Lexington and lived until 1854, carried his namesake to historical fame because the two were often confused. As the last survivor of the Minutemen, the nonagenarian became a powerful, but not too lively, prop at mid-nineteenth-century patriotic exercises.[75]

Appleton's work in behalf of the Harrington house went hand-in-hand with his opposition to a syndicate that tried to acquire land opposite the battlefield and demolish Buckman Tavern (c. 1690), where the Minutemen first gathered. He demanded its preservation "as a most interesting memorial of a thrilling incident in American history." In an era when the federal government had little concern for historic sites, he called it "a mecca of such importance" that the grounds should be preserved as "the Lexington National Memorial." A local historical society eventually acquired it, and enclosed it in a spacious three-acre park. Those threats finally encouraged the state to pass a constitutional amendment protecting historic landmarks in 1918. Years later, the federal government did create the national park. Appleton's work, as a result, was part of a long-term process of making the myth universal and slowly transforming Harrington's house from obscure to sacred.[76]

Obviously angered by the renovation of the Harrington house, Appleton knew that "what has happened here is all to be repeated elsewhere, and the sums required to prevent it, and the short time sometimes needed to raise them, make it evident how much we need a strong centralized organization." As he told a national officer of the DAR, "the very material alteration" of this house thus "precipitated the formation" of SPNEA. He acknowledged that the women's patriotic and ancestral societies, which accounted for most of the nation's preservation work, had limited abilities and interests in large-scale historic preservation. Breaking loose from that feminine pattern, he called SPNEA "a new departure in historic, patriotic work." He met with Bolton in December 1909 about creating an organization that could quickly and single-mindedly protect such sites.[77] Soon after, he founded SPNEA. It synthesized his Brahmin upbringing, his training at Harvard, and his work in real estate, "Boston-1915," and the patriotic societies. The work of SPNEA would subsequently revolve around the continuous loop shaped by progressivism and the Colonial Revival, as well as immigration, politics, and economic development.

3

"Preservation Must Depend on Private Initiative"

The Founding of the Society for the Preservation of New England Antiquities

When Appleton founded SPNEA in 1910, it was unlike any other preservation enterprise in the United States. Showing the imprint of progressivism, it assumed the task specifically of protecting endangered buildings and declared a commitment to scientific method, expert management, and the market economy. Organized as a regional movement from its corporate base, it also neatly interlocked with existing institutions. Appleton knew that historic preservation faced formidable obstacles. Many Yankees who possessed credentials that matched his own speculated on land and economic development. Lower-class residents, on the other hand, usually occupied the more ancient structures that had been abandoned by gentrifying Yankees. When Appleton formed SPNEA and enlisted his allies, he appealed not to these occupants, but to the upper classes with whom he had always associated. As was the case with the preservation movement in Virginia, this elite defined its interests as those of the region. With the sanction of the state, the commitment of progressivism, the independence of private initiative, and the blessings of wealth and education, they had the authority to define what was important in the past and, implicitly, in the future.

Appleton acknowledged that earlier preservation efforts had a very mixed record in New England, but he spotlighted the failures. "America's classic example of regretted destruction," he wrote, "must for all time be the house built in 1737 by Thomas Hancock on Beacon Hill" (Fig. 3-1). John Hancock had wanted the house to be given to the state, as did later owners who offered it below market value. That plan failed, and the land was sold for delinquent taxes. The new owners offered it to the city if it was moved from its valuable Beacon Street location, but the city declined. Appleton's uncle Greeley "came within an ace of securing the place for his home," but "was discouraged by the cost." One of the nation's masterpieces then fell to the wreckers. Oddly enough, Massachusetts savored its memory, and Appleton saw a replica at the Columbian Exposition.

FIG. 3-1 John Hancock House, Boston, before 1863 (Photograph by G. H. Drew, Courtesy, Society for the Preservation of New England Antiquities)

"When the citizen of Dakota or of Washington shall innocently ask what has become of the original," Drake worried, "that State pride, of which we possess our full share, must and will be heavily discounted."[1]

Hoping to rally traditionalists to his cause, Appleton devoted the cover of SPNEA's first *Bulletin* to the Hancock house and called its destruction "a classic in the annals of vandalism." The incident so aroused his emotion that a reporter mistakenly assumed that the yet-unborn preservationist had witnessed its demise. Tradition-minded Yankees prized its symbolism. It "taught history," said Drake. "It awakened patriotic aspirations; it stimulated honest endeavor. . . . Indeed, it was a charming old house—such a one as one's fancy delights to run riot in, and one's actual body aches to get into." Appleton derided those earlier Yankees who had been "wholly lacking" in their "appreciation of old buildings."[2] New Englanders did save some sites randomly linked to the Revolution, local pride, or an ancestor, but such patriotism, folklore, and filiopietism could not abate the destruction.

Even some tradition-minded Yankees accepted the fate of the wrecking ball for all but the most famous buildings. Drake, for one, saw change as inevitable. "In the very nature of things," he sighed, "nothing is, nothing can be permanent save the written record. Like every great city Boston is forever out-growing its old garments, and must be patched and pieced accordingly."[3] Since New England's businessmen had been cast as architects of progress, their self-aggrandizing designs forced his acquiesence.

SPNEA's founder did not know it, but the time was right for historic preservation in 1910. The recent drives associated with the Old State House, Park Street Church, and Revere home had raised the issue and created a cadre of activists and funders. The convergence of other factors, not the least of which was the Colonial Revival with its heady blend of nativism, antimodernism, and elitism, made the progressive era the opportune time for organized effort. Fixed in the Colonial Revival, animated by progressivism, and shaped to the methodological lines of an emerging professionalism, the modern preservation movement was set in motion.

Yet SPNEA occupied unique ground because Appleton's focus on architectural antiquities was so different from that of other conservation and preservation groups. In Massachusetts, for example, the Trustees of Public Reservations had been incorporated in 1891 as a public, tax-exempt body to publicize the necessity of protecting the state's scenic lands. Led by Charles Eliot, son of Harvard's president and apprentice of Frederick Law Olmsted, the conservation group pressed the legislature in 1892 to create the Metropolitan Parks Commission, America's first metropolitan park system, and one that Appleton would urge many years later to take on the role of preservation. It influenced the formation in 1895 of a similarly named group in New York, soon after called the American Scenic Historic Preservation Society (ASHPS). As stipulated by its charter, the ASHPS "endeavor[ed] to prevent the mutilation, destruction or dispersion of American antiquities." The ASHPS largely defined what was important by its use, however, rather than by Appleton's measures of antiquity and aesthetics. Like the Trustees, the ASHPS mostly protected the natural, instead of architectural, landscape.[4]

Appleton also joined the APVA when it was preserving Jamestown in preparation for the tercentennial celebration in 1907 of Virginia's founding. His first APVA *Yearbook* revealed what he considered a baffling range of tasks, and how SPNEA would soon differ. Characteristic of women's personalism and domesticity, and a consequent interest in a sentimental and patriotic history that would nurture upcoming generations, Virginians reported, for example, that they reinterred "the dust of five infant children" of Martha Custis (whose namesake would later wed Washington), placed granite memorials at several long vacant historic sites, and acquired the Rising Sun Tavern in Fredericksburg. The protection of extant architecture, on the other hand, would be the primary concern of SPNEA. Appleton would also diverge from the APVA's romantic and subjective restoration work. At first, however, he did similarly name his group the Association for the Preservation of New England Antiquities. He admitted later that his eventual choice of such an equally long-winded name had been "a great mistake." It was difficult to compress and many regarded its abbreviation as a "Chinese puzzle."[5]

SPNEA's brand of historic preservation was distinct also from the Society for the Protection of Ancient Buildings (SPAB, 1877). Shortly after he founded SPNEA, Appleton told his members that "there can be no doubt that the spirit of the work of the two societies is almost identical." In fact, there was a world of difference between SPNEA and England's SPAB, and it must be spelled out to show how the American pattern of preservation became so different.[6]

Steeped in the antiindustrialism of Ruskin and the arts-and-crafts philosophy of Morris, SPAB extolled the work of medieval craftsmen, decried the rape of industrialism, and demanded a loyalty to old forms. Like so many antimodernists who would influence SPNEA and try to reinterpret progress, Morris held that the degredation of Western society had begun during the Renaissance. Enamored of the medieval world that was displaced by the Renaissance and finally crushed by the Industrial Revolution, Morris hoped to replant its seed through historic preservation and the arts-and-crafts movement, which became "the chief joy of so many of our lives." Morris deplored the Victorian building boom that wreaked havoc on this heritage; he turned to socialism to protect both workers and artifacts.[7]

Warning modern capitalists, Morris declared in 1889 before SPAB's annual meeting that the old buildings of England "are not in any sense our property, to do as we like with. We are only trustees for those who come after us." He formed his "Anti-Scrape Society" precisely to protect "priceless" relics, such as England's medieval cathedrals, that were being destroyed in the name of restoration.[8] Yet his devotion to the Middle Ages did not deter him from pleading that England also preserve the great Renaissance architecture of Sir Christopher Wren. SPNEA differed from SPAB, therefore, not only in its attitudes toward capitalism but, as will be shown in Chapter 7, in its definition of preservation. Despite the claims of New England preservationists that they acted in the tradition of SPAB, SPNEA would have few ties to its English counterpart and worked more in the vein of Ruskin's apolitical aestheticism.

The preservation movement in Britain was also developing newer focuses. Partly inspired by the organization of the Trustees of Public Reservations, the National Trust for Places of Historic Interest or Natural Beauty was incorporated as a public company in 1895. Empowered by Parliament in 1907 to receive sites by gift or purchase, it pledged to maintain those historic grounds, many of which held old buildings, and to stay any compromising development. It worked "in close and happy accord" with SPAB, which remained active as more of a preservation society committed to medieval life, craftsmanship, and architecture. SPAB boasted, however, that it was "the only society in England which is interested in the protection of ancient buildings as ancient buildings." Appleton later claimed to have set SPNEA "in the footsteps of the English National Trust," but he narrowed his focus to buildings and aesthetics, just as the BSAC had diverged from Morris's focus on the producer to that of the consumer.[9]

Appleton could have heeded the advice of Charles R. Ashbee, an English preservationist, socialist, and advocate of the arts-and-crafts movement, who toured the United States in 1896, 1900, and 1908. This disciple of Ruskin and Morris hoped to spur the cause of preservation by forming an American National Trust, but found, as in his trip of 1900, a caliber of work not to his liking. Preservationists in Virginia were busy erecting memorials, a process that produced "barren" results. When Ashbee visited Boston, he received the help of Norton, Wendell, and Appleton's cousin Alice Longfellow. He spoke before such groups as the Colonial Dames and the BSAC, but came away regretting that Boston's "sense of self-satisfaction" led to a lethargy harmful to preservation work. He urged preservationists not simply to save historic sites but to protect trees, help settlement workers, promote the arts and crafts, and support legislation to restrict building heights and overcrowding. He wanted a broad-based program, not one that simply focused on old buildings.[10]

So different from the movement that did emerge in the United States, Ashbee criticized the evils of capitalism, the degradation of factories, and the anomie of cities. Like Morris, he recognized that the upheaval that so disordered the world was not in France in 1789, so hated by tradition-minded Americans, but the ongoing revolution in industry. But, as he realized, Boston's (and America's) conservatism and its mania for economic growth hindered his ambitious agenda. Yet it was not simply Brahminism, the boosterism of Boston, or, for that matter, the affinity between progressivism and capitalism that kept Appleton from Ashbee's notion of preservation. Progressivism and the elite organizations built during that era, such as SPNEA, also commonly stressed a specialization of tasks, not Ashbee's broad-focused approach. Within progressivism, such trans-Atlantic communication did reinforce reform programs, but in the case of preservation there was limited cross-fertilization. Although Appleton did talk "eagerly about European concepts of preservation," he learned eclectically from their work.[11]

Appleton insisted that private groups take the initiative in U.S. historic preservation, even though Boston had taken the lead in the nation by creating effective governmental organizations to develop metropolitan services for water, transit, and parks. This emphasis on private action also differed from the French model, where the government preserved much of the land's medieval heritage. Appleton's idea reflected not only the Brahmin custom of dispensing philanthropy through institutions they had created and could control but, more basically, his belief that governments (particularly ones dominated by immigrants) could not be trusted with a subject as sensitive and vital to the Brahmin's identity as history. If the populace was ignorant, the politicians corrupt, and the public's money misused, as Appleton believed, governments would be able to rewrite the record and strip the Yankees of their primacy. He was only too familiar with Fitzgerald's partisan use of history and knew that if preservation was in the hands of professionals, the public could be kept at arm's length. Professionalism thus represented not simply an avenue of meritocratic entry into the ruling class but also a means to separate this interest from the public, whether they be unwashed immigrant, unlettered Yankee, or unconcerned Brahmin.[12]

Only through private associations could the right Yankees protect their past. Writing in *Art and Archaeology*, Appleton claimed in 1919:

> Action by the nation or the states is in America peculiarly difficult of achievement and for some reasons not to be desired. That part of the public capable of appreciating a handsome building for the sake of its artistic merit, is small indeed, and the chance of obtaining support from the public treasury is too negligible to notice. . . . On the other hand, even if these were not the case, our political system with its almost total lack of responsibility, as well as widespread tendency to the spoils system, makes public action extremely dangerous. There can be no doubt but that for many years, at least, efficient action looking to the preservation of our best architecture must depend for its support on private initiative.[13]

Unlike New England's patriotic, ancestral, and historical societies, SPNEA's "exclusive object" would be the preservation of architectural antiquities. Specially formed preservation societies, such as the PRMA, generally acted too slowly, while family societies had even more limited interests, though the Fairbanks Family Association had splendidly preserved its ancestral home (c. 1636) in Dedham. Likewise, historical societies limited their acquisitions to one, or occasionally two, very select properties. Appleton thought, for example, that the seventeenth-century Roger Mowry house in Rhode Island should have been protected by a local group simply because it stood in "the days of Roger Williams." Yet Providence's local societies were quite typical, claiming that their purses had limits and their arms were full. As a result, the destruction of the Mowry house in 1900 "aroused but little notice."[14]

SPNEA tried to fill that void. It promised to take "aggressive action" and "act instantly wherever needed to lead in the preservation of noteworthy buildings and historic sites." It took as a special charge the houses of the earliest era, the medieval period in New England. Not only were these once prevalent buildings now an "utmost rarity," but historical societies looked askance at their primitive conditions. Such dwellings did not fit either the Colonial Revival's designs or the prevailing, mythical picture of colonial homes. Whatever the case, preservationists faced great odds. "Out of one hundred of the most worthwhile buildings still in private hands in New England," Appleton predicted,

> I suppose it would be safe to say that about a third would be wholly destroyed, a third altered beyond recognition and stripped of their attractive finish, and a third bought for preservation and after a fashion preserved by historical societies, family associations or special societies formed for the

purpose. The net result will probably be the loss within fifty years or so of two-thirds of any list of buildings that could be prepared.[15]

Unlike the case of the APVA where a handful of strong-willed women launched the organization, Appleton single-handedly provided the impetus for SPNEA's creation. He sounded out his ideas with Bolton, and soon asked him to serve as the society's president. The Athenaeum's librarian admitted he was "skeptical" of the project; others said it was "impracticable," as did the director of the Bostonian Society. In the long run, Appleton's "earnestness and his common sense" won Bolton's assent. Besides writing the charter, Appleton persuaded seventeen friends to contribute ten dollars and act as incorporators. All the while, he went on his daily business with the SR and "Boston-1915."[16]

Accompanied by a handful of supporters, he appeared before, and alone spoke to, a committee of the state legislature in February and March 1910 for the society's incorporation. As with the PRMA, Appleton added clauses that ensured SPNEA's tax exemption. Problems did arise. Just as Fitzgerald equated the Appletons with "the lords of the loom" who had exploited Irish labor, so, too, did others question the family name. Appleton knew that "there were those in the Legislature . . . who feared that we were not a real bona fide organization." Yankee traditionalists mustered their strength, however, and secured a quick approval.[17]

Appleton rented office space on Beacon Hill to serve as his headquarters (Fig. 3-2). For two years he built SPNEA in a single room that he shared with the Metropolitan Improvement League, a private organization that advanced the City Beautiful and "1915" movements.[18] In 1913 he moved to two rooms in the NEHGS building. At the time, he served on its Governing Council with Bolton as its treasurer. While they recruited friends from the genealogical society, Bolton did so at the Athenaeum.

Fig. 3-2   First office of SPNEA, 20 Beacon Street, Boston (Courtesy, Society for the Preservation of New England Antiquities)

An offshoot of Brahmin institutions, SPNEA slowly developed its own identity.

Appleton split his time between editing the *Bulletin*, recruiting new members, soliciting funds, running an office, and promoting preservation. As in the PRMA, he took what appeared to be a low-key position, Corresponding Secretary, but he actually shaped and led SPNEA. Some early newspaper accounts mistook his office as insignificant, and instead spotlighted Bolton as president. All of Appleton's cohorts nonetheless recognized him as the driving force. A lifetime bachelor once afflicted by neurasthenia, he immersed himself in what he later described to his Harvard fiftieth class reunion as "a congenial occupation . . . doing good for others." As one of his sisters politely explained, Sumner "was often lonely, but lost himself completely in his work." In the Brahmin tradition of service and philanthropy, he proudly told his Harvard classmates that he refused any salary in all his years with SPNEA. Moreover, he paid out of his own pocket "for all sorts of incidentals" to ensure that SPNEA became "a growing concern." Appleton's "incidentals" provided SPNEA with its lifeblood at times—contributing financially, purchasing library materials and museum curios, and even covering the annual deficit for most of the society's first decade.[19]

All the while, he maintained SPNEA's links with patriotic organizations. In the same breath that he formed a preservation society, he celebrated Patriot's Day by accompanying the SR on its ritualistic pilgrimage to the Old South Meeting House, and then marching to Revere's home, the Bunker Hill Monument, and John Harvard's grave. Those public acts were declarations of fealty to the ancients and spurs to newer residents to conform to sanctioned authority. Until 1913 Appleton served, moreover, as the chairman of the Committee on Cooperation in Patriotic Work and, like Bolton, also served as a director of the Bunker Hill Monument Association.[20]

Because of his weak voice and modesty, Appleton preferred to work in a retiring manner, but continually relied on his officers, trustees, and incorporators for assistance and advice. As a result, he chose Charles Knowles Bolton (1867–1950) as SPNEA's president (Fig. 3-3). Born in Cleveland, Bolton inherited an appreciation for the literary arts from his parents, both of whom were descendants of colonial New Englanders, mugwump reformers, and world travellers who published many books. At Harvard he wrote his thesis in History, studied Fine Arts under Norton, and reportedly received his B.A. cum laude, notwithstanding over a dozen C's and D's on his transcript. Before his graduation in 1890, he personally asked his parent's next-door neighbor from Cleveland, John D. Rockefeller, for a position as a private secretary. Rockefeller admired the Bolton family. He called Sarah Bolton "a philosopher and a Christian and a very good woman besides" and invited her family to use freely his Forest Hills estate. The younger Bolton respected him and deplored Ida

FIG. 3-3   Charles Knowles Bolton, 1918 (Charcoal drawing by John Singer Sargent, Courtesy, Boston Athenaeum)

Tarbell's muckraking account of his Standard Oil Company because it showed a "frenzy of hatred."[21]

Instead of working as a corporate secretary for a robber baron, Bolton became a librarian at Harvard and then in Brookline. Pulled by the currents of his era and family, he began to write history to educate the reading public. Knowing that New England's ethnicity was dramatically changing, he exhorted local communities such as Brookline to focus more attention on the Americanization of immigrants in their public schools. Writing in *The New England Magazine*, he suggested that historical societies show a "progressive spirit" by encouraging students to investigate local history, discuss their findings, and publish their class essays. Giving the example of an Irish-American boy whose project was to explore his town's role in the Revolution, Bolton discovered that such work produced "a healthier and happy community." It could "bind together an increasing number of people, through appealing to their local and social interests."[22]

From 1898 to 1933, Bolton settled in at Boston's Athenaeum, which Henry James called the "honored haunt of all the most civilized" in Boston's past. Unlike Appleton, whose social place was assured, Bolton courted power. His diary drops the names of those presidents and plutocrats with whom he attended a dinner, reception, or meeting. As the Athenaeum's director, he rubbed shoulders with the area's most distinguished gentlemen, writers, and historians. There he learned a fashionable skepticism toward history that was overly filiopietistic.[23]

Bolton used the library to write his own works. *The Private Soldier Under Washington* (1902) took an unflattering look at the motley and coarse Continental Army and the miserable conditions under which it fought the war. On the other hand, his *Scotch Irish Pioneers in Ulster and America* (1910) revealed an admiration for his ancestors. While many gentlemen feared that their own sense of manliness had been compromised by overrefinement, he praised those pioneers as "virile, earnest, and ambitious." With a strength of character and personal resolve, "utility was their law."[24]

Years later, *The Real Founders of New England* (1929) examined the hard drinkers and unscrupulous lot who preceded the Pilgrim and Puritan settlers. Bolton admired them as "men of courage in an age of adventure," but his work evidently ruffled the feathers of some Brahmins. Morison, for one, urged his friend James Truslow Adams in Gotham to review the book in 1929. Calling it "pretentious" and "silly" because it pictured this rough bunch as the founders, Morison said that "the book deserves to be slashed thoroughly, and of course you can do it better than any of us here who have to live with Bolton and see him every few days" at the Athenaeum. Adams obliged his friend in *The New England Quarterly*. Despite Morison's rebuke, Bolton's books left the clear impression that though such masses founded and defended the nation, they did not civilize it. His *Christ Church, 1723* (1913, rev. 1923), on the other hand, focused on the elite's civilizing role in politics and culture.[25]

Although he was institutionally well placed at the historical societies and fine arts museum, Bolton was not a rich Brahmin. He did own a house in Brookline and a ninety-six-acre home in Shirley, but in 1919 he still coaxed SPNEA into electing him an honorary life member by saying that he "had a gun for any who voted 'no.'" He told Appleton: "You will remember that I pretended . . . that I was so wealthy that I did not need to be free from the payment of dues, but the fact is that I am becoming so poorer that I actually shy at a tax blank." While Appleton lunched at the Union Club, Bolton offered instead to take him to an old Boston institution known for its inexpensive, informal setting, Huyler's cafeteria, "the scene of my wildest type of exploit." The Depression prompted him to retire from SPNEA in 1932 and the Athenaeum in the following year, but he still volunteered for the Works Progress Administration in 1935–36, supervising its survey of early American portraits in New York and New England.[26]

Appreciative of books and paintings, Bolton knew little about architecture other than that which Norton offered in Fine Arts 4. His interests lay mostly in history and the decorative arts. His *Christ Church, 1723*, for example, largely ignored design and craftsmanship, and seemed radically different from Appleton's preoccupation with the intricate medievalisms of colonial construction. SPNEA's president, however, learned on the job, as Appleton and others showed him the built landscape.

Because Appleton's role in SPNEA was so certain, it took some time for Bolton to exert his presidential presence. After one meeting, for example, he scribbled in his diary that "Appleton tried to cast dignity over me when speaking of Preservation Society affairs by calling me 'Mr. President,' but the dignity rolled off I fear."[27] Besides raising money and hobnobbing with literati, which he did very well, Bolton acted as Appleton's confidant and adviser. Like a Brahmin youth who required a trustee, Appleton's ambitions occasionally needed Bolton's restraining hand.

Appleton cast Boston as the hub of SPNEA's work. Juxtaposed with the APVA, which he thought had failed to balance the competing forces of centralism and localism, Appleton and Bolton pulled SPNEA's strings from the start. Mindful of New England's local organizations and traditions, Appleton selected his society's incorporators with much deliberation. Recognizing the customary role of women in the movement, he won the support of Edith Wendell (President, Massachusetts Society of the Colonial Dames), Adeline F. Fitz (Massachusetts regent and President General, National Society, DAR), Ida Louise Farr Miller (Founder, Faneuil Hall Chapter, DAR), and Alice M. Longfellow (Massachusetts regent, Mount Vernon Ladies' Association). His cousin Alice had a knack for philanthropy as well, having paid an architect in 1881 to restore and furnish Washington's library at Mount Vernon. At the same time, SPNEA tapped the select societies of gentlemen. In 1910 Waldo Lincoln served as president of the AAS, Worthington C. Ford as research director at the MHS, and Bolton, Julius H. Tuttle, and Ernest L. Gay respectively as librarians at the Athenaeum, the MHS, and University Club. Presidents of local preservation or historical societies joined the ranks of these incorporators. Perhaps William Crowninshield Endicott illustrated the institutional ties that SPNEA incorporators had or would have in the upcoming years. Besides working as SPNEA's treasurer from its earliest days, and as its president from 1932 until his death, he held the presidency of the MHS and the Essex Institute, and the vice-presidency of the Peabody Museum and the Isabella Stewart Gardner Museum.[28] SPNEA evidently anchored itself on a reef of supporting institutions.

Appleton and Bolton then chose a Board of Trustees and two vice-presidents for each New England state. Men and women of real influence, these officers held considerable social prominence, financial power, and public esteem in their communities. Appleton created a predicament for himself, however. Although he mostly set the agenda and regimen of preservation, he wanted these officers to take more responsibilities upon themselves. He admitted to Bolton in 1917 that "there is a need of finding a few people to help me shoulder burdens which are a little more onerous than I care to assume myself." The Board of Trustees had recognized preservation as Appleton's passion and usually took the position of "cheerfully voting, as it did at the last meeting, 'to leave the whole question to Mr. Appleton with full power.'"[29]

Less frequently, the trustees rejected or challenged a major element in Appleton's agenda, but there were enough cases to restrain him, as in the aborted acquisition of the John Bradford house or his piecemeal establishment of a folk arts museum. Generally, however, the trustees climbed aboard his bandwagon or absented themselves from deliberations.[30] In many ways, Appleton's corporate structure seemed typical for progressive-era organizations, whereby trustees set policy, but gave professionals some latitude to implement it. At the same time, SPNEA was old-fashioned in that Appleton's financial and managerial presence was so important that he could awe the trustees. He definitely wanted SPNEA run his way. He developed policies, which he recommended to other preservationists, whereby "unsatisfactory" trustees could be quietly removed and "absurdly low" quorums set, so that he and his coworkers could carry on their business.[31]

Appleton's criteria for selecting trustees and vice-presidents created the "leave it to Appleton" syndrome. More often than not, commitment to tradition came before experience in preservation. He looked for such credentials as social position, established wealth, propensity for philanthropy, connections to kindred societies, and a willingness to advertise the society. Sometimes he chose lawyers who specialized in handling trusts and real estate because they could offer practical advice. Many were financially well off. Connecticut vice-president Samuel P. Avery listed his profession as philanthropist, and the art collector and dealer did contribute generously to New York's museums. In fact, he helped William H. Vanderbilt and other Gotham millionaires form their private art collections. In one quick stroke Avery gave $10,000 to SPNEA during the world war, and "really put the Society on its feet." Only then did Appleton realize that he was "an excessively wealthy man." Discovering that he had founded the Avery Architectural School at Columbia University, Appleton thought that "there is no telling what he might do for our Society if we made him Vice-President." Although Avery was an invalid, he was elected.[32]

Morgan G. Bulkeley accepted the vice-presidency for Connecticut as well. Millionaire and former governor and U.S. Senator, Bulkeley had led the drive to preserve Connecticut's Bulfinch-designed capitol. Still another Connecticut vice-president, Morgan B. Brainard was "a gentleman of considerable property" who held the president's chair at Aetna Insurance. Bank presidents William B. C. Stickney and Henry Wood Erving held respectively the vice-presidencies for Vermont and Connecticut. Other officers or trustees included manufacturers, utility company executives, and brokers. Architect William T. Aldrich served willingly as a trustee. Grandson of an indolent mill hand, his father Nelson had turned his U.S. Senate seat into a multi-million dollar bank account, but still felt insecure about his social position. William felt grateful and readily lent his hand.[33]

Henry Ford even accepted a vice-presidency for Michigan in 1924, but his philanthropy never panned out. Apparently preservationists in both Williamsburg and Boston rubbed him the wrong way. In Virginia Rev. W. A. R. Goodwin told him that his flivver was to blame for the town's modern clutter and loss of quietude. Goodwin asked for his millions to restore Williamsburg, but received a cold reply. So, too, did SPNEA seek his money, but in the same breath openly asked its members to replace the society's Ford automobile with "a car of larger size and higher power." Instead of contributing his largess to Williamsburg or Boston, he spent it creating his fanciful Greenfield Village in Michigan.[34]

More than a handful of officers and trustees had political clout. Some had served in the Massachusetts legislature. Robert Ives Goddard, one of the wealthiest men in Rhode Island, had served in its state senate on the Good Government ticket. William Endicott's father had been Secretary of War, Heloise Meyer's brother an ambassador, and Waldo Lincoln's grandfather Attorney General in Jefferson's cabinet. Morgan Bulkeley set the model of service as governor of Connecticut. During his second term the legislature had refused to pass an appropriations bill and Bulkeley borrowed $300,000 on his own name to keep the government running. A direct descendant of the first minister of Concord, Massachusetts, he often tapped into and tried to preserve his Puritan traditions.

Appleton also selected his officers for their work in kindred societies. Edward J. Holmes served as director of Boston's Museum of Fine Arts, while Joseph G. Minot directed the Bostonian Society. Before his stint as SPNEA trustee, Worthington C. Ford had established a national reputation at the Library of Congress for his editions of the writings of Washington and the journals of the Continental Congress. SPNEA at times had interlocking directorates with the MHS and AAS, as well as the patriotic and genealogical societies. Appleton apparently tried to gender balance his trusteeships, but some women were appointed to get SPNEA within reach of their busy husbands. Other women did stand out for their own influence.

Clara Endicott Sears established in 1914 a museum at "Fruitlands," the site in Harvard, Massachusetts, where Bronson Alcott had founded a Transcendentalist commune in 1843. Sears's genealogical lines, like most of SPNEA's trustees and officers, descended from Puritan roots, in her case to John Endicott and John Winthrop, the first governors of Massachusetts. Described by her biographer as "unabashedly class conscious," she believed that "social bounds were not to be crossed" and took pride in her SPNEA trusteeship. Like so many, her apparent case of neurasthenia or extreme depression was cured by immersing herself in museums and preservation. As she absorbed Fruitlands' history, she took on the Transcendentalist's creative blend of nature, mysticism, and tradition. Inspired by both Fruitlands and a nearby Shaker village, she praised their sense of community and craftsmanship and believed that their union of body, nature, and spirit could be rekindled. She still felt the ideals of Emerson, Thoreau, and other Transcendentalists who had shared Alcott's table. "In this material age," she warned, "we cannot afford to lose any details of so unique and picturesque a memory." She resultantly devoted her life to farming, forestry, and historical studies.[35]

Sears's work revealed another pattern in Appleton's selection of officers. He chose women and men known for their expertise in arts and crafts. Three SPNEA vice-presidents (Avery, Erving, and George M. Curtis) and one trustee (Hollis French) had helped form the Walpole Society, an elite gentlemen's club of collectors of early Americana that similarly had been established in Boston in 1910.[36] Many SPNEA officers collected silver, furniture, porcelain, or books and manuscripts. Architect Lawrence Park, like Avery, was an expert in art, and the Cleveland Museum of Art appointed him a nonresident curator of colonial art. A few particularly lent their energies to public art education. Elizabeth Ward Perkins established children's art programs, while Simmons College president Henry Lefavour prepared his women students for teaching aesthetics.

The case of George Dudley Seymour (1859–1945) bears mention because it brings these themes together, and in particular the interconnections between historic preservation, progressive reform, and the civil religion. A prosperous patent lawyer from New Haven, a skilled collector of early American furnishings, and a true believer in Yankee ideals, Seymour boasted that his credentials also included the vice-presidency for SPNEA in Connecticut. He personally oversaw much of the work at the Thomas Lee house for SPNEA, but complained to his fellow bachelor Appleton that he was not a member of the "leisure class" like SPNEA's leader and could not commit endless hours to the task. He thereafter devoted his time to three passions: city planning, antiques, and the memorialization of Nathan Hale. He led city planning efforts in Hartford from 1913–24, and incorporated the past into those plans. With much fanfare, he asked the city to protect its elm trees, preserve historic churches on its green, and create parks and memorials to honor the state's heroes.[37]

Along those same lines, Seymour acquired an unaltered, but "a great deal abused," eighteenth-century farmhouse in South Coventry, Connecticut, in 1914. Erroneously calling it, "the birthplace of the patriot" Nathan Hale, he hired J. Frederick Kelly, who would later become a consulting architect to SPNEA, to restore the ten-room house. At a time when progressives were remaking historical figures to inspire children,

Seymour cast Hale as "the Nation's youthful hero and supreme symbol of patriotism, next to the flag." He preserved the home of the man who had been hung by the neck in 1776 as a memorial to "the martyr Spy of the Revolutionary War." Seymour's lifelong friend William Howard Taft visited the Hale Homestead and concluded that it was "well worth the devotion of a lifetime." The house later became a public museum.[38]

Seymour's zealotry became evident in other projects to honor Hale. After the federal government proposed relinquishing control of Fort Hale in New Haven, for example, he resisted its purchase by a syndicate that wanted to build an amusement park, as did earlier preservationists at Jamestown and Mount Vernon. He instead went to Congress, enlisted Chief Justice Taft to testify at hearings in its behalf, and eventually persuaded the government to create a memorial to Hale. He successfully pressed it as well to issue a postage stamp in Hale's memory in 1925. Almost three billion of those one-and-a-half-cent stamps were issued. In so many ways, Seymour's passion became a daily ritual for the public.[39]

Many SPNEA officers similarly preserved their own ancestral records and country homes as a statement of loyalty to the ancients. Bolton, for one, admitted that he longed to move back to Shirley, Massachusetts, "the town of my revolutionary ancestors." In the vein of Norton's lament, he looked forward to "replanting the old stock" at Bolton Farm because "we have wandered every generation and it is well that we return." Appleton likewise would purchase the homestead built by his great grandfather in 1756 in New Ipswich. Some even wrote their family histories. So unlike his grandfather and father, Appleton confessed, however, that he "hate[d] the genealogical end of antiquarian studies."[40]

A handful of trustees and officers were practicing architects who cemented SPNEA's ties to such organizations as the BSA. William S. Richardson was a member of McKim, Mead, and White, the firm most associated with the rediscovery of colonial forms in the late nineteenth century. Herbert W. Browne established a partnership with Arthur Little, and their firm propelled the Colonial Revival to even more popular acceptance. Steeped in the New England tradition, Browne freely offered his services to SPNEA when it acquired and restored the Bulfinch-designed Otis house in Boston as its headquarters. Theodate Pope Riddle served as vice-president in Connecticut for over a decade. One of three architects who planned the restoration of Bulfinch's capitol in Hartford in 1920, she also founded and built a medieval-inspired school at Avon, Connecticut.[41]

Ralph Adams Cram (1863–1942) served as a trustee, and his presence illustrated the power of antimodernism in Boston. A prolific writer and influential architect, he spent much of his life denouncing the inauthenticity of modern times. Maintaining that America had steadily declined after the election of Andrew Jackson, he claimed that the architectural product of that new democratic order, such as the Greek Revival, Italianate, and Second Empire styles, revealed a "vulgar, self-satisfied and pretentious" people. Those artforms placed architecture at a lower level than perhaps ever "in the history of human civilization" and reigned until the thinking of medievalists such as Ruskin and Morris came to the fore. A convinced mugwump as well, Cram is remembered not simply for his prominence as a cultural critic—for which he was placed on the cover of *Time* magazine on 13 December 1926—but the cynical elitism that premised those thoughts. His eccentricities also caught Boston's eye. He was a loyal Jacobite who imported Britain's ways to Boston. In 1907 he persuaded his Beacon Hill friends, for example, to sing carols on Christmas Eve and thus began a modern tradition.[42]

Descended from a line of Crams who came to North America in 1634, he most remembered his grandfather's New Hampshire farmhouse. Much like the medieval society that he extolled, it had a "unity of place and character" that held back any inkling of modernity and recalled the "human, personal relationship" of feudalism. Such a home, like Norton had said, was holy and "a direct outgrowth of the life within." According to Cram, nineteenth-century industrialism undermined that bond between person, society, and building, and he advocated a return to Gothicism. Although Wallace Nutting scoffed at Cram's fabled medieval culture, Gothic antimodernism entranced many disillusioned, but socially well placed, Brahmins.[43]

Architects, lawyers, corporate executives, and other professionals thus represented the occupations of SPNEA's male officers and trustees. Women came from the ranks of privileged families, patriotic societies, and select clubs. A collective biography of these men and women reveals many threads in the fabric of upper-class culture. Almost all preservation leaders listed the Unitarian or Episcopalian faiths as their belief systems, though Browne and Cram practiced Anglo-Catholicism. Men overwhelmingly had been educated at Harvard, but Yale and Brown Universities, Trinity College, and the Massachusetts Institute of Technology were represented. The vast majority of those in the Boston area were listed in *The Social Register* and participated in the constellation of groups and institutions that solidified elite society. As in Appleton's steady presence at the Union Club, these men usually belonged to a social club. They commonly were members of the NEHGS, a patriotic association, and a local historical society. More than a handful maintained the Brahmin custom of membership in the Massachusetts Volunteer Militia. Women commonly circulated within the ranks of such societies as the DAR, Colonial Dames, and Society of Mayflower Descendants. Not surprisingly, trustees and officers descended from the early settlers of Massachusetts Bay Colony. The Peabodys and Cabots were well represented, as were the Endicotts, Coolidges, and Crowninshields. Just as the Brahmins had long idealized nature, these officers frequently joined conservation societies, the Massachusetts Horticultural Society, or campaigns to eradicate billboards from country roads, preserve New England's forest land, or protect the simple town life of the countryside.

Similarly, these men and women served as trustees for countless philanthropic, cultural, or social service agencies. Just as Bolton accepted a trusteeship for the Boston Public Library, so, too, did Edward J. Holmes serve as treasurer for a settlement house. Whether it was a university, hospital, or museum, they lent their names and energies, as they did to the directorates of banks, utilities, and other corporate enterprises. Service had long been instilled in this leadership class. It had once been strictly defined by the locale, but the reorientation of life during the progressive era showed that service was given to corporate entities, defined by specialization of purpose and managed by newer experts.

When Appleton organized SPNEA, he faced a dilemma. Should it be an organization strictly associated with Brahmins, or should it seek support from a larger, though still select, community? Some friends proposed, and he found "much merit in that suggestion," that SPNEA follow in the footsteps of the MHS or the Walpole Society and limit its membership to an elite who would contribute large sums. In retrospect, he thought that "we would have been financially much better off under such circumstances."[44]

Like his earlier PRMA, and akin to Filene's philosophy in the "1915" movement, Appleton instead crafted SPNEA as an organization led by the select, but supported by a wider (but never large) constituency.[45] SPNEA would help educate and assimilate newer families of wealth and abilities into traditionalist culture. As Eben F. Thompson of the SR suggested, SPNEA would enlist the socially prominent ("The Aloof" in his terms) or those listed in *The Social Register*. Those who were "less prominent socially," but still "men of means" (whom he called "the Eager") would subsequently join. SPNEA as a result opened its ranks to all "who are by residence, birth, or in any way connected with New England." Traditionalists obviously would define New England's heritage, just as they would pass judgment on those who were "elected" to membership. Although founded by a Brahmin, SPNEA worked to define a broader based movement to protect old-time culture. Still, as SPNEA admitted in 1924, "there is probably no member of our Society whose ancestry doesn't go back in some line to some old town in England, Scotland, Ireland or Wales."[46]

In such a way, Boston's elite could incorporate newer members from business and the professions, as well as reinforce traditionalism within the ranks of the Yankee upper class. Such reinforcement was necessary. While many Yankees were demolishing or altering historic buildings, iconoclasts such as Henry Adams were calling the Colonial Revival "troglodytic." Even one SPNEA supporter found it "wearisome" to extoll New England's history continually. "The past is past," he said, "and though we may learn its lesson . . . it is never to be recovered with any backward footsteps." Always a restraint on Appleton's ambitions, traditional Yankees usually represented the major threat to their own heritage.[47]

As a result, Appleton and SPNEA carried their gospel to the relatively affluent, tradition-minded Yankee. As one who chiefly defined SPNEA, Appleton encouraged the middling classes to contribute. With preservation in private hands, traditionalists hoped to ensure their own cultural primacy in New England's identity. More effectively than those societies with limited memberships, SPNEA popularized that culture as it protected the most visible symbols of the colonial and revolutionary eras.

4

"A Mecca for Tourists and a Joy to All"

Preserving Antiquities as Symbols and Documents

During its first three decades SPNEA acquired forty buildings and aided in the preservation of many more. From the first days it acknowledged having an open-ended acquisitions policy. Henry Erving predicted that bankruptcy and disaster would follow. "I can but think, Mr. Appleton," he wrote in 1921,

> that the aims and desires perhaps of the Society are almost too ambitious. I don't think it possible for it to take up every old house that is offered however meritorious or otherwise. . . . My idea of the Society's function is that it should have two or three bits of property—the best obtainable—and do the very best thing—everything that is necessary in fact—to those particular places.[1]

Appleton retorted that his plans had been misconstrued. "We don't, by any means, aim to get a monopoly on the earth's surface," he wrote, "and are, on the contrary, only too glad when some other society offers to step in and take something which we would otherwise have to work on ourselves." Yet by 1940 SPNEA was the largest preservation society of its kind in the United States. The largess of Rockefeller and Ford could, of course, make their village museums titans in the field, but SPNEA had outpaced all others in its holdings. Even Appleton anticipated the difficulties that could follow and joked: "My ghost will very much enjoy seeing what the Board does with these various properties as they come to its attention and perhaps you and I will be able to join hands, above or below, and contemplate the situation together."[2]

In many areas Appleton set SPNEA on an uncharted course in preservation. Unlike earlier drives that reacted slowly to block a demolition, Appleton wanted SPNEA to take the initiative. Unlike the crusades to save historic sites such as Mount Vernon and Jamestown, Appleton heeded Norton's advice about the family home, added his own interest in its form and design, and subsequently focused on more common domestic antiquities. Unlike earlier campaigns in Boston that claimed a public trusteeship and allowed interior renovations, such as those in behalf of the Old State House or Park Street Church, SPNEA acted privately and pledged to act differently.

As Appleton explained, "the work of owning and maintaining a number of widely scattered old houses, and keeping them all as nearly as practicable in their original condition, is an experiment in this country. We have no sign posts to guide us and from the beginning have had to feel our way along." At the same time as the APVA was erecting plaques, tending graveyards, transcribing documents, and creating shrines and museums, its Yankee counterpart was acquiring one building after another and using them in more diverse ways. Appleton did want some sites "maintained soley as memorials," as was the custom. Unlike earlier groups, however, he planned to lease most of SPNEA's structures "under wise restrictions" to tenants for modern purposes.[3]

Even with his plan to reorient the movement, Appleton was moved by an ingrained ideology. He held the widespread belief that those early dwellings represented the unpretentious lives, rigorous thrift, and clear-headed resourcefulness of pioneers. Those buildings devolved from a medieval world that recognized the power of God, nature, and tradition. In it, change came slowly, artifact and artisan were one, and the ties between past and future were easily seen. What captivated Appleton were the nitty-gritty details of construction, the most masculine of all topics and one that illustrated Morris's belief that manly characteristics were those of simplicity and strength, whereas effeminancy was marked by luxury and waste. The building's medieval structure objectified Appleton's sense of the early Anglo-Saxon. Almost in a self-analytical way, he wondered about its massing and framing. Just as these buildings had been solidly built, constructed from local materials, and framed to withstand a hostile environment, so, too, did he think that his ancestors had borrowed from their Anglo-Saxon inheritance, but on the frontier created a new people, the Yankees. After all, such an explanation was a distillation of modern Darwinism, individualism, and pragmatism.[4]

The Yankee's traditional form of construction had blossomed in small communities where builders depended on custom and neighbors to construct their homes. To be sure, modern antiquaries idealized the early community as one of unity, harmony, and continuity. As the analogy went, just as mortise and tenon were interlocked in a building's frame, so, too, were Yankee neighbors in these communities. As antiquaries understood it, this medieval world slowly declined with the increased wealth, trade, and industry of the mid-1700s. The buildings of the late eighteenth and nineteenth century relied on a different heritage and belief system. An ornate Georgian mansion or a sober Greek Revival temple embodied not only the belief that humans could pick and choose from diverse cultures but the Enlightenment's conviction that they could gain ascendance and progress through reason.[5]

According to these antiquaries, the Industrial Revolution in the late eighteenth and early nineteenth centuries undermined a builder's traditional mastery. "The early craftsmen used the broad-ax with an admirable degree of skill," said Kelly. "They made no false strokes, for they handled their tools with deftness and precision." Industrialism brought in milled lumber, machine-made nails, and design books, however, and those innovations made possible a building boom with the standardized balloon frame in the nineteenth century.[6]

Appleton particularly wanted SPNEA to save the earliest homes. Reflecting a vibrant antiindustrialism, he loved their unworked materials, exposed construction, and other medievalisms that "gave the old houses an air of dignity so lacking in our modern work." In the vein of Ruskin, he saw within their earthen materials the individuality, creativity, and utility that was natural to their builders. Adding a racial dimension to Norton's dismay with the Renaissance, he also thought that "the 17th century [building] is the more strictly New England type, or I might say Anglo-Saxon type." Unlike that organic process, the later Georgian style was "an importation from the Latin countries, bringing with it the flavor of Greek and Roman civilization, with which our ancestral lines are not particularly connected. The 17th century work has the flavor of the soil and is the sort of thing our ancestors saw in their English homes, and I must say it makes a powerful appeal to me." While a Georgian house was "the work of the architect," he said, the earlier home was "the work of the builder" and often had "the supreme and fascinating interest attaching to the survival of truly mediaeval mannerisms in construction and detail."[7]

In fact, antiquaries generally put too much racial ideology and antimodernism into their reading of architectural forms. Appleton did not know it, but the personal self-reliance, local rule, and building type he so admired in early New England were waning well before the advent of the Georgian. Architectural forms of the seventeenth century, generally called postmedieval, may have still reflected his notion of medieval Anglo-Saxon forms, but their builders were witnessing instead a gradual emergence of the market, loss of independence, and rise of provincial authority.[8] What accounted for the widespread change in building was not so much a matter of race as it was the economy and technology. It was easy for antiquaries to focus on the Georgian style displacing their favored medieval, but market capitalism and a technology based on an abundance of wood and water power were the forces that brought the decline.

Appleton asked architects to help preserve those seventeenth-century buildings but, as Henry Charles Dean told him in 1914, they found those primitive dwellings insufficient. By training, they looked at the artistry of earlier architects and mostly focused on the ornament and design—"their proportion, mass, and the character of their surface details, and the beauty or simplicity of their plans." Dean, who restored a handful of SPNEA properties before his untimely death in an influenza epidemic, admitted to Appleton that "the elements & details of construction (especially those of a unique nature) have escaped my careful consideration." So typical for the education of architects, he conceded: "I have been led to look upon construction as a 'means to an end' rather than 'an end' in itself." As far as Appleton was concerned, that was the problem with that profession.[9]

Appleton's perspective was obviously not formed in a vacuum, and he learned from three antiquarian architects, Kelly, Chandler, and most of all, Norman Morrison Isham (1864–1943) (Fig. 4-1). As one who taught architecture at Brown University (1894–98) and the Rhode Island School

FIG. 4-1   Norman Morrison Isham (Photograph by *Providence Journal,* Courtesy, Rhode Island Historical Society)

of Design (1912–20, 1923–33), Isham not only authored (with Albert F. Brown) two seminal books on old buildings—*Early Rhode Island Houses* (1895) and *Early Connecticut Houses* (1900)—but, as a practicing architect, designed some notable Colonial Revival buildings, supervised restoration projects, and directed archaeological excavations. Influenced by a scientific regimen in analyzing the structure, materials, and environment of old buildings, Isham perhaps epitomized his generation's blend of antiquarianism, archaeology, and architecture.

Isham valued the earliest buildings of New England as expressions of the medieval world. Rhode Island had been settled, for example, by artisans who "were nearly all the descendants of the Mediaeval craftsmen." In England, meanwhile, the Renaissance classicism associated with Inigo Jones was supplanting the Gothic, but "our forefathers left England before it was finished, and had learned their trades . . . under men imbued with what was left of the Mediaeval spirit." Those carpenters and masons carried their medievalisms to New England, adapted their skills to the environment, and, taking on what Appleton called "the flavor of the soil," set a new tradition. Isham and Appleton searched not only for the surviving medievalisms but, true for Darwinism, for the first uniquely American features. They did not realize, however, that those early Yankee builders maintained what one historian called "a carpenters' grapevine" with their trans-Atlantic peers through which they learned of and borrowed from each other's changing work and fashion. Isham and Appleton shared the antimodernist premise that individuality and diversity of form were to be prized, but ironically they were looking for the beginnings of uniformity with an American style.[10]

Like Appleton, Isham praised those seventeenth-century artisans who preserved "the traditions of their trades." Correcting the prevailing belief that those pioneers had been "wasteful and clumsy," he called them "good workmen" who were "economical" and "skilful in handling their material." Just as the English crafts movement had praised the roughness, irregularity, and variety of preindustrial carpentry, so, too, did Isham refute the charge that the work of early Yankees was ugly, haphazard, and barren. Those early craftsmen had been "artistic," he said in his own twist of Horatio Greenough's adage "form follows function," because they "solved the problem before them in the simplest manner, with logical use of the material which they had at hand, and with good arrangement of line and mass." Unlike his own day, those buildings were simple, but "simplicity, as we are just beginning to see, is the cardinal virtue in architecture."[11]

Isham's thinking reveals some of the paradoxes of antiquarianism. Yankee preservationists of his ilk held a subterranean streak of populism, mixed with antimodernism, in their admiration of this folk tradition. Not coincidentally, their cohorts were founding at the same time ethnological museums, as well as the American Folklore Society and American

Anthropological Association.[12] All the while, these antiquaries were a world apart from those architects who were experimenting with a confusing range of Classical, Renaissance, and Colonial revivals that showed more panache than restraint, more machine-made decoration than an artisan's soul. Meanwhile, Isham and Appleton were laboring to save the medieval vernacular, which had been shaped by common men and revealed, unlike academic work, a building's intimate contact with the soil, the times, and the craftsman's hand. Paradoxically, while Isham was praising those earlier artisans who had clung to their traditions, New England's workers were being robbed of their own customs and skills by profit-minded corporate managers who promoted Americanization, social order, and business efficiency in the name of progressivism.

When Appleton founded SPNEA, his attention was naturally drawn to such buildings as the seventeenth-century Jackson house in Portsmouth. Yet Appleton eyed ornate Georgian homes, despite SPNEA's unique focus on postmedieval buildings. He confided to his diary in 1910, for example, that SPNEA "must have" the brilliantly executed Pierce-Nichols house (1782) in Salem.[13] Designed by Samuel McIntire, it eluded his grasp and was later acquired by the Essex Institute.

SPNEA's first significant work did occur in Salem and showed how progressivism and preservation could easily mix. Over the past half century, the once-Puritan city and seat of Essex County had attracted countless newcomers. In 1906 Henry James took a "pilgrimage" to the House of the Seven Gables in search of "the New England homogeneous," but found instead the "flagrant foreigner" congested in its tenement neighborhood. The Seven Gables won his sympathy for its "simple dignity" and "solid sincerity." He wanted the house's "preserved and unsophisticated state" to teach Yankee "social 'values'" to these immigrants.[14]

Salem reformers did labor on many fronts to teach Americanisms. When the Essex Institute opened its period rooms in 1907, local residents immediately saw the museum's relevance. Those immigrants, said one native in the *Salem News*, "already hold the balance of power in city politics, and if they are not given the hand of fellowship and assimilated and inspired with respect for American ideals and American institutions, they will get absorbed and go to swell the columns of socialism, militant laborism, and other worse isms." At the same time in Worcester, a Playground Association was formed by Yankees to teach patriotic songs and Anglo-American folk dances to children. New England's factory owners feared the power of immigrants and labor, promoted Yankee traditions, and called that work, as did SPNEA supporter Henry Hornblower, one of "self-preservation."[15]

As a student of Ross, Appleton had surveyed the architecturally rich town and knew it fairly well; he combined historic and self-preservation in 1911. Modernity was symbolically threatening a medieval vestige when the owner of the Hooper-Hathaway house (c. 1682) sold the plot to a developer who wanted to build a movie theater, a more popular means of Americanizing the immigrants. "Already the harpies are gathering," George Dow of the Essex Institute told Appleton, "among them being a violin manufactory looking for the old timber." Dow wanted only a few of the overhangs from what was called the Old Bakery, but he told Appleton that the building could be purchased for $500, and the purchaser "would have no difficulty in securing permission to remove [it] to a new site."[16]

Appleton most admired the oldest work in the building—its overhangs, summer beams, and chamfered posts. The sophisticated progress of 1911 seemed a world apart from the Old Bakery. "The work was done in a slapdash sort of way, almost brutal in its simplicity, and the timbers vary in size in an amazing way," he said. "The whole work is essentially mediaeval, and the decorative motives are of Gothic extraction." He was intrigued by it, and bought the building himself. Since in situ preservation was impossible, he readied to "move the older part or take it apart and store the timbers," but then persuaded SPNEA trustee Caroline Emmerton to buy the house.[17]

Despite Dow's predictions, Emmerton had to battle the City Council to move the Old Bakery (in three pieces) to a site one mile distant and adjacent to her other medieval dwelling, the House of the Seven Gables (1669, before 1680). Like Hawthorne, she saw these buildings as anything but inanimate piles. As part of the Transcendentalist's attempt to bridge soul and nature, Hawthorne had viewed the Seven Gables as "a human countenance, bearing the traces not merely of outward storm and sunshine, but expressive also, of the long lapse of mortal life, and accompanying vicissitudes that have passed within."[18] In 1909 Emmerton hired Chandler to restore the house. She wanted him not only to equip the building as a settlement for immigrants but to find its long-lost gables and emulate the novelist's setting of the 1840s.

Born in Plymouth and descended from the Pilgrims, Joseph Everett Chandler (1864–1945) had graduated from the Massachusetts Institute of Technology with a degree in architecture in 1889 and, after his work at the Revere house, became one of the region's prominent restoration architects (Fig. 4-2). An admirer of colonial aesthetics, Chandler said that "the homes of our forefathers bespoke a fearless honesty characteristic of themselves—a lack of pretense and sham, but with a diffident expression of a love for the beautiful which, if somewhat severe and subdued, was their rightful heritage." Critical of modernity, he thought that "they builded better" in those days when "life was richer and fuller." His cultural politics and imagination became apparent as he spoke openly about the simplicity and humility that such seventeenth-century houses should teach. It would "be well to-day," he said, "if the rank and file of our nation could return in a marked degree toward this simplicity and again live a life approximating the sane life of our Colonial forbears." Ironically, the House of the Seven Gables did not reveal his notion of simplicity

FIG. 4-2 Joseph Everett Chandler (Photograph by Alfred Wayland Cutting, Courtesy, Society for the Preservation of New England Antiquities)

but, according to a recent interpreter, "the architectural refinements enjoyed by the mercantile elite" of the late seventeenth century.[19]

Seven Gables served in 1910, as did the Old Bakery after 1911, as a settlement house. Within that industrial and tenement quarter, Emmerton predicted that the Puritan house, Yankee novel, and settlement work "must surely help in making American citizens out of our boys and girls." There immigrants learned housekeeping, sewing, and even sloyd, a preindustrial carpentry of Europe that was hardly practical in the new environs. When Prohibition came, they also learned "why they can't have beer any more." Appleton publicized SPNEA's role in linking self-preservation and antiquities, and even persuaded Emmerton in 1916 to as-

sume his option on another postmedieval-style Salem building, the extant
half of the Retire Becket house, which she moved and incorporated as an
ell on the Old Bakery in 1924.[20]

While SPNEA assisted such efforts, it grew anxious to acquire its own
building. It had been offered options on high quality structures at mod-
erate costs, but fiscal conservatism aborted the process. The Lippincott
family, for example, offered moneys to purchase (but not to restore) the
seventeenth-century Major John Bradford house in Kingston, Massachusetts. Contrary to the connoisseur tradition of Erving, Appleton thought
that a simple dwelling associated with "one of the best-known Pilgrim
families . . . must be the very kind of house" that SPNEA should protect.
Other houses, such as the ancient Bunker Garrison in Durham, New
Hampshire, nearly fell into SPNEA's hands, but strapped finances were
again the problem.[21] These frustrating experiences explain how a second-
rate building became SPNEA's first acquisition in May 1911.

Appleton had earlier inspected the Swett-Ilsley house of Newbury,
Massachusetts (Fig. 4-3). When built about 1670 by an Anabaptist cord-
wainer, it possessed one room on each of its two stories. Appleton thought
the house was "very interesting," but "lacked sufficient historic association and architectural merit to justify the Trustees in making a purchase."
Precisely because it was of second-rank quality, however, he worried
about its fate. Picturing a worst-case scenario, he predicted that "some
person may find it profitable to destroy the building and erect a three or

Fig. 4-3   Swett-Ilsley House, Newbury, Mass., 1917 (Photograph by The Halliday Historic Photograph Co., Courtesy, Society for the Preservation of New
England Antiquities)

four family tenement house on the site." What brought the house into his hands, then, were its below-appraisal price and, more important, an offer by a New York businessman (and relative by marriage to the Ilsley line) to hold the $1,200 mortgage. A local newspaper reported the acquisition as one made by a society "composed of wealthy Bostonians whose purpose is to save these famous landmarks of the early settlers."[22]

Appleton was most interested in its craftsmanship, simple features, and the revealing look that it provided at colonial life. The summer beams, fireplace, and chimney were "first-class." Mixing historical fact, sentimental statement, and realtor's sales pitch, he said that its fireplace was the "largest I know of" and probably one of the largest in New England. It measured approximately ten-feet wide, five-feet high, and two-and-one-half-feet deep.[23]

The romanticism of Americans swelled when picturing close-knit families around such hearths (Fig. 4-4). As centrifugal forces seemed to pull families apart, Frank Lloyd Wright, for example, centered the open floor-plan of his Prairie homes around a massive fireplace. Nutting likewise used a sketch of an old hearth to introduce his *Massachusetts Beautiful* (1923). He said that a fireplace best captured "the flavor of the old life" and connected moderns with "the founding of the human family." He thought that it was "nothing short of a disaster to history and to romance" when Victorians removed those hearths. In fact, he went so far

FIG. 4-4 Fireplace, Swett-Ilsley House, 1932 (Photograph by Arthur C. Haskell, Courtesy, Society for the Preservation of New England Antiquities)

as to advise SPNEA that the "main thing" to look for in "a very ancient house of the cottage type" was its fireplace. When Bellamy pictured Boston in 2000, there were ironically no chimneys along its skyline and no hearths for a family gathering. All in all, the Swett-Ilsley house's "long, low rambling appearance" and its setting in a still-sleepy town created an "extremely picturesque" portrait of old New England. It was not a gem, and lovers of the colonial would regret that its mid-eighteenth-century alterations "deprive[d] it of much of its seventeenth-century appearance," but it was still a fitting symbol of olden days.[24]

In the following year, SPNEA acquired the Samuel Fowler house in Danversport, Massachusetts, largely through the benefaction of Heloise Meyer, a consistent friend of SPNEA and sister of the wealthy investment banker George von Lengerke Meyer. SPNEA's second acquisition caused quite a stir because it had only been built in 1809 and its style was quite common (Fig. 4-5). William Endicott, SPNEA's treasurer, told Appleton that he did not "think very much of this house." He wanted instead to acquire The Lindens, an ornate mansion in Danvers that tycoon J. P. Morgan had offered to purchase for SPNEA shortly before his death, but the owner declined the bid. Some in SPNEA even claimed that the elegance of such Georgian architecture corrected "the errant fancies of the colonial craftsmen."[25]

Appleton acknowledged that the Fowler house paled in standing when

Fig. 4-5   Samuel Fowler House, Danversport, Mass., 1913 (Photograph by The Halliday Historic Photograph Co., Courtesy, Society for the Preservation of New England Antiquities)

compared with such an opulent mansion. "To be quite frank," he said, "only those who appreciate the finer touches of early 19th century work [are those] who see how good that house really is. Others are apt to be disappointed that it is not ornate." Reporting the acquisition to his members, he claimed that the two-story brick home "reflects the simple tastes of its owner," a style that was "as severely simple as it could be." Accordingly, and in tune with his idea of proper values, "the principal features of the house may be said to be simplicity, good taste, solid construction, splendid preservation, and homogeneity."[26]

In a case of very selective documentation, Appleton accented Fowler's life as a role model. Quite typical for Chandler, Kelly, and Isham, he believed that architectural forms embodied the values of its builder. Fowler was the son of a soldier who had served on 19 April 1775 at Lexington, and in turn became a patriot, good citizen, and successful industrialist. In rags-to-riches terms, but illustrative of a proper Yankee, his simple tastes began when he was "educated in the village school" where "his seat . . . was but a rude bench and his desk a portion of board placed across two barrels." Those humble beginnings instilled values that ensured his rise to prominence.[27]

Surely a model for the modern age when privatism and materialism had corrupted many Yankees, Fowler was pictured as "public-spirited and ever ready to aid financially such enterprises as tended to improve the village and town." His personal habits, moreover, had been impeccable, as he was "strictly temperate" and very religious. He invested his money in processing mills, began the area's first tannery, and introduced machinery to card wool. Appleton had nothing but praise for the Yankee who "rose regularly at four in the morning, winter and summer . . . to superintend the beginning of the day's work." Fowler's disposition, furthermore, matched that of the ideal Brahmin; he had "a kind and generous temperament, gladly helping others to help themselves, which was to his mind the wisest charity." He drew happiness from his apiary and orchard. His life fit the appearances of his home, in which there "is nothing lavish or ostentatious."[28]

SPNEA acquired the Fowler house under the condition that it also grant a "life occupancy" to two unmarried Fowlers. Apparently the first case in American preservation of such a life interest, Appleton saw its advantage as the ladies agreed to bear part of the upkeep. Within a few years, Appleton decided as well to open the downstairs as a period display of early nineteenth-century life. Fowler's stature obviously did not match that of a Hancock or Adams, but when his home became a museum, SPNEA elevated this relatively obscure businessman to the status of an icon. This was not so much a case of fabricating an imaginary hero, but remaking for modern purposes those Yankees who industrialized New England.[29]

Tradition-minded Yankees later practiced many of those traits, urged newcomers to adopt them, but failed to see their irrelevance. Just as Fowler's work ethic had little meaning for wage-earning workers who toiled before lifeless machines, so, too, did his love of horticulture have limited bearing in the urban economy. It had been emulated earlier as an antidote to materialism, but held meaning only for those gentry who could cultivate suburban yards or rural pastures. It became more of a personal therapy and class habit to tired Yankees than meaningful symbol of an alternative life. Those rural values still defined New England, however, as Cram and others extolled the village life.[30]

In 1912 SPNEA purchased the Cooper-Frost-Austin house (c. 1689) in Cambridge (Fig. 4-6). Known for its great college, Cambridge had become one of New England's many factory towns with a mixed population. Lever Brothers' Soap Works, the New England Glass Company, and countless businesses employed many more humble workers than those elite students who attended Harvard. Norton had lamented in 1905 that "it has been a pathetic experience for me to live all my life in one community and to find myself gradually becoming a stranger to it." No better symbol of the town's Anglo-Saxon roots could be found than this house that was, according to Appleton, "architecturally one of the best worth preserving" with its massive pilastered chimney and saltbox rear.[31]

SPNEA trustees wanted such a relic so badly that, despite the society's strained finances, they voted in 1911 to "get possession of the house in whatever way may appear most feasible." Appleton hinted that others might demolish the postmedieval building, and Cambridge friends came out in force to fund SPNEA's drive. Preservationists also stressed the fam-

FIG. 4-6   Cooper-Frost-Austin House, Cambridge, Mass. (Photograph by The Halliday Historic Photograph Co., Courtesy, Society for the Preservation of New England Antiquities)

ily histories of earlier residents. Its assumed builder, John Cooper, had been a leader in church and state, having served eleven years as a selectman of Cambridge and thirteen years as deacon of First Church. Not only did he hold "offices of trust" in the community, he was "prominent in all town affairs."[32]

Appleton evoked the sentiment of family and hearth, obvious concerns of Yankees who knew that homelife was threatened not only by a divorce rate that had doubled since 1890 in Massachusetts but by the prevalence of child labor among immigrant families who depended on young breadwinners for their daily sustenance. Appleton asked the support of ancestral organizations that longed to establish a hereditary home in New England. The Frost Family Association, for example, donated funds "to redeem this handsome inheritance." Its president waxed sentimentally about "the days when Hannah and Sarah Cooper as little girls flitted about those spacious fire-places and climbed the great stairways."[33]

With the house so close to the intellectual seat of Brahminism, SPNEA took added steps to ensure its visibility. It held an opening-day party that attracted over 500 Cambridge supporters, hired Chandler to begin the restoration, and bought the adjacent lots to keep away modern clutter. Those Yankees gave generously. Within the first few months of the drive, two dozen residents donated $100 each, as did the Elevated Railway Company of Boston, recently the focus of suspected franchise abuses. In 1912 $100 was no paltry sum; it provided about three months of essentials for those at the very minimum of living conditions.[34]

Another seventeenth-century dwelling, the Bennett-Boardman house, was acquired in 1913 (Fig. 4-7). Once a remote farm, its fate seemed tied to the expanding industrial center of Lynn. Ever since the introduction of the nation's first shoe sewing machine in 1848, Lynn had attracted wave after wave of immigrants. Although Puritans had founded Saugus (Lynn) in 1629, three centuries later it was a confusing patchwork of ethnic neighborhoods. The house was rented by poor Italians who regarded it as a hovel.

Typical of Yankee preservationists was Nathaniel Hawkes, a local antiquary and parks commissioner in Lynn who spurred the drive to remake the memory of the Boardman house and laid the goundwork for SPNEA's campaign. Like many wistful traditionalists, he personified the home. "This place has all the cool, calm attributes of serenity," he wrote. "It just stands there with never a thought of time, never a fear for the future." Caught in medieval time, it would be able to teach lessons about the simple life, the work ethic, aesthetics, and craftsmanship. Hawkes evidently regretted not only that the Industrial Revolution had debilitated craftsmanship but that his own contemporaries stressed a man's outward appearances, not inner strengths, as the keys to success. "Some houses, like some people," he thought, "boast of beauty and strength by outside boldness. This one is built massively, but its impressive sturdiness is only seen in the interior, whose chamfered American oak timbers put to the

Fig. 4-7   Boardman House, Saugus, Mass. (Photograph by The Halliday Historic Photograph Co., Courtesy, Society for the Preservation of New England Antiquities)

blush the skill of modern artificers in wood." It greatly surpassed those "parvenue villas of [nearby] Melrose."[35]

The Boardman house would serve, moreover, as a means to strengthen ties with Britain. Tourists would appreciate its calm and be reminded, Hawkes claimed, "of leafy, rural England." It would become a counterweight as well to the "anglophobists" of Boston. "American demagogues, in the demand for newly-made Irish votes, pretend to dislike England," he explained, "but underlying this the true American has all along imitated and reverenced his Mother England." The Boardman house, as a result, brought the Yankee closer to "the cradle of his race." The campaign for the Boardman house subsequently evoked its Anglo-Saxon character, preindustrial workmanship, and role as a hereditary home. Even the mayor of Melrose, an Adams with old roots, admitted that Appleton's publicity barrage proved its worth.[36]

Appleton highlighted one episode in the history of the Boardman house. It embodied, he said, the industrious immigrants who had won wealth and freedom through hard work and perseverance. Calling it the "Scotch"-Boardman house, he claimed that it was "doubtless the most interesting building in America to all persons of Scottish descent." Appleton broadcast that the house had been "built [in 1651] to house Scotch prisoners taken by Cromwell at the Battle of Dunbar and shipped to America to work for a term of years as indentured servants for the Undertakers of the Iron Works at Lynn." Consequently, "to these humble and pathetic beginnings thousands of our present Americans must trace their ancestral lines." Judging recent immigrants by implication, as in the case of those who joined the IWW at Lawrence, he claimed that these Scots, on the other hand, "were a worthy and cleanly lot" and had been "carefully selected as being best calculated to help [the iron works'] development." Moreover, they "seem to have been an orderly and law-abiding lot and a distinct addition to the community in which they settled." They confirmed their worth by respecting the local culture, intermarrying with Puritan neighbors, and showing their patriotism in the War for Independence. Those Scots and Wobblies stood a world apart.[37]

SPNEA acquired the Boardman house and its surrounding lots, but acted secretly out of a fear that the Italians would torch it in revenge. Igniting a long-running conflict, Appleton evicted the destitute occupants from the shabby building. His monument to the acculturation of immigrants failed to suade the Calabrian neighbors who, he said with twisted humor, were "not famous for their good behavior." They then walked away with his building materials, and he wanted "an unclimable fence." It was "absolutely essential," he said, "that the house be occupied every instant on account of the Italians in the vicinity." He had difficulty finding "a responsible American" caretaker, however, because he wanted no modern improvements in the building. Local boys used the vacant dwelling to test their rock-throwing abilities and broke eighty lights of glass.[38] Whether this vandalism was a malicious prank by idle children or a conscious act of revenge against Yankee outsiders, it was evident that the old house occupied hostile ground. Historic preservation was one battleline in a wider conflict.

Preservationists experienced an even more difficult time raising money to fund the project. At first Appleton sent a circular to every Bennett or Boardman in New England's telephone directories, a select number since less than fifteen percent of Bostonians had a telephone. He soon conceded defeat along this line and, contrary to his picture of industrious, thrifty Scots, concluded: "The trouble seems to be that none of this particular line of Boardmans ever made a cent." Even a Cambridge bank president, a man who must have had *some* money, sent only $2, "sufficient," he said "to save two shingles on my respected ancestor's house"! A dozen Bostonians, ten of whom were listed in *The Social Register*, did contribute $100 each, but could not fund Appleton's ambitious plan. Meanwhile, Saugus celebrated its centennial in 1915, spotlighted the Boardman house, and even persuaded Senator Lodge to speak.[39]

As a result, he cast a different line. Playing up the idea that Scots had come to establish the iron industry in Saugus, he tapped a Scots-American known for his iron and philanthropy, Andrew Carnegie. He wrote an acquaintance of Carnegie and suggested making the house "The Carnegie Memorial to the Scotch in America." It showed their "humble beginnings," he said, and "when contrasted with the present prosperity of the Scotch among us today, [it] should be an inspiration to young America and a proud memorial to the perseverance of the Scotch race." He then wrote Carnegie and declared it "peculiarly appropriate" for him to fund the memorial as he had "built the industry to its present world commanding position." He lauded his Protestant work ethic and individualism.[40]

Appleton's interest in the medievalisms of the Boardman house and his appeal to Carnegie reveal a telling paradox, however. The late-nineteenth-century cult of the medieval, led by the likes of Ruskin, Morris, and Norton, had essentially romanticized the era as a means to critique the changes wrought by the Industrial Revolution. They objected to the degradation of labor, the materialism of capitalism, and the alienation of urban civilization. Corporate tycoons such as Ford, Rockefeller, and Carnegie ushered in those changes, but Appleton had lost part of the philosophical connection between artifact and medieval society that Norton, Morris, and Ruskin had seen. As he asked Carnegie to pay tribute to the preindustrial world, Appleton showed how many antimodernists were reaching an accommodation with the industrial economy. Despite his Gospel of Wealth, Carnegie said no.[41]

Appleton did turn the hovel into the "Scotch"-Boardman memorial. What is to be questioned, however, is the origins of the "Scotch" connection, particularly after SPNEA acknowledged almost forty years later that the house had actually been built about 1687, well after the collapse of the Iron Works. In *Hearths and Homes of Old Lynn* (1907), Hawkes had ascribed the home to a wealthy Puritan; in *The Homes of Our Forefathers* (1880), Edwin Whitefield had dated the house's construction at 1690. Despite this documentation, Appleton and a local antiquary fostered a myth that it had been built for those Scots. Appleton first aired the claim in letters to Carnegie and his associates in 1916.[42] As he lured the philanthropist, Appleton remade the Boardman house as a shrine to the Scots and the iron industry.

At the same time, and spurring Appleton's imagination, Nutting was restoring the Appleton-Taylor-Mansfield house in Saugus. The Ironworks house, as it was called, likewise paid tribute to those early manufacturers, but the house had so changed over the years that Nutting speculated on details such as the long-lost pinnacles and gables. The more Appleton inspected Nutting's remade house the more he became convinced that his "Scotch" house once had similar Elizabethan features, such as facade gables and a projecting porch. Nutting's conjecture, however, paled in dimension and invention to the so-called "faithful replica of 'Hammersmith' " that was later created by the American Iron and Steel Institute, and which the National Park Service inherited when it established Saugus Ironworks National Historic Site in 1968.[43]

While the European war dragged on, SPNEA acquired two buildings that contrasted dramatically in tone and setting, the Laws cottage in

Sharon, New Hampshire, and the Otis mansion in Boston. In 1915 SPNEA accepted the very simple, but "quaint and picturesque" cottage (c. 1800) as a gift from a long-time neighbor who so identified with the landscape that she wanted to protect the setting. Another friend donated funds for restoration. As in the case of the Fowler house, however, a split occurred between preservationists who only wanted ornate mansions and those who sought a wider range of buildings. Bolton later lampooned the thinking of the first group as:

> We are the best selected few
>   And all the rest are damned;
> There's room in heaven for me and you
>   But we can't have heaven crammed.[44]

Typical of that split were the differences between Emily Eliot Morison and her son Samuel. SPNEA would have refused the gift had not Emily donated the restoration funds, and she admitted to Appleton: "My son was so 'down' on the Society for buying 'those little wooden houses' in the country, like that at Sharon, instead of preserving a large, handsome house like the former Otis house. He little knows that I was responsible for the Sharon house."[45] These divisions were only natural when preservationists held different ideas about New England's past. While Appleton held the factions together, he clearly sided with those who favored relatively simple, rural cottages. Sam Morison knew that, and when Appleton asked him to serve as a trustee, he declined. Ironically, twenty years later he gave SPNEA his own family's little cottage in the New Hampshire countryside, "Bleakhouse" (1796), near the artist colony founded by composer Edward MacDowell.[46] With the nearby Laws house and Appleton's own ancestral home at New Ipswich, Hillsboro County held the rural roots of Yankee culture.

SPNEA did acquire the Harrison Gary Otis house, thanks in large part to the generosity of his descendants, the Morisons. An imposing mansion designed by Charles Bulfinch and built in 1796, it symbolized upper-class traditionalism in Boston. It was "almost as familiar to the oldest Bostonians as the Old South or the Old State House," the *Globe* reported, "for it is one of the few local historic buildings that has undergone almost no outward transformation since it was put up." That was not the case, however. Three stories in height, the large brick dwelling had first flaunted its Adam Brothers' decoration in its central bay—a delicate entry, a second-floor Palladian window, and an attic story with a semicircular light— but all had been lost over the years (Fig. 4-8).[47]

In a sense, geography had dealt the building a bad hand. One who made a fortune in land speculation, Otis abandoned this house in 1801 for newer quarters that he built on Mount Vernon Street, then a pasture on Beacon Hill. In the mid-nineteenth century, owners subdivided the first Otis house. Appleton had even inspected the rooming house in the late

Fig. 4-8   Harrison Gray Otis House, Boston, before restoration, c. 1916 (Published by Frank Cousins Art Co., Courtesy, Society for the Preservation of New England Antiquities)

1890s while working for a local realtor. Shortly after, Woods predicted that the West End "will pass quite fully into the possession of the Jews," many of whom, he claimed, had fallen into "an inhuman sordidness." Appleton repeated his fear as he searched for money. He wrote Harrison Gray Otis, conservative editor of the Los Angeles *Times* and a known anti-Semite, and claimed that the house was "threatened" by "a Jewish corporation which plans using it, after extensive remodeling, as a home for aged women. I have no doubt," he said, "that in the course of time the house will be pulled down."[48]

SPNEA campaigned not simply to purchase the Otis house but make it the society's headquarters. It occupied important ground and defended Beacon Hill's flank against the newcomers. It also stood adjacent to West End Church, designed by Asher Benjamin in 1806, but since converted into a library for those immigrants. As was common, the Otis house also had storefronts that held such enterprises as a shoe-repair shop and a Chinese laundry.

Traditionalists rallied to aid the drive. Edith Wendell gave the Colonial Dames' money, in return for rights to use the house for its meetings. A handful of Brahmins essentially funded the acquisition. Bolton took to the telephone, and four friends gave $5,000 each. In the next year, a half-dozen Yankees, all listed in *The Social Register*, contributed another $9,000 to remove the row of businesses in front. Women from old Puritan families such as the Cabots, Eliots, Hunts, and Whites contributed almost the entire purchase price. That amount paled in comparison to the $130,000 that SPNEA would raise to move the house a decade later when Cambridge Street was widened. Morison helped the drive by providing press materials, speaking before the members, and raising money. One who revered the house's symbolism and aesthetics, and even possessed the Otis family papers, he had also written a two-volume biography, *The Life and Letters of Harrison Gray Otis* (1913).[49]

Boston traditionalists admired this nephew of James Otis as a man who was devoted not simply to business and family, as in modern privatism, but to public service, having served as a Massachusetts legislator, U. S. Senator, and Boston mayor. Writing in SPNEA's *Bulletin*, Morison set him in the context of Federalism and its commercial elite. As was the case in modern Brahminism, he had "loathed democracy, and . . . believed that the country should be governed by men of education and wealth." His picture of Otis as an enlightened public servant contrasted dramatically with the Brahmin's caricature of Mayor Curley. The latter, however, did not speak kindly of Otis, who was like most Yankee mayors of the period, "an aristocrat who did little for the average citizen." Curley pictured the lot as "Yankee overlords" known for their "inhumane numbskulduggery." Morison's hagiographic piece for the *Bulletin* also omitted mention of Otis's shady real estate dealings while in office, as well as his near-traitorous role at the Hartford Convention during the War of 1812.[50]

A seventeenth-century house that showed the simple roots of this Yankee stock simultaneously captured Appleton's eye. The Norton house (c. 1691) on Moose Hill near Guilford, Connecticut, "interested me extremely," he wrote in 1914 (Fig. 4-9). This one-room stone house with a garret was "one of the crudest survivals of colonial architecture that has come down to us." Standing inside, he felt "it was as though the entire frame was exposed to view without stirring from the spot." It would have made a splendid "archaeological document" as it was "one of those houses almost unspoiled by the hand of time, that has come down to us in its crude, almost brutal, simplicity, in a way that so few have done." It was vacant, dilapidated, and isolated, however, and he feared that "the passing small boy" might torch it.[51]

Appleton tried to interest the community, but Guilford already had a museum at the Whitfield house (1639), a state-owned stone dwelling with a hall-parlor design that made the Norton house appear slight in stature. He negotiated with the Polish immigrant who owned it, but he was much like the frugal Yankee who would rather be called a miser than a patsy. The building fascinated him but, remembering his days in real estate, he thought that the price of an old building was determined by the value of its land. Rejecting such speculation, a tradition in the vein of Otis, Appleton thought that "the price . . . seemed larger than the case warranted and nothing was accomplished." Instead, the Pole demolished the garret

FIG. 4-9 Norton House, Guilford, Conn., before renovation (*Old-Time New England* 24 [July 1993]: 30)

for its timbers and used them to rebuild the dwelling in a different form (Fig. 4-10). As Appleton saw it, "this ignorant foreigner has destroyed it." What caused the tragedy was not his own stubbornness, he said, but "the difficulties involved in trying to do business with a foreigner, whom fortune had made for the moment the custodian of a really interesting New England antiquity." Years later, he juxtaposed photographs of the ancient structure and the modern dwelling to remind the readers of *Old-Time New England* how "the Polish owner destroyed an American antique of few rooms" because it was "to his mind inconvenient" and did not match "his taste."[52]

One who took a special interest in the Norton house was J. Frederick Kelly (1888–1947). After graduating from Yale University in 1911, he studied in England, Italy, and France. Kelly went into private practice and earned his sustenance by designing residences and buildings for Connecticut's wealthy. Won over by Seymour's Hale Homestead, he shifted his interest to antiquities, and in 1915 began a fifteen-year project compiling architectural data and photographs of Connecticut's old buildings for the Colonial Dames. In 1924 he published the authoritative *Early Domestic Architecture of Connecticut*. An associate of Appleton who, like Isham and Chandler, was appointed by the Board of Trustees as a consulting architect to SPNEA, Kelly outlined the significance of historic buildings.

FIG. 4-10   Norton House, renovated (*Old-Time New England* 24 [July 1933]: 31)

While Isham saw simplicity as architecture's cardinal virtue, Kelly deemed it to be truth. As in the case of the Norton house, the buildings of an era were documents that "reflect[ed], faithfully and without distortion, the economic and social conditions out of which they sprang." As a result, he concluded that "the early domestic architecture of the American colonies" was

> unmistakably pure and virile. . . . Its building is honest, straight-forward, devoid of affectation and sham. The early Colonial houses were true in two respects, both of crucial importance. First, they expressed with entire simplicity and directness the conditions which produced them. Secondly, and hardly less important, their implication was always intensely intimate, *domestic*. They were true to their *milieu*; and they were equally true to their purpose.[53]

Kelly held professional credentials, but his sentiments were shared by die-hard romantics such as Nutting. So apt for their antiindustrialism, Kelly believed that the true "dignity" of postmedieval structures stemmed from "a rugged and vigorous integrity due in large measure to . . . the crudity of their construction." He thought that the "barbaric massiveness of their framing" should "delight anyone possessed of the smallest amount of architectural sense. A feeling of boundless strength, of security and steadfastness, as well as a notable kind of dignity, is inseparable from the ponderous timbers which go to make up these mighty frames." In a modern era of impermanence and flux, he wanted his contemporaries to look "with satisfaction upon that which is substantially and enduringly built."[54]

Those beliefs led him to focus even more on the Norton house. Influenced by the ideology of Darwinism and progress, Kelly thought that the one-room house with a side chimney represented the first, and most primitive, stage of Anglo-Saxon building in New England. The second stage was the hall-parlor design. Appleton thought, too, that those houses with one room had been "the smallest permanent houses of the poorer settlers," and though enlarged over time were "extremely picturesque." Although Kelly's schema fit theories of his day, it has been refuted. His focus on the Norton house, however, was warranted, but too late, because most antiquaries preferred the more substantial hall-parlor design. They usually neglected the one-room houses and, as Appleton feared, lost important pieces of the archaeological puzzle of early New England.[55]

SPNEA acquired a different stone-end, seventeenth-century dwelling as a gift in 1918. When built about 1687, the Eleazer Arnold house in Lincoln, Rhode Island (Fig. 4-11), was "so far into the wilderness as to have been called 'at the end of the world.'" That image dovetailed with an earlier Puritan description of the land as a "desart" populated by ignoble savages, thus rationalizing the conquest. Though such a description was more myth than reality, it was repeated and became generalized fact.

FIG. 4-11   Eleazer Arnold House, Lincoln R.I., 1928 (Photograph by George Brayton, Courtesy, Society for the Preservation of New England Antiquities)

Having served in town and colonial government, Arnold erected what Appleton called "one of the very grandest houses in Rhode Island—something of a seven days' wonder." Such an edifice now stood, it was said, as an extant symbol of those strong, virile colonists who transformed the wilderness into a garden.[56]

By 1918 Appleton thought that the Arnold house was one of "the least changed of those still standing" from the era. Enhancing its appeal, publicists said that it was heavily timbered and built with a stone end "so as to be considered bullet proof in case of an attack from Indians." Such an image of garrisons, particularly with overhangs, was based on a myth that even Kelly would demolish. "Very obliging Indians they must have been," he joked, "to march up to the *front* of a house in order to be scalded or shot, when they might as easily have attacked the *rear*, where no form of framed overhang ever occurred!" Its massive stone wall also harbored a fireplace that measured almost eleven feet across, five feet high, and nearly four feet deep. Appleton concluded that it "must ever remain the finest example of the 'stone-end' house in Rhode Island," and he knew of "nothing to equal it in the United States."[57]

A seventeenth-century dwelling whose fate came to obsess Appleton like no other was the Abraham Browne house in Watertown, Massachusetts. He described it in 1915 as "one of the very best old houses still standing in New England," but the Otis house campaign drew his attention. Over the next few years, billboards hid the house from the road, and it turned even more ruinous. Not only did the local historical society accept its demolition, but town authorities condemned it. Appleton even admitted that "the hole in the roof of the house was large enough to drive a crowded Ford car through." One of the summer beams had also decayed, and brought down the garret with its collapse. The owner allowed such ruination because he planned to sell the lot for suburban development.[58]

SPNEA's Board of Trustees told Appleton that it was beyond help and voted against its purchase. Appleton tried to find some descendants to buy the house, but failed to find "a single Brown who has more than car fare or two in his pocketbook." He gave up in late 1918, but planned to measure the building, buy the parts, and reerect the building near the Boardman house. In the final week before the demolition, the owner dropped the price, but a telephone strike fortunately kept Appleton from contacting his Board of Trustees. On his own initiative and with $3,000 of his own money, he purchased the lot and building in April 1919. As he later told one of his sisters, "between you and me and the corner lamp post . . . [the house] is my own personal monument and the fact that it is now standing at all is simply because I got mad and decided that it shouldn't be pulled down, but I would hate to tell you how many thousands I had to risk paying myself had my efforts failed. At one time it seemed as though I would have to sell everything I owned."[59]

After a few years of his own restoration work, Appleton gave the house to SPNEA but passed on a large mortgage. Concurrent with his attempt to raise that money, Appleton tried to generate publicity. One Boston newspaper helped the effort and went so far as to claim that Abraham Browne, Sr., who was originally thought to have built the house, had been the first to utter the phrase "No taxation without representation" and could therefore "be called the father of the revolution." Quite a different picture of Browne's importance emerges from later analyses, however. He had been an ambitious speculator intent on consolidating land, expanding the market, and bringing in the new order.[60]

Appleton was drawn to the Browne house by its Anglo-Saxon roots, archaeological evidence, and stark simplicity. He thought it had been built as early as 1640, but SPNEA later attributed it to Abraham Browne, Jr., and dated it between 1694 and 1701. Appleton regarded what originally had been one room on each of two stories plus a garret as one of the earliest types of dwellings. He advised that "our Preservation Society should particularly aim to save [such simple houses], because no other agency seems to care." Though enlarged over time, the dwelling was unique as it was "practically in its original condition, unspoiled by later changes of the old work, such as are to be found in practically every other old house." If properly restored as a museum, the Brown house "would be of the greatest educational value—a Mecca for tourists and a joy to all."[61]

After committing itself to eight buildings in its first decade, SPNEA increased its pace by acquiring twice that number in its second. Half dated before 1700 and showed Appleton's preference for postmedieval buildings. The acquisition of the Richard Jackson house (c. 1664) was a case in point (Fig. 4-12). He had first seen the Portsmouth house in his freshman year at Harvard. He found it "open and unoccupied" and inspected its interior. Although his "ignorance of old New England architecture was as great as anyone's very well could be," he liked the place "very much in a perfectly ignorant way." He visited it again in 1913, but failed to gain entry because it was "too filthy, with a large accumulation of rubbish." Its nearby owner evidently used it as a garbage dump.[62]

Appleton wanted the building, and he persuaded Bolton and Edith Wendell to inspect it the following spring. Barrett and Edith Wendell lived nearby and took interest in preservation, but Barrett most voiced "the conviction that our civilization . . . is fatally ill." Believing that the gentry suffered from "over-refinement," he found his own therapy by restoring his ancestral home. While Bolton and Edith inspected the Jackson house, however, he stayed home and napped. Bolton, typical for the literati, described New Hampshire's oldest dwelling as "history-less but picturesque."[63]

The house's owner, Nathaniel Jackson, credited the house with even less. "There is nothing beautiful about the old house," said the descendant of the original builders, "but it was built at a time when our forefathers thought more about shelter and refuge from the Indians than they did

FIG. 4-12   Jackson House, Portsmouth, N.H. (Photograph by The Halliday Historic Photograph Co., Courtesy, Society for the Preservation of New England Antiquities)

about ornamentation." An official in the United Brotherhood of Carpenters and Joiners, Jackson illustrated the chasm that separated modern craftsmen and medievalist antiquaries. Appleton regarded the clapboarded structure as "extremely interesting, in fact one of the most interesting" in New England. He took particular note of its plank frame (including walls framed with vertical planks), its collar beams, and its original materials. The saltbox addition at the rear sloped gracefully to almost ground height, and inspired many artists in New England. Some claimed, in fact, that the Jackson house compared favorably with the Fairbanks house in its picturesque qualities.[64]

Appleton wanted the Jackson house badly, but not so much as to interfere with the Harvard-Yale football game, "one of the big days of the year." As he negotiated the terms of sale, other obstacles arose. Jackson only wanted to sell the house with sixteen feet around it, so as to keep a cottage that he rented. He warned Appleton that this small hovel next door held former slaves who were "about as shiftless as the usual run of Negros." Eventually Appleton bought both the larger lot and adjacent cottage to preserve an Anglo-Saxon shrine. SPNEA's purchase came in the immediate wake of Portsmouth's tercentennial celebration, at which a grand pageant pictured the town's history from the Puritans to independence. Not surprisingly, this Yankee blood had been substantially di-

luted as the town had turned to industry, but the Jackson house, along
with the Aldrich Memorial, celebrated a time before "a wild motley
throng" had entered "the Unguarded Gates."[65]

Through the 1920s SPNEA maintained a steady pace of growth, re-
ceiving most houses as gifts from affluent members or sympathetic friends.
In 1927 it even purchased the Salem home of a merchant prince, the
Richard Derby house (1762). Perhaps the most interesting acquisition of
this lot was the Rebecca Nurse house in Danvers. The public most associated the dwelling with Rebecca Nurse, the fourth woman accused by
Tituba in the witchcraft delusion of 1692. Then seventy years old, Nurse
had protested her innocence, but was hanged at the gallows as a witch.
A group of descendants organized the Rebecca Nurse Memorial Association, purchased the home, and erected monuments and held pageants
vindicating their ancestor as a defender of freedom. In 1909, they hired
Chandler to restore the large clapboarded home with a massive central
chimney along the lines of the claimed date of 1636. Two decades later,
however, Appleton complained that "the somewhat thorough-going ideas
of the time" had led him to damage it through overrestoration. After the
group disbanded in 1927, SPNEA received the building.[66] Those many
steps represented the long process of remaking Puritan history.

The roll of acquisitions went on. By the outbreak of World War II
SPNEA had a string of thirty-eight properties that were valued well over
$500,000. "Peace and rest and quiet are of the graveyard but not for
living, growing organizations such as ours," Appleton explained. "It was
that great librarian, Justin Winsor, who said that the only library with
room enough was a dead library, and the same remarks applies to an
antiquarian society." SPNEA had difficulty using and restoring its buildings, however. Only a few years after its purchase, for example, Appleton
wanted to unload the Swett-Ilsley house. Always cash-strapped, he post-
poned maintenance until the neighbors complained about its "shabby"
appearance. SPNEA had not "markedly improved" it, he admitted, and
it was not "an attractive feature to the public." Although rented out for
commercial business, it was still "a somewhat costly proposition to run."
The building lingered and, as late as 1941, required extensive repairs.[67]

The Laws house in New Hampshire, for another, went unoccupied for
many years, and only in the late 1940s did SPNEA find a useful tenant
who established a local arts center. Maintenance was another matter, and
usually first ignored by a financially strapped society. Appleton admitted
that SPNEA's houses, whether used as a tearoom or a museum, bore a
"harder usage" than resident-occupied homes. Committed to the policy
of leasing buildings to tenants for commercial or residential purposes
whenever possible, he advertised the Cooper house in 1913 for $500 per
year and the Browne house ten years later for $600, but pledged for the
latter that those moneys would be used to repair and enlarge the house,
and make it suitable for a residence or tearoom. Committed to this pay-
as-you-go financing, he did not confront the fact that such tenancy might

prove destructive to an ancient building. Sometimes a tenant's plan did raise his eyebrows, however. When two "lady artists" asked to rent the Cooper house in Cambridge for a tearoom, art studio, and sleeping quarters, he thought that it was a "rather promiscuous" mix. "I forgot who was going to use the garret," he said, "—but it was not the servant."[68]

Appleton launched SPNEA with the expectation that annual dues would fund his acquisitions. Quite early, he learned the error of his thinking. In 1916 he wrote the president of the APVA and asked how it "could succeed on only $1 annual dues" when an active member paid $5 to SPNEA. Lora Ellyson confidently replied: "The answer is, in numbers there is strength."[69] By that time, SPNEA had over 1,500 members, as did the APVA. More accurately, the APVA acquired most of its landmarks by gift or conveyance, did little in the way of costly restoration, and relied on the volunteer labor of each chapter.

To escape SPNEA's financial impasse, Appleton acquired and restored the society's buildings through individual campaigns, bequests from loyal friends, and special accounts. In 1912 he created an "Emergency Fund," in effect a revolving fund for those crises when urgency was needed. His concern for bottom-line financing ultimately led to a policy of asking that donations of property be accompanied by moneys for restoration and upkeep. As one who lived off the annuities of a trust, Appleton knew its workings and asked members to create endowments. In an age of conspicuous consumption, he promised that "the results of such benefaction would be apparent to everyone." Those buildings already in SPNEA's hands would be underwritten by drives to generate an endowment, while dues simply covered the daily operations of the society. For example, the annual appeal of 1921, raised to endow the Arnold house and pay the mortgage on the Otis house, garnered over $9,200, seventy-five percent of which was given by 114 members.[70]

Despite these obvious financial limitations, Appleton's business acumen and Yankee friends put SPNEA on relatively secure footing. Those benefactors saw its work as a defense of their traditions, heritage, and continuing influence in a remarkably different twentieth century of flappers, flivvers, and fads. SPNEA had evidently struck a sensitive nerve. So tied to the Colonial Revival, its image of the past did serve modern purposes since there was a reciprocal relationship between traditionalism, preservation, and the remaking of history. The work of preservationists was not so much a case of falsifying the record as it was of selectively preserving and interpreting it. Whether or not Fowler was the community-minded industrialist, the Scots the ideal immigrants, or Otis the enlightened statesman was not so much a clear-cut matter of the record as it was a case of wishful thinking about their own society. The past would reconfirm what they needed in the present: tight-knit families around the hearth, strong-willed patriots to defend the land, and industrious newcomers who would be loyal and disciplined. Historic preservation was no sentimental affair; it had much to do with power in the present.

5

"A Gospel of Further Acquisitions"

Defining a Preservation Movement

As the economy and society fell into line during this period of quick-step modernization, the canons of the United States resembled more and more the principles of the boardroom. It took an enterprising Yankee to say it, but "the business of America was business." Historic preservation was no exception, and Appleton worked to shape a movement governed by the principles of hierarchy, efficiency, and bottom-line financing. Publicizing the necessity of forceful action, he prodded smaller societies, amateur collectors, and local and state governments to follow SPNEA's precepts. His campaign remade the movement in significant, and perhaps unforeseen, ways. As Appleton incorporated the axioms of business and science into preservation, not only were women slowly pushed to the margins but the powers of the state were significantly increased.[1]

During its first thirty years, SPNEA acquired forty buildings but, as Appleton admitted, it was "an unbalanced list of holdings." With three-quarters of its holdings in the Bay State, SPNEA only had three edifices in New Hampshire, three in Rhode Island, two in Maine, two in Connecticut, and none in Vermont. But SPNEA "bought almost nothing" and acquired largely what its members gave. The residents of Massachusetts, particularly metropolitan Boston, gave generously.[2]

Rhode Island was a different case. In 1923, for example, Appleton admitted to Isham that the Cyrus French house in Kingston was "one of the most beautiful houses in that section of the state." The house was linked to one of New England's revolutions, but it was the *wrong* one if he wanted to use patriotism to boost preservation, as General French had revolted against Boston's merchant oligarchy in Shays' Rebellion. "Horribly neglected," it deserved protection, but when asked to buy it, Appleton replied: "Not a chance in the world." His decision to let the house slide further into dilapidation, as well as the society's lopsided list of holdings in Massachusetts, resulted not simply from the Bay State's hold on SPNEA but from Appleton's policy of encouraging local societies to undertake their own preservation efforts. SPNEA had been incorporated in Massachusetts, and its initial legal standing and freedom from taxation were limited to there.[3]

In Connecticut SPNEA tried to avoid owning property. Its activity generally followed the pattern set in the Hiland-Wildman house (attributed to c. 1660), another postmedieval dwelling in Guilford. Appleton admired its chimney and staircase, but its chamfered girts captured his attention. "Practically unchanged since its erection," it was "preeminently worth preserving, being almost perfect throughout," he said, "and its destruction would be a decided loss in Connecticut and New England." Such a prize was threatened by so-called progress as an automobile garage wanted its land, but SPNEA declined a chance to buy the house. Joined by a former Connecticut governor, Appleton pressed local residents to form a house association, but only after the owner had hired a wrecker did they find success. They then loaned the group part of the purchase funds. As a result, Appleton described SPNEA's role not as a purchaser, but as a publicist. It had broadcast the importance of the house, sparked a drive, and in the hands of the Dorothy Whitfield Society, the house became a museum to honor the Puritans.[4]

Appleton followed the Brahmin tradition of self-help by bestowing his knowledge freely, advising others on the best means to succeed, but expecting them to assume their own burdens and perform the necessary work. A decade after SPNEA's incorporation, for example, he estimated that it had already been "a deciding factor . . . in the preservation of some three or four dozen" houses. Appleton had chosen not simply to establish his own society but to lead a movement. One student of Rhode Island preservation later credited his "astute guidance and persevering leadership" in giving "direction to New England preservation efforts."[5]

From the start Appleton created a society centralized in Boston where he could pull the strings. In many ways "the Hub" claimed New England as its own, and Boston traditionalists defined their past as Yankee history. As one trustee told Bolton, SPNEA should develop a regional approach where "state lines" would "be obliterated." Critical of decentralized movements, Appleton cautioned a southern preservationist that if her group worked "through chapters scattered all over your state," as in the APVA, "your energies will be frittered away quite hopelessly." Any true Yankee knew that the region's inhabitants prized their local identities, however, and Appleton tried to reinforce those sentiments through landmark preservation.[6]

He also could have modeled SPNEA on the ASHPS, which worked in New York but was hardly a movement. Although its honorary president was magnate J. P. Morgan, and its trustees were also impressive, the ASHPS had only 522 members by 1912. By then SPNEA had already outpaced it with 642; by 1915 it had 1,500 members; by 1922 over 2,400; by the outbreak of the Depression, almost 3,000.[7] Appleton wanted his members to prod their local historical and patriotic groups to join the movement. "By far the greater number" of those societies, he complained in 1914, "are content to sit tight and let the gifts of various kinds dribble in one by one as may be." He recommended that such a society keep "always a little ahead of what it thinks it can accomplish." So much depended on the commitment of individual leaders. "But for weak knees in many directions," he lamented to antiquary Henry Chapman Mercer, "fully twice as many fine old houses would today be standing in New England." Consequently, he advocated "a gospel of further acquisitions," whereby each local group would emulate the Lexington Historical Society or Essex Institute with a variety of holdings. "The more signs of ambition and life" that a society displayed, he thought, "the greater the support it receives from its friends and the public."[8]

By 1913 SPNEA realized that its resources would have to be used to encourage those local societies. It created "state accounts" that returned part of a member's dues to local work. Instituting the practice of matching grants, SPNEA was "more or less in the position of the philanthropist who draws his check for a fund provided the remainder is raised by other persons who are willing to give their appropriate amount."[9] This particular philanthropist had a shallow purse, however, and Appleton yearned to catch a millionaire to fund an endowment for preservation. In 1919 he contributed a lengthy article to *Art and Archaeology*, his principal literary piece outside of SPNEA's magazine. With help from University of Virginia professor Fiske Kimball, he set his bait to catch a benefactor who, hoping to elude the new income and inheritance taxes, would endow a foundation to fund not only SPNEA but the APVA, ASHPS, and Archaeological Institute of America.[10]

He continued that elusive search for the rest of his life. In 1926, for example, he wrote a well-placed New York judge who knew the Rockefeller family. John D. Rockefeller, Jr., had not yet committed himself to the reconstruction of Williamsburg and would eventually contribute some $400,000,000 to philanthropy. Appleton made his case by predicting that in the next half century approximately two-thirds of the historic buildings then in private hands would be either demolished or radically altered. He suggested that "a national fund for the protection of all the best work anywhere in the country should appeal as strongly to a man of young Mr. Rockefeller's tastes as a gift of $10,000,000 he recently proposed to the Egyptian government for a museum at Cairo." Whether it concerned the endangered walls of Constantinople or Bacon's Castle in Virginia, Appleton wanted to shape a hierarchy in preservation work, at the top of which would stand the Archaeological Institute of America. With Kimball, Appleton served on its Committee on Colonial and National Art, alongside such Bostonians as architect Lawrence Park, collector Francis Hill Bigelow, and Harvard professor Charles Moore.[11]

Interest in these antiquities was increasing. Not only had the Metropolitan Museum just opened its American Wing in 1924, but Ford would soon launch his project at Greenfield Village. Unfortunately for Appleton, Goodwin won Rockefeller's largess for Virginia's second capital. Continuing his search, he focused more on activating and funding the professional associations of archaeologists and architects for such preservation work. He even suggested that the one-house societies, patriotic organizations, and local historical associations be excluded from any such endowment because they did not reflect the gist of his professionalism[12]

While local societies worked to conserve their community's particular identity, Appleton increasingly used SPNEA to protect properties that possessed regional, not simply local, interest. In effect, he tried to define a New England identity through material culture. When asked to acquire the Bodwell house (c. 1708) in Lawrence, Massachusetts, for example, he admitted that it was "a good one," but thought that it was "not of the grade of excellence to justify its being of interest to the whole of New England." At the same time, he told the residents of Brighton, Massachusetts, that the Noah Worcester house did have historical worth, but lacked structural distinction. Therefore, its loss was "chiefly theirs and no future building however fine can ever give them back what they lost in the Worcester house."[13]

Although Appleton tried to define what was meritorious in New England's material identity, few of its local societies shared his concern about a building's construction. Most patriotic societies, as Chandler complained, showed more interest in placing a bronze tablet commemorating their noble work than in securing a restoration "actuated by the fitness of things." In 1914, for example, the Newburyport Chapter of the Daughters of the Revolution considered spending $1,000 to build a memorial. At the time, Appleton was searching for moneys to pay the mortgage on the nearby Swett-Ilsley house and suggested this as a "more profitable use" of their money. The ladies deemed it "more appropriate" to erect a granite memorial with a bronze tablet that "honor[ed] the memory of a patriotic citizen," but he eventually won their aid. He later recoiled that "much valuable effort and money" was wasted when those societies erected "memorial tablets stating that this, that and the other had at one time stood here or been done there."[14]

As Appleton groomed preservation according to the male professionalism of archaeology, architecture, and business, that reorientation slowly displaced women from their once-prominent standing in the field. The pattern occurred elsewhere, as in Virginia where the women of the APVA would be losing ground in the late 1920s to newer organizations in Williamsburg and Jamestown.[15] This is not to say that these men lacked any sentiment about old-time buildings. Instead, they channeled their feelings and ideology through the ostensibly scientific study of artifacts as historical documents. What was innovative about Appleton's course was that preservation was shifting its orbits from romance to realism, feminine to masculine, and personal to professional.

Just as Norton's sense of personalism required earthy materials to which human affection could cling, many female preservationists believed that historic houses could kindle a personal bond between modern visitors and earlier residents. "Every house has a life and personality of its own," said Jenny Arms Sheldon. "The closer we come in touch with this life, the more we love it, the deeper the impression it makes upon us." Sears admitted as much when seeing Alcott's Fruitlands; she felt its "ghost of the Past" and found herself reciting Longfellow:

> We have no title-deeds to house or lands;
> Owners and occupants of earlier dates
> From graves forgotten stretch their dusty hands,
> And hold in mortmain still their old estates.[16]

Women were still well placed in the movement. In Connecticut, for instance, preservation emanated from women's domestic sphere. George Munson Curtis, a founder of the Walpole Society, warned Appleton to remember those gender divisions. "Work on old houses . . . is especially in the hands of the Colonial Dames," he said in 1913, "and I am sure you will get more help from them than you will from the men." They administered the Whitfield house in Guilford, for example, after the state, town, and Dames had purchased it to establish a museum.[17]

The work of Celeste Bush reveals some of the many angles of women's interests. A school teacher who had moved to enjoy the quiet of rural East Lyme, she proposed forming a historical society around the turn of the century, but her "friends laughed at the idea." A handful did succeed in taking care of an ancient cemetery and placing tablets on historic spots. She most valued the Thomas Lee house (c. 1660), a postmedieval home with a saltbox, because it represented the "ideals [that] seem most necessary to preserve" in the modern age (Fig. 5-1). Voicing her own per-

FIG. 5-1   Thomas Lee House, East Lyme, Conn., 1924 (Photograph of Spencer Studios, Courtesy, Society for the Preservation of New England Antiquities)

sonalism and filiopietism, she thought that Yankees "must honor our fathers and mothers if we are to live long in the land." She feared the imminent demolition of "this beautiful old mansion" in 1914. Beautiful was hardly the case, however. What Appleton encouraged her to see was an archaeological document of rough hewn, timbered framing. It was a seventeenth-century dwelling that had "escaped that touch of mediocrity" associated with later renovation. Bush won SPNEA's financial aid and publicity, as well as that of the Colonial Dames and Society of Colonial Wars, in her campaign to save the Lee house.[18]

Appleton gave Bush other advice to set her work in his mold. In 1915 she told him of her idea to reorder a graveyard and reinter the remains in new coffins. At the time, female preservationists in Virginia commonly reinterred the "sacred ashes" of their forebears in new plots and used those rituals to regenerate traditionalism. In Boston, earlier Yankees had rearranged several old burial grounds, but the response was quite different. Oliver Wendell Holmes deplored the practice as "the most accursed act of vandalism ever committed within my knowledge."[19]

Appleton repeated that admonition. As far as he was concerned, the only remnant there having "permanent value" was the gravestone. Virginia ladies sought sacred ashes, but Appleton warned Bush that she would instead find "a thin layer of slime over the bottom of the vault, and in that a few metal buttons." Such a difference in perspective cannot simply be attributed to the lingering sentimentalism of southerners, but as much to gender attitudes. The era's professionalism increasingly stressed science, not sentiment. Appleton did not shift direction in one fell swoop, however. SPNEA still interpreted those gravestones not only as reminders of the importance of religion and character but as symbols of "the humanity-old controversy between tradition and innovation."[20] Ironically, SPNEA's focus on materials showed that it was verging toward innovation.

When Appleton spoke before historical societies, or even committed his hand to those groups, his advice sometimes unsettled preservationists. One case in point concerned the John Howland house (1667), a two-and-a-half-story clapboard building with a gabled roof and central chimney. In 1912 Lillie B. Titus, treasurer of the Society of the Descendants of Pilgrim John Howland of the Ship *Mayflower*, asked SPNEA to help preserve "the last house left standing in Plymouth whose walls have listened to the voices of the passengers of the Ship *Mayflower*." She had formed the Howland House Association to restore it "to the style of the olden days." Even tight-fisted Appleton countersigned a financial note to encourage the group but, as the project evolved, her sentimental, ad hoc approach to the restoration represented everything he opposed in the movement. He gave advice on the carpentry, but she turned a deaf ear. Without the guidance of a skilled architect, she ordered that much of the old work be ripped out of the building.[21]

When Titus proved unable to repay the note, Appleton asked his attorney to bring the matter to court. Rumors abounded that the house would be sold at a sheriff's auction, and indeed one was scheduled. Some members of the association publicly accused Appleton of pulling a fast one; he allegedly had engineered the default so that SPNEA could acquire Plymouth's premier house. Appleton diplomatically responded by praising the "good friends" who had come to the house's rescue. He welcomed this challenge because "the more publicity that is given the conduct of the Howland Association . . . the better I shall like it." Appleton knew that the publicity could be focused on her restoration and management. Just as men in major art museums were challenging the feminization of culture that had occurred over the years, so, too, did he question her sentimental, unscientific hand.[22]

Appleton ran into Titus two years later in a fray over the Shirley-Eustis house (1748) (Fig. 5-2). Once a grand mansion of colonial governors, the three-and-a-half-story, wood-framed Georgian building in Roxbury was topped by an elaborate cornice, dormered roof, and cupola. Like a roller coaster, the building had been periodically renovated after years of decline. Vacant in 1911, it was a patchwork of Georgian, Federal, and Victorian pieces. The spacious interior that once had greeted "almost every celebrity who visited Boston," including Lafayette, had been carved into "wretched tenements" for immigrants. It still was, he said, "the shell of the most magnificent colonial house now standing in New England." Preservationists acted when they did because the area was "rapidly going over to tenement houses." In fact, the congested neighborhood was a fire

FIG. 5-2   Shirley-Eustis House, Roxbury, Mass., before 1915, East garden front (Courtesy, Society for the Preservation of New England Antiquities)

trap, and Mayor Curley's buildings commissioner threatened to tear the structure down.[23]

Thinking that SPNEA's hands were already full, Appleton had pressed local Yankees in 1912 to form the Shirley-Eustis House Association (SEHA). As in Americanization campaigns elsewhere, he asked SPNEA's members to support "an opportunity for inspiring patriotic, historic and social work" in Irish-dominated Roxbury. When properly outfitted, it would be "of increasing interest to the older residents and of increasing value to the newer arrivals." In 1915 Appleton also interceded with the legislature to secure passage of an act exempting the house from the city's building codes.[24]

What complicated matters for Appleton was the role of Titus as the SEHA's secretary. While his interest in the house revolved around aesthetics and cultural politics, she was moved by personalism. Titus had roots in the neighborhood, having grown up there and even shared Sunday teas with Madam Eustis. A loyal defender of Yankee culture, she remembered her "grief" when "seeing strangers handling" the house and its contents so poorly after her death in 1865.[25] Yet in her administering of the SEHA, Appleton counted three strikes: She had mishandled repairs, failed to win financial supporters, and blundered when the group's charter was first written. The words "for charitable purposes" were apparently omitted, and the SEHA was not exempt from taxes.

A new charter had to be written in 1917, and Appleton, citing his professional standards, used the occasion to reconstruct the SEHA. According to Titus's account, he "very cooly informed me that he did not intend to have me serve any longer as secretary, [and] that he intended to have some 'new brooms' for the offices." Appleton's membership in the SEHA had allegedly lapsed, but he "proceeded to nominate a list of officers for election." He excluded "a very much embarrassed" Titus. She interpreted her ouster as a vendetta. "It must be clear," she wrote, "that he wanted to get square with me for showing him up to the public, when he tried to get possession of the old Howland House." She was also put off by his way of doing things. "No one wants to work with Appleton," she contended, because "he is so domineering." She dismissed SPNEA as imperial in its ambitions and tactics. "Appleton intended to try to absorb this house," she claimed, "as he has tried to do with others."[26]

In subsequent years Appleton held the SEHA together, despite the suspicions of Irish-American neighbors and the all-too-common indifference of Brahmins. Scrambling to win funds and support, he apparently remade the house's history. In 1924 he boasted to a public relations agent that its grand Palladian window had inspired Washington to reproduce it at Mount Vernon, but the extant record does not support his claim. Without adequate funding, the house museum closed during part of the Depression. Recognizing the impasse, Appleton compromised his long-held opposition to a federal hand in preservation and tried, unsuccessfully, to persuade the National Park Service to acquire the dwelling. His friends in the Colonial Dames of America opposed that takeover, however. Like Titus years earlier, they prized the house as their legacy from the grandees. To counter Appleton's plan, they even considerd moving the house out of the slum into a more parklike setting in the Fenway.[27]

The contest over the Shirley-Eustis house begs for explanation. Titus surely held a grudge against Appleton, but her accusations should be taken seriously. Rather than simply dismissing Appleton as domineering and manipulative, as the cold standards of professionalism would appear to many, her ouster represented one phase of what would become a dramatic shift within the ranks of preservation, as organizations slowly, but increasingly, regroomed themselves along the lines of SPNEA. Unlike the era's arts-and-crafts movement where women found a personal and profitable niche producing textiles and jewelry, the leading preservation organizations would thereafter be constructed in a corporate pattern, be business-minded in their dealings, and advocate scientific principles derived from disciplines as diverse as archaeology and business.[28]

Another dimension of that shift was an increased accent on architectural aesthetics, as in the case of the Sargent-Murray-Gilman house in Gloucester. Appleton spotlighted the house in 1916 and revealed the various threads of interpretation. "To all Harvard men," said this graduate of 1896, the house "is forever endeared as the birthplace" of Rev. Samuel Gilman, author of the ode "Fair Harvard." Here also lived Rev. John Murray, called the founder of American Universalism for challenging the power of the state-supported Congregationalist church. His house became associated, therefore, with "one of the most important legal contests in the history of freedom of conscience in America."[29]

Yet Appleton admitted that his real interest was drawn by artistic details. "The mantels in the two parlors," he said, "are also of such an astonishing degree of elaboration that it was largely on their account that lovers of New England architecture so frequently hoped this house might be preserved intact." He suggested further that preservationists purchase and remove two nearby wooden houses, recreate the original lot with its view of the ocean, and thereby create "a beauty spot in the business centre of Gloucester." If the aesthetics of architecture and landscape were of prime importance to Appleton, he only incidentally mentioned that the house had been built about 1768 for Judith Sargent Murray. Though slighted in her own day, Murray was later recognized as a chief theorist of women's education, perhaps the nation's first feminist, and one who had challenged men's use of tradition to manipulate women. At the very moment when women were campaigning for suffrage in 1916, her significance could have been highlighted through preservation, but aesthetics prevailed.[30]

Appleton's neglect of Murray and spat with Titus were not isolated encounters. He even tangled with good friends, such as Edith Wendell. Motivated by domesticity and personalism, she would freely restore the McPheadris-Warner house (1716) in Portsmouth in 1931 after wresting it from the grip of the Metropolitan Museum. She disregarded Appleton's repeated suggestions on the work, however, and he complained that she was "a dangerous woman" who was unable "to appreciate anything that isn't spic and span, neat and clean and lovely and beautiful, according to her own ideas of what she would like to live with."[31]

Whether it was Bush, Titus, or Wendell, Appleton worked to replace their personalism and feminine interests with his professionalism and aesthetics. Of course, the financial clout of some women or their tightly focused localistic ambitions enabled them to hold on in the field. Other prominent contemporaries, such as Mary Wingfield Scott in Virginia and Susan Pringle Frost in South Carolina, were able to blend personalism and professionalism, but their thrust was noticeably different from that of Appleton. Like many later advocates of a neighborhood-based preservation program, they were concerned first with community and second with architecture. For many years to come, professionalism, on the other hand, would stress architectural tastes, business sense, and scientific method. Certainly it was not the case pictured by historian Charles Hosmer, who did note that men were becoming dominant in preservation, but explained that "women apparently were not so enthusiastic about the field of architecture." More a case of insensitivity than misogyny, Appleton's professionalism helped to marginalize those who had been the pioneers of the movement.[32]

Those preservationists who were setting the profession also modeled their structures on the corporation. Like many progressives in the historical profession, they pictured society as an organic system in which elite organizations and their trained professionals held sway. Darwinian in its workings, the strongest of that fold would be self-assured, business-minded men who cast a hierarchy of command, preached scientific operation, and touted their expertise. Created during the progressive era, as was the National Park Service, SPNEA manifested this pattern within the preservation movement. These models and perspectives would shape organized activity within trans-Atlantic society. As SPNEA removed preservation from women's sphere, it limited the sentimental appeal and made alliances with those who held power. As a result, the Boston Chamber of Commerce did regard SPNEA with favor. "In the past," a chamber spokesman wrote, "many men had thought preservation a matter to be discussed only at Women's Clubs. . . . But, times have changed and men see the wisdom of preservation." Men recognized that it "serves as an instructor, acts as an inspiration and pays as an investment."[33]

Appleton publicized these precepts through SPNEA's *Bulletin*, a serial he began in 1910 and edited during the next decade. From its first days, the *Bulletin* was distinct in the field—the publications of kindred societies looked tedious and clumsy in comparison. The *Bulletin* revealed that the iconographical revolution transforming the publishing industry had hit the more specialized professions. He not only selected a wide range of photographs and architectural drawings to sell antiquities to his audience but subordinated them to a narrative that underlined the importance of energetic action, professional management, and accurate work.

He faced a dilemma over the proper balance in the *Bulletin*. Should he appeal to the populace, evoke their outrage, and shake their pocketbooks loose for his cause, as was so common in an era of muckrakers? Or should he produce a highly detailed, scholarly journal that targeted a small audience? Hoping to avoid the limits of both extremes, he took a middle road. "It is very hard," he wrote in 1915, "to strike an even mean which avoids too much technicality in wording and at the same time makes such articles worthy of being put into print." Scorning the sentimentalism that prevailed, he said: "I have the greatest contempt for the popular trash that is so often printed about old houses and would rather print nothing than something of only contemporary interest."[34]

At times, SPNEA did print nothing, rather than create controversy. Whether the issue involved somewhat dry details about the history of an old building or openly derogatory comments about the inability of Italian farmers to cultivate what was once Puritan soil, Appleton looked askance at anything that might alienate potential donors and friends. "We have made it our policy," he told one forlorn writer, "to avoid anything controversial."[35] Of course, SPNEA did publicize the virtues of traditionalism, a cultural package that was distinctly controversial, but only in the context of competing, alien traditions.

SPNEA expanded its *Bulletin* in 1920, gave it an even more appealing format, and renamed it *Old-Time New England: A Quarterly Magazine Devoted to the Ancient Buildings, Household Furnishings, Domestic Arts, Manners and Customs, and Minor Antiquities of the New England People*. Dow joined SPNEA specifically to launch this quarterly, and, as will be shown in Chapter 8, his perspective influenced much of its content. He worked for SPNEA until his death in 1936, and used *OTNE* not only to promote its brand of preservation but to advance the new scholarship in the social history of early America. Packed in between those messages, *OTNE* also promoted the collection of Yankee antiques, a connoisseur tradition so appropriate for Dow, Isham, and their friends in the Walpole Society. Such a topical blend was appealing, and one English preservationist described it "as well produced a publication of the kind I have rarely seen."[36]

Whether in the pages of *OTNE* or in Appleton's daily preaching, SPNEA regularly advanced the tenet that professional societies should manage the preservation of these antiquities. "The most casual knowledge of the fate of old buildings," Appleton wrote in 1919, "shows the uncertainty of such private tenure" by churches, clubs, and descendant families. Even historical societies committed acts of destruction when they altered or modernized their landmarks. Although his mentor Norton had called for the protection of family homesteads, Appleton distrusted their descendants to the point of questioning even the Adams family with the family homes in Quincy. For another, the Platts-Bradstreet house in Rowley, Massachusetts, had apparently suffered under the hands of a descendant who chopped a summer beam in half and, as Appleton said, it represented "the worst case of vandalism I have yet discovered." By custom, those families had a proprietary right to their homes and rarely acknowledged any community interest. The obstacle was Sir Edward Coke's notion that "A man's house is his castle," or, as Curtis put it, "The owner is, of course, Monarch of his Domain."[37]

Private corporations acted similarly. As affluent Yankees retreated from the city to seek the seclusion and camaraderie of country clubs, they acquired and altered to their needs one-time mansions of New England's elite, as when Waltham Country Club purchased the Governor Christopher Gore house (1799–1804). Even Harvard University did not stop after demolishing the home of Oliver Wendell Holmes. In 1928 it planned to demolish the John Hicks house in Cambridge, the home of a man who sacrificed his life nearby on 19 April 1775. True to the Yankee civil religion, Appleton wanted it instead preserved and "forever dedicated" to the memory of that "strenuous day" in American history. The college ironically wanted to replace it with a swimming pool for flaccid moderns! Again, Appleton compromised, especially with this Goliath, and worked successfully to move it from the site. Another preservationist complained that "too few Universalists," such as those who governed the college, "have sufficient respect for old houses."[38]

Just as Appleton looked suspiciously on private corporations, so, too, did he learn to question ambitious entrepreneurs in the increasingly popular business of history. At first, SPNEA helped assist the most adventurous one-man project of the era in preservation, the attempt by Wallace Nutting (1861–1941) to form a Colonial Chain of Picture Houses. Born amidst the poverty of Maine, he had become a minister but, like Appleton, suffered a nervous breakdown in 1904. His therapy was an immersion in antiquarianism, first as a photographer of old-time scenes for national magazines, then as a furniture collector and restorer, and finally as a businessman. Tapping the era's antimodernism, his business produced ersatz antiquities for Colonial Revivalists because he thought that authentic "antique furniture in a modern house is like a jewel of gold in a swine's snout."[39]

Nutting pledged to establish a new form of house museum by providing accurate restorations and artifact-rich interiors. Critical of what passed as "restoration" in his day, Nutting visited over seventy-five houses and claimed that "in every case they have been nearly ruined" by clumsy architects or daffy designers. What those buildings further lacked, and he would include, would be everything from period hardware to antiques. Unlike Appleton who reveled in the intricacies of a house's framing, Nutting thought that "the house is the shell and the furniture is the meat of the nut." He gave Appleton the unlikely line that his museums did not represent "a business venture" but an attempt to teach New Englanders about their roots.[40]

In 1914–15 Nutting acquired five houses for his Colonial Chain. They ranged from the Iron Works house (c. 1680) in Saugus to the opulent Wentworth-Gardner house (1760) in a rundown waterfront neighborhood of Portsmouth. "Without the knowledge of the Society's work," he complimented Appleton, "I should probably never have done any of this." The expenditure of "some hundred thousand dollars or thereabouts on good old homes and old furniture," he said, resulted "from pure love of good lines and the old American feeling." He pledged that he would own these houses "like the brook [that goes on] forever." Appleton applauded Nutting's "labor of love" and called him "a first class friend of New England antiquities."[41]

Nutting's fortunes turned sour, however, during World War One. Dependent on the visitor's twenty-five-cents admission fee, he complained to Appleton, who covered SPNEA's deficit with his annuity, that he did not have "invested funds to live upon like most persons who cultivate the passion for antiques." His brook ran dry, and he offered to sell all five houses and their furniture for $125,000 to SPNEA, but Appleton replied that it had committed all funds to the Liberty Loan. He privately said that Nutting was "an impossible man to deal with." He knew that Nutting's restorations had been idiosyncratic, and suspected that he was trying "to unload the property on us at a decided depreciation."[42]

Nutting blamed SPNEA for his losses and accused Appleton of persuading him to buy houses that SPNEA did not want. "The houses which I learned of through your society," he said in 1920, "were sold at a tremendous loss." Pressed for cash, he sold not only the Wentworth-Gardner house to the Metropolitan Museum, knowing that it planned to strip the interior, but much of his Georgian-era furniture to Wanamaker's department store. Appleton complained that it would "hereafter masquerade in various private houses of New York as of 'Dutch' or Southern origin." In 1924 Nutting sold his Pilgrim furniture to J. P. Morgan, Jr., but scoffed that he "didn't know any more about the value of an antique cupboard than a hole-in-the-wall."[43]

If elite Yankees or indifferent immigrants failed to advance the preservation movement, who would protect a community's heritage? Appleton certainly did not look to the federal government. When rumors abounded that Monticello, the long-neglected home of Thomas Jefferson, might be acquired by the U.S. Government, he predicted that if its fate was held by Congress, it would become "the foot ball of politics." Appleton called himself "an ardent Jeffersonian in his principles," and claimed that "Jefferson would turn in his grave at the mere suggestion that the Federal Government should buy his home by right of eminent domain." What Appleton wanted instead was ownership by a private organization, as was the case with the Mount Vernon Ladies' Association. He predicted in the Boston *Herald* that "a calamity" would follow once "the public assumed complete ownership and charge through some commission or federal department." So typical of Massachusetts reform in the progressive era, preservationists cast doubt on federal authorities intervening in local affairs.[44]

Tradition-minded Brahmins also held little confidence as well in the government's deciding questions of aesthetics. Boston possessed, for example, a handsome Greek Revival Custom House (1837–47), designed by architect Ammi B. Young. By 1913, however, the federal government required more room for its operations. As "stingy" as the government could be, Appleton complained, it chose not to construct a new building, but instead only "appropriated enough money to ruin the ancient Doric temple." Not bound by Boston's building-height limitations, it erected between 1913 and 1915 a 498-foot, sixteen-story tower from inside the building and created what he called "one of the fiercest architectural aberrations in America."[45]

State officials could show a similar ignorance. Both Massachusetts and Connecticut had capitols designed by Charles Bulfinch, master architect of the Federal Period in New England. In Connecticut in 1913, preservationists confronted developers who wanted to erect an office building on land occupied by the Old State House. Ever since the state had designated Hartford as the sole capital and commissioned Richard Upjohn in 1878 to design a newer capitol in the Victorian Gothic style, the future of the state's two earlier capitols was in doubt. In 1889 the state demolished a grand Greek Revival-style capitol (1829–31) in New Haven. Hartford's landmark (1796), one of the great pieces of Federal civic architecture, became a city hall. Set in a booming business district, the capitol could have been demolished, like its neighbor the one-time home of Chief Justice of the Supreme Court Oliver Ellsworth. "As usual," Appleton complained, "many so called 'practical' persons were unable to gauge the financial possibilities of attractive antiquities." He told Curtis, who represented SPNEA at public hearings, that he could easily generate a movement to prevent its demolition.[46] Shortly after, however, Appleton failed to persuade SPNEA's trustees to challenge the Massachusetts government when it planned to add marble wings to its own Bulfinch-designed, red-brick capitol (1795–98). The trustees took a narrow view of preservation, did not consider the compatibility of those additions, and ruled that "the new wings are in no way antiquities themselves."[47]

Activists increasingly did turn to the government during the progressive era to achieve what had been unachievable beforehand. Most commonly, progressives chose governmental action because they expected that their efforts in lobbying, publicizing, and vote-getting could protect their interests. Historic preservationists generally lacked such confidence in the federal government until the 1930s, however. For example, archaeologists and conservationists had persuaded Congress to pass the Antiquities Act (1906). As a broad-based bill that focused on archaeological landmarks in the West, it could have been applied to architectural antiquities in the East, but little was achieved.[48]

Bolton and Appleton held a states' rights perspective that placed the focus of such activity on local and state authorities. Appleton so lauded the roots of state government, for instance, that he was willing to "overlook the artistic failings of the Old Constitution House" in Windsor, Vermont, and urge its preservation as such a memorial. Appleton knew, however, that "in the matter of state and civic action" New Englanders were "vastly surpassed by the states and municipalities of Europe—especially France and Germany." In fact, a preservationist from the Royal Arts and Crafts Museum of Berlin visited Salem in 1914 and toured the historic neighborhoods, most of which would escape the town's devastating fire in June. He told Appleton that such landmarks in Germany "would all be listed and protected by law, and their owners allowed to make no alterations except by consent of the government." England was another matter after the courts undermined the Ancient Monuments Act (1913).[49]

Appleton had long opposed the U.S. Goverment using eminent domain but, consistent with his states' rights philosophy, he wanted local governments to fill the void. What brought fruit to his proposal was the calling of a constitutional convention in Massachusetts in 1917. Before its Judiciary Committee, Appleton single-handedly pressed an amendment "represent[ing] the work of the Preservation Society" to protect historic sites through eminent domain. As eventually passed (Appendix B), it declared that "the preservation and maintenance of ancient landmarks and other property of historical or antiquarian interest is a public use." Crossing his own Rubicon, he had challenged Sir Edward Coke. Writing every SPNEA member and historical society in the Bay State, he appealed for support. At a time when the suffrage was limited to men, he calculated that if all those men voted in its behalf, and women "influence[d] their men folks to do so," those 25,000 ballots would be "ample to insure adoption of the amendment." He did fear that there was "a lot of dead wood" in those groups, but almost all endorsed his drive.[50]

Appleton's proposal, the first ever to a state constitution, was introduced through a friendly delegate. In some ways, the convention picked up the progressive mandate of the "Boston-1915" movement when it passed amendments that restricted public billboards, established zoning, and protected natural resources. At the same time, it showed its business-minded conservatism by rejecting such proposals as a minimum wage and "one day's rest in seven" for workers. It rejected moves to enfranchise women and abolish capital punishment, but passed amendments creating the initiative and referendum.[51] Like a broad estuarial river, Bay State progressivism held many streams, some of which were at cross currents. The convention's rejection of social legislation to protect workers revealed the upper hand of business. Amendments to enhance natural conservation and historic preservation reflected another phase of progressivism whereby professionally trained elite received a public charge to protect the community. On the other hand, the direct democracy of the initiative and referendum mirrored the belief that "the people" should take power from "the interests." Just who was whom was a matter of opinion.

Encapsulating the debate that SPNEA had instigated, tradition-minded delegates broke into two camps over the landmarks amendment. Robert P. Clapp, the Lexington delegate who embraced Appleton's idea, had first drafted the amendment, which the Committee on Public Affairs revised but approved unanimously. When debate began in June 1918, he recalled Lexington's own battle to save the sites associated with the April 19 skirmish. He moved unsuccessfuly to revise the amendment's wording so that the powers of eminent domain could be exercised not only by the state and local government but by "any incorporated historical society in such city or town."[52]

Edmund G. Sullivan, a Salem delegate, endorsed the amendment and reiterated Appleton's argument. He told the assembly that close to 50,000 tourists visited Salem each year to see some fifty places, one of which was the "Witch House" (1675) made memorable by the witchcraft trials. Over the years, however, the building had been enveloped by additions. "Look at it now," Sullivan told the convention,

> with a wart on one side with a Chinese laundry in it and another one with a restaurant baker's shop in it. . . . It is liable to burn up any day. . . . It would be impossible to replace that particular landmark which thousands of people go to see every year, and yet the present owners of it will not do anything to restore the building to its original form. They simply drag down the money from visitors for entrance fees to see the interior upstairs and get the money out of the stores and other tenants of the additions and "sit tight." We ought to have it within our power to preserve that particular landmark and other historical buildings for the benefit not only of the people within our own State but the thousands who come from all over the Nation. . . . It is part of their education to be able to do so.

A few years earlier, the owners of another Salem landmark, the Grimshawe house made famous by Hawthorne, likewise rebuffed preservationists and sold it to "some aliens." Sullivan lamented that it had been converted into "a third-rate rooming house" for immigrants who "have but little knowledge or regard for our historical ideals . . . about which every boy or girl attending the English grammar schools in this country is familiar." Every town in Massachusetts held such landmarks, he said, but often "the people who own them or hold the title to them" were simply "not interested" in their preservation.[53]

Some delegates wanted to protect different Yankee traditions, however. Roland D. Sawyer of Ware took umbrage with the issue of eminent domain. "This resolution violated my Anglo-Saxon sense of justice," he told the convention, because it transgressed on the rights of private property, as did the amendment restricting billboards. Another delegate, Lincoln Bryant of Milton, warned that a certain elite was using the name of the community to advance its own special interests. He feared that the state was empowering "a few individuals, members of a hastily organized society, which very possibly does not admit to its membership anybody who wants to come in."[54]

Augustus P. Loring, a delegate from Beverly, further claimed that those societies were, like a horse-leech, continually asking for money. They were "a menace to this country." Hitting preservationists for their allegedly misplaced priorities, this delegate from a shoe-producing town where available land was scarce warned with much exaggeration:

> Look at China. There . . . two million people have to die of starvation every year on account of ancestor worship, because one-quarter of the arable land is taken up by the burial places of their ancestors. Are we going to reduce this country to that condition, where every old house that somebody thinks is interesting and will draw tourists to the town is to be preserved and kept standing, to the detriment of the health and the general welfare of the community?

According to Loring, the state had already given too much to those societies with an exemption from taxation and, if the amendment was passed, it would further drain the public coffers through the costs of eminent domain purchases. Ralph S. Bauer of Lynn concurred. Describing his industrial city as one that wants "to let the dead past bury its dead," he wanted to spur the economy.[55]

The delegates considered the state of Bunker Hill Monument (1825–42), a 221-foot granite obelisk built and maintained by a private association, on whose board Appleton and Bolton sat. Oddly enough, Charles Francis Adams, president of the association and delegate to the assembly, knew little about its plight. John J. Mahoney, who resided in and represented Charlestown, excitedly rejoined that its condition was "a disgrace to the city." Its sidewalks were nearly impassable, the grass had grown wild, and the government did nothing. "If there is any place in this State that ought to be honored and respected," he said, "it is Bunker Hill Monument."[56]

Massachusetts voters overwhelmingly ratified the amendment in 1918.[57] Even though he took credit for the idea, Appleton apparently did not give much effort to empowering the vaguely defined measure. Upon his petition, the General Court tried unsuccessfully to extend its authority through enabling legislation in 1919, and succeeded only many years later. For example, the bill in 1919 would have "authorized and directed" the Metropolitan Parks Commission, a haven of traditionalists, "to acquire in behalf of the Commonwealth, by eminent domain or otherwise, any other monuments or structures, together with the grounds pertaining thereto, which mark historic places, or commemorate historic events in the Commonwealth . . . for public uses and purposes." Bolton admitted that the proposal was "very sweeping" but "deserving of very serious consideration." Tradition-minded elite strove particularly to protect those memorials that defined the region as Puritan and Yankee so that, as the president of the convention put it, they could "tell their inspiring story to the generations that follow us."[58] He had in mind such memorials as Plymouth Rock, the Myles Standish Monument in Duxbury, the Pilgrim Monument in Provincetown, and Daniel Chester French's Minuteman statue at North Bridge in Concord. With this Colonial Revival the state would remind newcomer and native just who had established America.[59] Ironically, Appleton did not press other New England states to follow the example of Massachusetts. His amendment did inaugurate another phase of preservation activity years later. Although Appleton had wanted private societies to act, what followed was action by local and state governments. By that time, those agencies would be groomed in the professionalism that SPNEA had instituted during the progressive era.

6

"To Transform Dead Property into a Valuable Asset"

Destruction, Development, and SPNEA's Paradox

Whether it involved the "Witch House" or Plymouth Rock, preservationists packaged their antiquities in the era's fashionable wrapping. As a result, they fell into the paradox of looking back on a romanticized past, fighting cultural and economic battles in the present, but all the while trying to plan for an uncertain future. Historic landmarks and landscapes subsequently served as their platforms to prepare for war, fight radicalism, and boost the economy, as well as sell the Colonial Revival, develop parks, and acculturate immigrants. Controversy never ended as past and present became one.

While Appleton was campaigning for the landmarks amendment, he ruminated in his *Bulletin* about the effects of World War One on antiquities. In the United States preservation ground to a halt as "everybody's attention was centered on war work of one kind or another," while in Europe the annihilation tipped the balance in "the eternal conflict between the forces of destruction and the forces of preservation." Just as the Parthenon had been destroyed during wartime in 1687, or the Hancock house demolished in 1863, so, too, did antiquities suffer when the guns of August erupted in 1914. The German juggernaut rolled into France in September, and Europe's centuries-old landmarks were literally caught between a rock and a hard place. Just north of the Marne River, for instance, the medieval city of Reims with its ancient cathedral lay in the German path. Designed about 1210, and once the center of French civilization, Reims Cathedral stood as a powerful testament to the Gothic vision of God and man intertwined through architecture. Norton had encouraged countless Harvard students, including Appleton and Bolton, to appreciate its beauty and symbolic meaning. The defending French forces used it as a lookout, however, and the Germans retaliated. Its destruction, said Bolton, "enraged us all."[1]

The ravages of Europe's war further tore Boston apart. While the press questioned German tactics, Bolton wondered if their "brutality" stemmed from "Nietzsche's philosophy that it is weakness to be kind to the help-less." By 1915 he thought that "German hate has reached the point of childish rage." However, some Yankees, including Bigelow, did support the German cause. At the same time, many Irish-Americans anticipated Eire's independence with England's defeat, as did Martin Lomasney, a machine politician in the West End.[2]

Most revealingly, Appleton showed more than forbearance for the Germans. The Second Reich had broken the peace by invading Belgium, but Appleton thought that both sides were to blame for the ensuing de-struction. Moreover, when belligerents militarized landmarks such as at Reims, retaliation was "perfectly justified." He admitted holding a cul-tural sympathy for the Teutons. "My feeling is," he told A. R. Powys of SPAB in September, "that any German village is worth several dozen French or Belgian villages in antiquarian interest," and he hoped that war's destruction would not spill over into western Germany. In fact, those villages were not significantly different architecturally, but notice-ably different in ethnicity and culture.[3]

The shelling of Reims also forced preservationists to cross a major threshold. Assuming an international duty, SPNEA's trustees instituted and passed a resolution in October (Appendix C) lamenting the loss of "our most precious heritage" and calling on President Wilson to intervene diplomatically in the fray. SPNEA asked him to persuade the belligerents to avoid those landmarks and transport their moveable artworks to America for "temporary safe keeping." SPNEA circulated its petition within the ranks of New England's patriotic, historical, and professional groups, and "well over one-half of the societies . . . memorialized the President along the same lines." Some of the more professional organi-zations, in many ways hallmarks of the progressive era, turned a deaf ear, however. "Judging from their actions," Appleton told Barrett Wendell, "the architects and the large museums don't care what happens and would be perfectly ready to see all these cities [such as Bruges, Ghent, and Brussels] with their wonderful architectural monuments consigned to the ash barrel. Personally I should consider that the world had lost a great deal of what makes life worth living if these monuments were lost."[4]

Wilson failed to acknowledge those petitions. Appleton immediately asked the help of Senator Lodge, who as a youth had seen Hancock's house demolished. He told the member, and soon-to-be chairman, of the Foreign Relations Committee that American diplomacy could tip the bal-ance, as was the case at Antwerp. Apparently, its landmarks "were saved owing to the American consul putting into the hands of the attacking German commanding officer a plan of the city with every important mon-ument directly marked, so that the guns could be turned to avoid them." If the American consul had acted similarly at Reims, Appleton said con-fidently, "the Germans would have spared the building." Appleton, in fact, wanted "the American flag" flying over all such buildings and entire towns to make them "neutral territory." When Wilson failed to act, Appleton fumed. "Nothing that he has ever done," he told Wendell, "shows the least reason for believing that he personally cares a snap for any architectural monuments, or even knows the meaning of the word."[5]

Appleton's willingness to commit America's flag to the European theater in 1914 gradually turned to an acceptance of American entry into the war by 1917. Not all Yankees who held a Puritan pedigree and Harvard degree took this route, as was the case with antimilitarist Roger Baldwin. At the same time, Appleton rebuffed the peace movement. As the war dragged on, however, neutrality became more untenable for the Wilson Administration. Germany resumed unrestricted submarine warfare in January 1917, and Bolton expressed "great relief" when the United States broke off diplomatic relations with the Kaiser. The United States declared war in April, and he expressed glee that it would finally use "the fist in pacifist." A month later, Appleton also rebuked Mary Northend, a popular writer on New England antiquities. After American bankers had loaned billions of dollars to England and France, and U.S. manufacturers had provided the wherewithal for war, Northend lamented that it was "a war of greed . . . brought about by Wall Street and politatians [sic]." Appleton "wholly disagree[d]" with her opinion.[6]

Progressivism, preparedness, and preservation mixed quite easily. Not only had Teddy Roosevelt, the embodiment of the progressive era, rushed off to Plattsburg in 1915 to prepare for war, so, too, did Lynde Sullivan, who resigned from his position as SPNEA's Recording Secretary in 1917 to attend the Plattsburg training camp. Similarly, Edith Wendell led female preservationists with wartime work, serving as president of the Massachusetts Special Aid Society for American Preparedness. Even the example of Harrison Gray Otis was used to argue the case. During the European wars of the 1790s, a time amazingly similar to that of 1914–17, said Morison approvingly, Otis "helped to push through President Adams' policy of preparedness" and pushed a "naval policy which made the Stars and Stripes" respected on the high seas. Like its counterparts, the preparedness movement played on fears that social bonds were unravelling. George Creel, director of the government's Committee on Public Information, said accordingly: "When I think of the many voices that were heard before the war and are still heard, interpreting America from a class or sectional or selfish standpoint, I am not sure that, if the war had to come, it did not come at the right time for the preservation and reinterpretation of American ideals."[7]

Progressives demanded this regeneration more vocally after world war had turned apparently to world revolution. When Bolton heard that the Russian Czar had been toppled in 1917, he admitted: "No one in the future can know the chill at one's heart that such words [as 'revolution'] bring in these terrible times." His fears intensified that same day when the Athenaeum shook from "a severe bomb explosion" at the Suffolk County Court House. Bostonians thought that the revolution had come,

as rumors circulated of a "black hand" anarchist plot. He felt "an un-
dercurrent of terror" in the city.[8]

War's end brought little peace to progressives who saw America crum-
bling before their eyes. Massive strikes hit the nation in 1919 as hundreds
of thousands of workers challenged the status quo. In Lawrence, textile
workers successfully struck for a forty-eight-hour week with no loss in
pay. Bolton saw "threats of soviet" rule when workers demanded economic change; he feared that these "crippling" strikes were "the entering wedge of revolution." Tradition-minded Yankees of his stripe
"shiver[ed]" when the Boston police, ostensibly the defenders of law and
order, went out on strike. SPNEA's president even felt endangered around
his Athenaeum. "The masses of idle men keep one's nerves on edge," he
wrote in September 1919. "The mall opposite Park St. was alive with evil
looking fellows all playing 'craps' or some other gambling games. Many
plate glass windows on Tremont St. are shattered." During the strike,
Appleton hired "well armed" ex-servicemen to protect the Otis house,
and only "the arrival of the military" relieved his anxiety. The militia,
including members of Appleton's Union Club and Harvard graduates,
used force to disperse the throng, killing half a score and wounding hundreds.[9]

As the Red Scare led to mass arrests and coercion, the continuous loop
uniting imagined history and present reality became even more apparent.
Shortly after, Bolton took to the pages of *Old-Time New England* to
praise the steadfastness of his ancestors who "were ready at all times to
face realities. . . . If they wanted safety they were willing to strike terror
into the hearts of possible evildoers." Parents, for example, had taken
their children to a public execution of two African-Americans in Cambridge in 1775. While the man was hung, a woman burned at the stake.
As children watched they supposedly "learn[ed] respect for the law by
witnessing the horrible results of its transgression." In spite of these "grue-
some" happenings, Bolton thought that "'the good old days' were doubtless better than ours in many ways." In New York, preservationists also
feared that "society at large is suffering . . . from the criminal proclivities
stirred up by the war." Bolton moaned: "Oh for a month of Grover Cleveland!" Traditionalists went a step further and elected a modern Puritan
as Massachusetts governor; Bolton declared "a great victory for Coolidge,
law and order."[10]

What Calvin Coolidge most valued about old New England was not
its antiquities, but its use as a model for a "progress" that was defined
by business-minded elite in their boardrooms. In many ways, Yankee
preservationists felt comfortable in this world of Coolidge, corporations,
and Colonial Revivals. That feeling derived from the lingering hope of
progressives that their reforms would strengthen such respected values as
stability, order, and rule by the betters. No better architectural symbol
could be found for their mindset than a Colonial home, whether real or

revived. Steeped in the myth of the good old days, it symbolized a world without strikes, wobblies, and immigrants. Remarkable differences occurred in the ranks of preservationists, however, over just what was to be revived in the revival.[11]

The Colonial Revival represented a mixed blessing for preservation. It did increase interest in old-time architecture, particularly those Georgian homes whose artistry and large massing appealed to the era's wealthy, and their obvious roots to a parvenu in need of a pedigree. Yet those homes only found favor if remote from the uncomfortable hustle and bustle of the city. As culture became more and more commodified, preservationists stressed that one who owned such a historic home could gain distinction, find a sense of individuality, and be at peace in the roar of the 1920s. With the ascent of the Colonial Revival, Appleton was flooded with requests for information and feared that SPNEA was "in danger of becoming an amateur real estate office."[12]

Yet the Colonial Revival also distorted the preservation movement. Sometimes the case involved well-off urbanites who retreated from Boston and other cities to small towns where they fostered myths about the glories of the countryside. Those Yankees who sojourned along the coast or in the countryside associated those landscapes with a simpler, cleaner, and more wholesome life. They cringed as they watched Boston change. Though they won financial blessings amid that uncertainty, the Colonial Revival evoked the peace, stability, and cultural continuity of old-time America.[13]

While progressives often adopted the Colonial Revival home to represent the values of earlier Americans, architects did not generally depict the rough-hewn carpentry, irregular outlines, and simple plans of post-medieval dwellings. So much a part of the remaking of memory, new designs generally mimicked the clean lines and ordered plans of Georgian homes. The public resultantly perceived the colonial era as one of grace, stability, and comfort. Stylish, cozy, and roomy, the interior of a Colonial Revival home offered a full range of contemporary amenities. In some ways, it was a safe middle ground between the palatial, Neoclassic estates of the robber barons and the bleak, crowded tenements of immigrants. The irony of the style's design is most telling. Progressives associated those two-story, central-hall homes with enterprising yeomen who clung to their traditions, but they had often been built by calculating Yankees who won wealth by breaking into the market economy. So, too, did the Colonial Revivalists maintain a mythical hold on the past while entering the corporate economy.[14]

Preservationists divided over the worth of Colonial Revival architecture. As early as 1893, Drake had regretted its hypocrisy and pointed to the demolition of landmarks such as the Hancock house. He lambasted "our architects, those indefatigable purveyors to public caprice" who concocted "a fetich before which our national pride loves to prostrate itself." He warned Americans not to deceive themselves. "Reverence for the shadow is in this case a vicarious atonement for our sins against the substance. To use a popular phrase—a vile phrase indeed—there is money in it."[15]

One who did make that money was Cram. Deploring the nation's experiment with Greek and Italian styles during the "dark ages" of the nineteenth century, he applauded the Colonial Revival as a symbolic return to Yankee roots. In 1896 the highly popular *Ladies' Home Journal* even included one of his essays with blueprints on how to build "A $5,000 Colonial House." As the Colonial Revival gained even greater momentum, Isham joined the bandwagon, as with his essay on the colonial homes of Providence for *The White Pine Series*, published by an industry trade bureau to promote the use of its wood in Colonial Revival reproductions.[16]

Other preservationists took exception with the revival's fresh touch because it made the authentic colonial look pale in comparison. Those small, unsophisticated homes that survived from the early colonies, Appleton explained, "lend themselves with great difficulty to the average person's idea of a comfortable home." As a result, they were enlarged and renovated, and he deplored the resultant "mediocrity." Any one of those original dwellings, he thought, "seems in every way better than anything intended for similar purpose that our modern architects and builders are able to produce."[17]

In many ways, the Colonial Revival home contrasted dramatically with the postmedieval. Antiquaries of Kelly's mindset looked at the old framing with oak timbers measuring 16 to 18 inches thick and imagined the vigor of yore. Modern society seemed flimsy and weak. "The frame house of to-day, built as it is of 2-by-4 [inch] studs which must be sheathed with inch boards to impart to the framework the practicable modicum of rigidity," he thought, "seems pathetically, not to say ludicrously, frail." Focusing on ornament and plan, Chandler contrasted the handcrafted original with the machined counterfeit. He claimed that even a layman could "discern that the earlier product is the more quiet and contained, while its supposed imitation . . . is too likely to bristle with features with the sad inclination to be unstudied, badly proportioned, and generally uncomfortable in disposition." SPNEA's task, said the Boston *Evening Transcript*, would be to revise that sense of aesthetics. "Merely as an educator and corrector of taste in domestic architecture," it reported, "such an organization pays its way." SPNEA, like the BSAC, found one niche as a tastemaker in a consumer society.[18]

A little-noticed aspect of the Colonial Revival was the attempt by preservationists to protect the New England town and village. As the region grew by leaps and bounds, and as the automobile and interurban transit encouraged mobility, these small towns faced a crisis. Horace Wells Sellers, an Anglophile architect, addressed the danger in *Old-Time New England*. In an essay entitled "Preserve the Charm of the New England Village," he cited the warning of British Prime Minister J. Ramsay Macdonald, the leader of the Labour Party, to protect the "quiet peaceful settlement" and ancient cottage as "sanctuaries for the human foot and human mind." As was so typical of the therapeutic bent of antimodernists, Sellers prized New England's own villages as models of an era "when heart and hand went into the production of everything" in home life.[19]

According to Sellers, those villages in old England and New were threatened by "uninstructed, ill educated" workers who were escaping the industrial city and carrying "with them all the most detestable characteristics of the detestable civilization from which they flee." They were introducing "their bungalows and stereotyped improvements" and destroying "the very thing they have sought." He raised a tocsin, but revealed the attempt of elite Yankees to maintain the countryside as their reserve, while abandoning the city to the working classes. Compounding that irony was the obvious fact that, as far as preservation was concerned, the "stereotyped improvements" included the Colonial Revial home of affluent urbanites.[20] Preservationists who extolled country values lent a philosophical reason for that urban exodus.

As in the case of Wethersfield, Connecticut, these small towns were at the same time losing many of their old homes through demolition or conversion into tenements and businesses. Regretting the waning of the small town's face-to-face community and the waxing of the impersonal city, Appleton warned that Wethersfield was "fast losing its individuality." It was "necessary" to conserve those homes, he said, "if New England is to preserve its old-time flavor." Dow also voiced his concern for those villages, and called them "the noblest accommodation of man's life and actions that I have encountered." More optimistic than Sellers, he deemed them alive and well.[21]

What increased the wear and tear on those villages was a trend promoted by preservationists, tourism. Well before the dawn of the twentieth century, tourism had begun to develop in New England, first at natural attractions and then at historic ones, as Yankees sought refuge from the city. Although nineteenth-century preservationists had commonly denounced commercialism, their successors began to hawk their ancient wares to a wider audience with the advent of car culture. When SPNEA campaigned to preserve the Jackson house in Portsmouth, for example, Appleton penned a circular, signed by a local businessman, and predicted that commerce would boom with such "drawing cards" as that and the Aldrich Memorial. "Every dollar spent in adding to this heritage from the past," it was said, "will come back to us many fold in the business brought by the constantly increasing tide of summer motor travel." SPNEA's vice-president for New Hampshire bluntly told Appleton that historic sites had to be "money-makers" for the town. "You will find much interest here in material things," he advised, "but very little in sentimental."[22]

So, too, did Boston's businessmen seek those dollars. Their Chamber of Commerce had earlier estimated that summer tourists spent $60,000,000 or more in New England. SPNEA's work obviously did not set "growth versus beauty," as one historian pictured it; instead, it promoted such growth to finance the protection of beauty. Those revenues could be significant for the empty coffers of preservation organizations. Almost 30,000 tourists paid the twenty-five-cents admission fee in 1924 at the House of the Seven Gables, for example. That money-making did not impede the museum's message. One visitor still saw within the "wood and plaster" of the house "some vision of the old America and some idea of the manifold duties of the new." Moreover, and at a time when the Maine Publicity Bureau was repackaging that depressed state as a haven for visiting naturalists, a corporate executive said in *Old-Time New England* in 1929 that the goal of preservation should be "to transform dead property into a valuable asset." Historic sites and a landscape with century-old trees created a "material scenery" and an "atmosphere" that drew tourists. Even Isham advised towns that held "a wealth of colonial work . . . to exploit their riches."[23]

Just where boosterism ended and blight began was difficult to establish. Few preservationists glimpsed the other side of the tourist coin, not only the resultant overdevelopment of neighborhoods and towns but the strain that thousands of tourists put on fragile old buildings. Few anticipated the impact of the car and its culture on the settled past. For example, Appleton wanted SPNEA to acquire a Samuel McIntire-designed house in Salem and saw only the dollar's lure. "Its location on the main highway," he wrote cheerfully, "insures the maximum automobile traffic during the tourist season." Cars encroached on the once-impenetrable wilds as well. Appleton was asked in 1913, for example, to help protect the Sturbridge Trail, and he suggested that the state acquire "some fine trails" for public enjoyment. Pandora's box opened, however, when he suggested that they also be maintained as "driving roads."[24]

At the time, Ford Motor Company was successfully advertising its cars as the American dream. Appleton, who did not drive, confidently predicted that the creation of house museums would bring thousands to Portsmouth. He even speculated that it would make "Portsmouth a pleasanter place to live." The city did faintly try to boom tourism through pageants and museums, but its fate resembled the plight of all-too-many towns that failed to appreciate their past. Commercialism, elite withdrawal, and so-called urban renewal by business-minded leaders left it with old neighborhoods that increasingly had less character and more traffic-driven development. The trend intensified with the years, and Appleton later recounted the story that Prime Minister Macdonald had cancelled a trip to New England because gas stations and modern trappings were replacing too many of his favorite old houses. "Multiply this experience by several thousand every year," he warned, "and figure the loss to New England—a real tangible money loss in failing to keep the travellers."[25]

Rather than interpret preservation's accommodation to business as a Faustian deal, it is more appropriate to set it in the context of the movement's class leadership and progressive-era norms. Appleton typified the mold. Boston's elite had long recognized business as the primary mover of society. As Santayana admitted, Boston was "a commercial community" where "weight in the business world was what counted."[26] It must be remembered, however, that the allure of the dollar was hardly incompatible with the cultural politics of traditionalism and the Colonial Revival. Preservation found its niche therein.

The tercentennial commemoration of the Pilgrims' landing is a major case illustrating those themes. New Englanders had anything but forgotten the founders, but if the Pilgrim Monument at Plymouth was typical, any memorialization had to be well organized and financed. The monument's construction had begun in 1859, but it was only dedicated thirty years later. Many other memorials were laid in old and New England to draw the hearts and wallets of patriotic tourists. In the 1880s Plymouth Rock was sheltered under a canopy, partly because relic-hungry visitors had been chipping at it.[27] After founding SPNEA, Appleton petitioned the General Court to celebrate the Pilgrim Tercentennial. By 1920 it meant different things to different people, but SPNEA helped to bridge the gap. As Americans, including the President and Vice President, came to honor the Pilgrims, preservationists used their legacy to fight radicalism and internationalism, promote conservatism and tourism, and refurbish Anglo-Saxonism.

SPNEA booster Charles W. Eliot headed the Pilgrim Tercentenary Committee. While the tremors of the Red Scare were still reverberating, the former Harvard president used Plymouth Rock to buttress conservatism. "The people must be taught," he warned, "the insidious dangers that threaten and be encouraged to combat the dogmas of ultra-radicalism—anarchy, Bolshevism, communism—and other misleading sophistries which now attack the very life of our Republic." As in the elitism of Harvard or "Boston-1915," he called on a select group of "forward-looking men" to serve and "guarantee that all things necessary shall be done effectually to controvert all unsound, un-American dogma or propaganda." His celebrants pledged to Americanize the newcomers by fostering such virtues as self-denial, patriotism, and respect for law and order.[28]

While government authorities undertook their witch hunt, Eliot pictured the Pilgrims as truly American heroes who lived the simple life, worked hard, and worshipped God. Funded to the tune of over one million dollars by the national, state, and local governments, the tercentennial became an opportunity to "create in the hearts and minds of our people the love of liberty and an allegiance to those tenets of a free republic first instituted by the Pilgrim Fathers." Eliot's interpretation fit into a long tradition. In the Revolution, patriots had used the rock to "encourage the slackers"; Whigs of the 1830s used it to combat Jacksonian Democracy; and even in 1907, at the height of the new immigration, President Roosevelt laid the cornerstone for the Pilgrim Memorial Tower in Provincetown. In 1920, Yankees consequently pressed the newcomers to "make a vow to preserve the honor and integrity of this country, given to us by our English ancestors."[29]

In 1921, SPNEA brought Appleton's friend and mentor to speak before its annual meeting. Eliot took to the rostrum and predicted that SPNEA "would become a permanent institution and one of the powers for good in New England." Declaring that "the preservation for posterity of the memorials of its ancestors was a work of piety," he applauded its work of education.[30] Piety turned to politics that same year not only when Congress enacted the first quota to restrict immigration but the state convicted Sacco and Vanzetti in a heated wave of xenophobia. Traditionalists had repeated the myth of the Puritans as defenders of freedom, but neglected to mention that their freedom was based on the intimidation and persecution of dissenters. In a cruel twist, the case of Sacco and Vanzetti was indeed part of the Colonial Revival.

During the tercentenary, preservationists in nearby Marshfield declared their own acts of piety. "We are planning to live over again in pageant," they said in *Old-Time New England*, "our settlement of this country." Uncomfortable in a nation of newcomers, social mobility, and cultural critics, especially those like H. L. Mencken who attacked the Puritans as kill-joys and frauds, Marshfielders claimed that they "know and preserve their traditions, and they know and preserve those places from which the traditions spring. They give local pageants and entertainments which have their origin in local history. They simulate local personages in order that it shall not be forgotten that such distinguished people contributed to their own village." Accordingly, they preserved the Winslow house, a late seventeenth-century "Gothic" home whose central chimney symbolized those roots. Left unmentioned was the fact that its builder had little regard for preservation and had cannibalized an earlier Winslow dwelling for his materials. Marshfielders also enshrined the Winslow Burying Ground, in which rested the remains of Daniel Webster, the ultimate nineteenth-century symbol of Yankee public service.[31]

Whether it was the physical material in that "Gothic" home or the stone on Plymouth's shore, it acted as a magnet for that pride and Appleton urged its protection. Despite the cloud of uncertainty that hung over Plymouth Rock as the actual point of arrival, for example, he said that "the Rock stands as the visible symbol of the permanent landing." Praising the Colonial Dames for enshrining the stone, he considered it appropriate that it was transferred to "a far more pretentious and beautiful canopy" with many columns and a balustrade. Such reverence soon turned to outrage. One dark night, someone painted Plymouth Rock red. At first, locals blamed the Communists whom Eliot claimed were all about, but the culprits proved to be Harvard pranksters. Many of those youth also saw the rock as a symbol, one that represented so much of what was wrong with the traditionalism of their prudish parents.[32]

SPNEA also committed itself to more practical pursuits during the Pilgrim Tercentennial. It did offer its podium to kindred souls to circulate their ideas, but it mostly promoted its own agenda. Bolton, for one, wanted the celebration to generate good publicity and new members. In the midst of a fiscal crisis, Appleton focused on *money*. "Personally I think that cultural exhibitions," he wrote in 1916, "sound like a lot of poppycock nonsense, and rather tend to believe in the kind of fair that brings most people to Boston, and booms business most effectively."[33] He wanted tourist dollars, endowment funds, and more dues-paying members.

Although the Chamber of Commerce regarded the promotion and preservation of history as investments, many business developers disregarded such advice and forced Appleton to blink when some antiquities stood before the wrecking ball. As the Boston chamber aptly described SPNEA's policy, its preservationists "endeavor[ed] to place equal stress upon the idealistic and the practical. They would not preserve where impractical. They would not stand in the way of commercial growth. Where expansion demands that a place of little historic importance be torn down the officials do not hold off and insist upon its remaining." Indifferent owners failed to keep up the Timothy Paine house in Worcester, for example, and its fate was uncertain. Sentiment had made the house famous, for while visiting there John Adams allegedly had said that he would also drink to the devil if asked to toast King George III. Despite his long standing role in the SR, Appleton admitted that he was "very lacking in enthusiasm for the house," and thought that "the best use to which the land could be put would be for the erection of a mass of three-deckers."[34]

Three-story apartment buildings did not replace the Paine house, but a developer's plan to build a row of shops in Cambridge ran like a juggernaut over the Watson-Davenport house. Appleton valued the house not simply because it was in perfect condition but for its "associat[ion] with the stirring events of April 19, 1775." Just as SPNEA used the Cooper-Frost-Austin house to reestablish Cambridge's identity as a Puritan settlement, so, too, did Appleton want the Watson-Davenport house as a memorial to the Revolution. Developers had a different identity in mind, and SPNEA abandoned the building to its fate.[35]

Similarly, Appleton dared not condemn too boldly those developers who wanted to build a tall office building on the Boston site where stood the remains of Province House (Fig. 6-1). Erected by Peter Sergeant in 1679, it had been acquired by the colony as a governor's house about 1715. Destroyed by fire in 1864, the house still had three walls and a massive double chimney in the early 1920s, and Appleton deemed it superior to Bacon's Castle as an Elizabethan manor house. At the behest of the governor, he asked the developers to move the chimney and, when that failed, accepted measured drawings by Thomas T. Waterman as a form of preservation. Years later, one of his successors recognized "the startling importance of this imposing seventeenth-century mansion," and

FIG. 6-1   Demolition of the Province House, Washington Street, Boston, Mass., 1922 (Negative from the W. K. Watkins Collection, Courtesy, Society for the Preservation of New England Antiquities)

wondered "whether or not its loss was indeed to be reckoned first among all others."[36]

What prompted Appleton's action was one of his unwritten rules, "Don't bite the hand that feeds SPNEA." Boston had defined development as the primary goal, particularly after New York had supplanted New England's influence. But, as the economy became more competitive, the New England Tercentenary Club, a band of historical and commercial boosters, worried that Boston was losing its historical identity. Deploring commercialism, it warned in 1920 that "the spirit of New York is the crushing power that broke the Roman Empire and we must overcome it here in Boston."[37] Within the limits imposed by corporate capitalism and Brahmin culture, preservationists did confront those who threatened historic properties and seemed most to violate their conception of a proper Yankee. As a result, new immigrants, insensitive bureaucrats, and self-centered speculators bore the brunt of preservationist pressure. It must be underscored, however, that the ambivalence and indifference of Yankees themselves were to blame for much of the destruction.

Those Yankees had been abandoning older neighborhoods for suburban quarters, and newcomers rushed in. As the ethnicity of Boston changed, for example, Bolton murmured in 1916 when he filed the papers for the Otis house that "the Registry of Deeds was crowded with Jews and Italians." All over New England, preservationists challenged poor immigrants who failed to appreciate their tastes. In the countryside, immigrants moved onto the abandoned farmlands of the Puritans. What happened to the Norton house in Guilford was repeated in East Haven, Connecticut, when two Italian builders demolished the seventeenth-century Moulthrop house and built "a two-family tenement on its site."[38]

Bradley Tavern (1738) was another case and, according to Appleton in 1914, "distinctly worth preserving." The evolution of Haverhill, Massachusetts, from remote frontier to booming shoe factories had gone hand-in-hand with the tavern "going down hill, ending with a quite unsavory reputation." Its owner—"a foreigner"—dismantled the building to sell its sheathing, bricks, and timbers, prompting Appleton to mourn that a responsible Yankee "with courage and enterprise" had not acted to save Bradley Tavern. Haverhill also held other imperiled antiquities, such as the Hazen Garrison (then attributed to 1680–90). Appleton called it "the most interesting brick house in New England" and "a gem of very first rank" because it gave "so good an impression of a small English manor house."[39] The house ironically was later damaged and devalued by Nutting's overrestoration.

Appleton ran into immigrants elsewhere. In Boston's congested North End, the Dodd house (c. 1800–10) had been "practically unchanged" over the years. Its residents had even recently cooked over an open hearth with an old-fashioned crane. The Salem Street dwelling had "excellent" examples of woodwork, moreover. Whether immigrants resented the fact that Yankee antiquaries showed more interest in an old building than the plight of the newcomers, or felt indignant that playgrounds were few and far between, it is difficult to say, but the unoccupied house "promptly became the prey of local vandals who smashed windows, doors and other woodwork." Unwilling to commit his hand in such surroundings, Appleton dismissed the house as "doomed." The MFA, SPNEA, and other "appreciative hands" stripped its woodwork.[40]

In Gloucester, where Anglo-Saxon seafarers had given way to Italian and Portuguese fishermen and factory workers, the Stanwood house fell to a similar fate. Again, a skirmish over the fate of an old building revealed an underlying contest for power and a deep cultural clash. A preserved house from Puritan forebears could become a claim on the neighborhood that would identify not only its past, but implicitly its future. SPNEA tried to gain custody of the house, but negotiations stalled while Appleton haggled over the price. He called the seventeenth-century dwelling "picturesque," yet it remained vacant and dilapidated. It was then burned to the ground by what he called "a gang of hoodlums who have been doing much damage in that part of Gloucester." This vandalism should not be casually attributed to the allegedly irrational impulses of unthinking foreigners, however. Facing ethnic and class discrimination and relative economic deprivation, these youth most likely lashed out at what they could reach, and the victim was a building. Perhaps one man's artifact was another's eyesore; one man's symbol of worthy ancestors was another's tenement owned by outsiders.[41]

Nearby in Gloucester, the Davis-Freeman house (c. 1709) possessed those medievalisms that seemed to catch Appleton's eye—a hewn overhang with carved posts and a very simple wood frame. This "peculiarly interesting and valuable house" fell victim to two different types of alterations. First, Nutting stripped it of its hardware. Then its African-American occupants tried to improve what remained. As Appleton told antiquary Donald Millar, "the entry doors on the chamber floor were interesting until the darkey family got rid of one for something wholly modern."[42] As was so typical, one man's improvement was another's curse. Appleton said little about Nutting's brand of vandalism, however, because SPNEA sometimes acted similarly.

Preservation in such cramped, immigrant neighborhoods was increasingly difficult for Appleton, as was the case with the West Roxbury Meeting House (c. 1773) (Fig. 6-2). After its congregation moved to escape the immigrants and find safer quarters, the meeting house declined. Edward Everett Hale, the noted Boston clergyman, led a drive to repair and purchase the building, but it was abandoned about 1890 and the next generation of preservationists would not maintain the momentum. When offered to SPNEA in 1912, it was encumbered with a large mortgage and the trustees declined. What most miffed Appleton and violated his ethic of individual responsibility was the fact that "perhaps the wealthiest Unitarian in the country" held the mortgage. "If she cared so little about this building as to let it be pulled down," he wrote, "the rest of us were entitled to care even less." Trustees such as Cram, moreover, held little favor for what he called those "barren" meeting houses. In his "revolt" against Puritan society, he designed All Saints' Church (1894) in nearby Dorchester to accord with his Gothic Revival aesthetics. Lacking sufficient friends, West Roxbury Meeting House was demolished in 1913.[43]

A similar roll of the dice faced First Parish Church, Roxbury (1804), in whose tower hung a bell cast by Revere. Nestled on a green, it overlooked the encircling homes and presented a comfortable, if not mythical, picture of an old-time village. After Roxbury had been taken by Boston in 1868, the congregation dispersed. The neighborhood was "invaded by

FIG. 6-2 West Roxbury Meeting House, West Roxbury, Mass., 1892 (Photograph by Charles M. Seaver, Courtesy Society for the Preservation of New England Antiquities)

foreigners of all creeds" and became Curley's political base. Crowded
apartments occupied the once-rural land, and Appleton successfully asked
SPNEA's members to fund an endowment to protect the building.[44]

Local governments similarly threatened antiquities, as in the case of
the Benaiah Titcomb house in Newburyport. Appleton admired not only
its medieval overhangs but its Jacobean staircase. The city offered it to
SPNEA if it would move the structure, but the trustees declined, based
partly on the peculiar logic that Isham had already measured the building.
Scavengers meanwhile "removed the best portions of the interior," and
SPNEA took the doors and entire staircase for its museum. According to

Appleton, "the building was then abandoned to its fate." The house was taken apart by an antiques dealer, and reerected in 1917 in Essex with its doors and staircase on loan from SPNEA. It did not satisfy Appleton's archaeological standards, but he found it "amazing to see the old building put together again in any form."[45]

Not only did city governments require more space for their operations, so, too, did they adopt building codes and implement town planning for public needs. In each case, old buildings often stood in the way. An "ancient pair" in Newport, Rhode Island, caught Appleton's attention in 1924, for instance. In the nineteenth century, the city's quaint neighborhoods with their narrow streets and cramped quarters had markedly deteriorated. One of those buildings was of "first-class importance," Appleton claimed, but it was "in the run-down condition so much disliked by fire departments and boards of health." The buildings were condemned, but he did not understand "just what may be the danger from either fire or plague due to the mere fact that a residence is empty and somewhat out of repair." These bureaucrats were indeed biased against older dwellings, but again public standards conflicted with antiquarian tastes.[46]

Changing standards also prompted cities to create urban playgrounds and parks. Proposals repeatedly aired in Boston, as during the "1915" movement, to demolish significant parts of the North and West Ends to build those facilities, and revealed so much about Boston's progressivism—its fears about the underclass, its hopes for improved housing, and its belief that patriotism could bond a fractured populace. Many progressives were also revolting against not only formalism in the university but the architectural remnants of the discredited old order. In 1919 Millar encouraged Appleton to consider a proposal aired by city officials to create a park around the Revere house. "Many buildings will be torn down to give space for yards and streets," he cheerfully told him, and those included eighteenth-century houses. "They have an attractive sketch showing the Paul Revere house standing free in the park. How fine that would be," he thought. Those plans were revised, but the city commissioned Shurcliff to build Paul Revere Mall in 1933, a full city block of cleared park in the midst of the crowded North End. There, Cyrus E. Dallin set his equestrian statue of Revere on his fateful ride.[47]

The immigrants, often from peasant cultures where land was more plentiful, did need land for recreation. As was the case in Salem, a city whose population was mostly foreign, young boys ended up playing in old cemeteries. A cultural clash followed when John Robinson of the Peabody Museum tried to remove them and raised their ire. He asked SPNEA for help in 1915. "In their vigorousness," he wrote, "they are now deliberately smashing headstones. I got two wheelbarrow loads of them (headstones, not boys—I wish it was the latter) this afternoon and had them put in the museum cellar." Appleton wanted residents to act "as extra police officers to arrest immediately at sight any children who might be misbehaving in the cemetery." As the Second Reich was mauling its enemies in the war, he ironically praised "the good behavior of children in Germany" where tight discipline was maintained. Those children in Salem, on the other hand, were "heedless of the rights of others," and he wanted the culprits to be forced to work "as a boy or girl scout force" for the community. After all, the Scouts represented one means to build traditional values in impressionable youth.[48]

Progressives sometimes found preservationists in their way, however, when they tried to build parks. In the Boston suburb of Arlington, officials condemned a parcel of land in 1923 for a park. Appleton tried, but failed, to spur the local historical society to save the site's two old houses. Nearby Reading faced the same issue when it considered the fate of Parker Tavern (attributed to 1694). Town fathers first decided to demolish the ancient home, but preservationists forced the city to relinquish the building for $100, providing that it was restored and opened as a museum. Appleton made the argument, as he so often did, that "a well-restored and well-maintained colonial house" enhanced the total value of the town's real estate, particularly when the house, like Parker Tavern, was in "parklike surroundings." Ironically, it sometimes became difficult to distinguish between colonial buildings in a park and Colonial Revival homes on suburban lots. In fact, the premise was similar. Home and land would rest in an ordered harmony, and contrast with the chaos of the city. A metal marker at Parker Tavern made the antimodernist point: "The simple home of an ordinary man, not wealthy, not particularly distinguished, but a type of the God-fearing yeomanry. . . . As Ephraim Parker left it, it remains today an unchanged relic in the midst of a changed world."[49]

Speculators were another threat. During the war, for example, Appleton worried that the seventeenth-century John Balch house in Beverly, Massachusetts, would "almost certainly be bought for transformation into a three-family house" for factory workers. Vacated by the last of the Balch family in 1914, the dwelling languished. Appleton prized the appearances of this many-gabled, asymetrical home that originally was a story-and-a-half cottage with a room on each floor. It was believed to be as well "the only remaining house built by an 'Old Planter,' namely, by a man who settled New England before the arrival of the Winthrop group which founded Boston." SPNEA chose not to acquire the house while the nation was at war, however. Appleton, Bolton, and a handful of friends purchased it in a holding action, but felt strapped by taxes and mortgage. Hoping to unload the building, Appleton advertised that it was on a busy corner and could be converted into a tearoom or gift shop. Eventually a local society remade the house as "one of the most hallowed shrines of America."[50]

Both land speculation and a lack of government oversight threatened a site closer to the heart of SPNEA, Beacon Hill. Brahmin traditionalists subsequently rallied to defend what had long been the symbol of proper tastes, good breeding, and class leadership. Ever since the Gilded Age,

Beacon Hill had deteriorated in stature. As a preservationist, Appleton therefore worked to keep the Brahmins at home and the immigrants at bay. His first opportunity came with the Parker-Inches-Emory house (1818) at 40 Beacon Street. Alexander Parris had designed both 39 and 40 as a pair, and highlighted the bow-fronted brick townhouses with imposing, temple-fronted porticos and brilliant fanlights. When 40 Beacon Street went on the sale block in 1913 for $160,000, Appleton devoted ten pages of his small *Bulletin* to "one of the most interesting and beautiful houses in Boston." Its imminent sale, he said, could threaten "the future character of Beacon Street on the hill." Should it give way to new apartments, as was rumored, "the artistic unity of this, the best portion of the street, would be lost forever." He wanted the house as SPNEA's headquarters, but the Women's City Club bought the pair, a telling statement about what Walter Firey called the "decidedly 'feminine' character to organized neighborhood activities on Beacon Hill."[51]

What pinched SPNEA was not only that organized preservation depended in great part on the pocketbooks of those ladies but that Appleton did not trust them with his landmark. "No one who knows anything of the vagaries of club house committees," he wrote in 1919, "can for a moment look forward to the club ownership of such a house with any feeling of confidence in the future." All the while, SPNEA did tap the assistance of Beacon Hill residents, particularly its women, many of whom were unmarried or widowed. They prized the Hill, as did Cram with his personalism, as "a closely knit, intimately sympathetic community, with a real unity in tastes and ideas."[52]

After SPNEA acquired the Otis house on the Hill's backside, Appleton could better watch the neighborhood's daily affairs. All was not too his liking, however. When Brahmins moved out, land values fell and the neighborhood attracted diverse occupants, including antique shops and artist studios. As it took on a Bohemian flavor, many tradition-minded Yankees cringed, and one warned in 1923: "Beacon Hill is not and never can be temperamental, and those seeking to find or create there a second Greenwich Village will meet with obstacles in the shape of an old residence aristocracy whose ancestors have had their entries and exits through those charming old doorways for generations."[53]

Appleton's campaign to acquire 40 Beacon Street represented a significant countermove in the revival of Beacon Hill. Its regeneration had begun in 1905 when Frank A. Bourne, a prominent architect, preserved the exterior of his home, while modernizing its interior. Such renovation was exactly what Appleton feared with the women's club. In 1922 Bourne and his allies formed the Beacon Hill Association, a group favoring interior modernization and clashing with Appleton's preference for authenticity. In this case, SPNEA was swimming against the current. In 1925, for example, *The House Beautiful* ran a story on "Reclaiming Colonial Landmarks" on Beacon Hill. Salvaged from the past, those old homes offered the "soul-inspiring . . . influences emanating from the Colonial

environs." Catering to modern tastes associated with privacy and mate-
rialism, their renovations included extra closet space, double baths, and
separate entrances for servants. Along with this gentrification, African-
Americans were forced to move from an area near the former Charles
Street Meeting House, which had reverted to the First African Methodist
Episcopal Church.[54]

Committed to Beacon Hill and its traditionalism, Appleton fell into a
paradox of untold proportions when a proposal was aired to rebuild
Hancock's home on the Hill. There was no better symbol of everything
he valued than the house that fell in 1863. Between 1916–17 two proposals for its rebuilding converged, one from architects R. Clipston Sturgis and Robert D. Andrews, who supervised the capitol's enlargement,
and the other from the Bay State's patriotic societies. The former wanted
a mansion for the governor, but the latter lobbied for a memorial and
museum. While the preparedness and Americanization campaigns were
heating up, the time seemed right for a memorial, but Appleton admitted
that he was "not over sanguine about its projected restoration." He was
troubled by the fact that the bill only authorized an "approximate" reconstruction. He appeared before a legislative committee "and told them
that nothing that was 'approximate' was worth doing." Instead, he voiced
his belief in scientific method by suggesting that "an exact restoration of
the main house" be undertaken, to which wings could be added for the
museum. The whole would then become "a mecca for tourists." He was
concerned about the museum's coffers and told Walter Gilman Page,
chairman of the state art commission, that it should extend "the length
of time every visitor to Boston spends within her gates in order that there
may be a still greater amount of money spent here by visitors."[55]

Appleton knew that the project would have dramatic repercussions on
Beacon Hill. The rebuilding of Hancock's house and terraced gardens,
construction of a new museum, and ample room for its future expansion
would have required a large parcel of land and the demolition of existing
houses on Joy and Beacon streets. When pressed to choose between the
neighborhood and museum, Appleton chose the patriotic course and "favor[ed] the rebuilding." He recognized that the deterioration of Joy Street
had allowed encroachment from the West End, but the remaking of Hancock's gardens would create a small buffer zone. "To my mind," he told
Page, "none of those buildings have the slightest value of any kind, sort
or description, and the sooner they are got rid of the better. It is absolutely
essential that they go if the Hancock house is to be rebuilt." Attitudes
have surely changed since that time, and one architectural guide suggests
that "the little stretch of Joy Street from Beacon to Mt. Vernon street is
particularly charming." The cleared zone would have included not only
houses designed by well-known architects Alexander Parris and Cornelius
Coolidge in the 1820s but a cultural fabric that interwove human spirit
and material form in the neighborhood. Appleton's bid to remake history
was indeed a pandora's box.[56]

The outbreak of war stalled the drive, and Appleton complained in 1920 that "the extra taxes imposed by the state veterans' bonus" put the project on hold for four more years. The proposal came up again in 1924, and SPNEA was again asked to choose between promoting the civil religion and preserving a neighborhood. Torn by indecision, it did nothing. The *Evening Transcript* reported in a headline that SPNEA was "Non-Commital on Demolishing Present Buildings or Erecting War Memorial." It still favored "the reproduction of the Hancock house," but washed its hands of the consequent demolition. Millar explained in *Old-Time New England* that SPNEA wanted "a real restoration rather than a pretty bit of stage-setting."[57] Having pushed scientific method as preservation's only course, Appleton balked at the idea of approximating Hancock's home. That restoration never came, and all that remains today is a marker on the site.

Such a paradox showed how the precepts of progressivism had placed real limits on SPNEA and was gradually changing the orientation of the preservation movement. Whether it involved the Hancock house or the "ancient pair" in Newport, preservationists who demanded scientific method and archaeological accuracy were defining their interests as those of a unique and separate profession. What was actually occurring was the shaping of a new preservationist agenda. Scientific in method, business-minded in appeal, defensive in posture, but still traditionalist in culture, SPNEA's canon was thoroughly a product of progressivism.

7

"DO NOT TEAR THE HOUSE DOWN!!"

Establishing a Scientific Method in Preservation

As far as Appleton was concerned, the work of preservation had resembled for too long that plan to rebuild the Hancock house—it was idiosyncratic and downright inaccurate. SPNEA instead felt the pull of progressivism toward scientific method. Yet an innovative nostalgia still premised that work; the very notion of preservation was based on the remaking of history through restoration. To understand why Appleton accepted the practice, it is necessary to examine the alternative models of preservation that existed when he founded SPNEA.

William Morris, for one, influenced a long line of cultural critics from Norton to Cram. Though they held him in high esteem and cited his example, few Americans were willing to implement his philosophy, whether that of socialism or preservation. Upon founding SPAB, he reiterated Ruskin's lament that almost all restorations were in some way destroying the artifact. "If the present treatment of them be continued," he warned, "our descendants will find them useless for study and chilling to enthusiasm." Setting one model, SPAB decreed that buildings that were artistic, picturesque, historical, or antique were not to be compromised one iota. Ones that were dilapidated could be stabilized, as long as repairs were unobtrusive and did not imitate any style. Restoration, however, was a "most fatal idea," because "its very name implies that it is possible to strip from a building this, that, and the other part of its history—of its life that is, and then to stay the hand at some arbitrary point and have it still historical, living, and even as it once was." By its "very nature" restoration "compels them to destroy something and to supply the gap by imagining what the earlier builders should or might have done." As far as Morris was concerned, the remaking of history that resulted was "a feeble and lifeless forgery."[1]

His "Anti-Scrape Society" was the polar opposite of the French school shaped by the *Commission des Monuments Historiques* (1837). Eugène Emmanuel Viollet-le-Duc, an architect who became its most prominent inspector, had used preservation metaphorically as a weapon to defend the Gothic against its foes in the Renaissance-minded *Ecole des Beaux-Arts*.[2] Believing that Gothic antiquities spoke the mind of the medieval world, he wanted to hear one voice and suppress later echoes. His aggressive restoration policy, based on subjective cut-off dates and the erasure of subsequent material change, was condemned categorically by Morris. Widely popular, but very controversial, Viollet-le-Duc literally reinvented the Gothic for native and tourist alike in France. In 1909 Appleton saw his work and was evidently impressed. For example, he called his restoration of the walled city of Carcassonne "glorious." Isham too admitted a great debt to Viollet-le-Duc.[3]

Appleton knew of these antithetical models, but he was also acquainted with others, including the work of the APVA. Its use of the past was largely metaphorical and, in the spirit of Viollet-le-Duc, it even allowed the hypothetical reconstruction of Jamestown's seventeenth-century church. Yet it was inconsistent, as its first acquisition, the Powder Horn in Williamsburg, stood in disrepair thirty-five years after its purchase. Having no need for a scientific regimen, the APVA single-mindedly protected traditionalism and used buildings allegorically within that context.[4]

New England's patchwork record in preservation influenced Appleton even more. Like their counterparts in Virginia, tradition-minded Yankees wielded artifacts to fight immigrants, iconoclasts, and modernists. But another style of preservation was slowly developing in the gulf between Morris and Viollet-le-Duc. In the decade before Appleton's first campaign, Isham advanced that approach by writing innovative studies of New England's antiquities. SPNEA quickly departed from the courses set by SPAB, the APVA, and most others, and slowly set what would become a primary trend in America—an acceptance of restoration guided by modern archaeology and scientific method.

Appleton learned about preservation empirically and intuitively. Unlike Isham who approached architecture from an academic perspective, his education prepared him little for his eventual duties. In SPNEA's early years he fell back upon some basic principles, such as Norton's philosophy of archaeology, but then eclectically borrowed ideas and practices, adapted them to an individual situation, and revised them afterwards. Strongly opinionated, his ideas further devolved from his Brahmin upbringing, his European travels, and his committed sense of ancestry. Just as he was exact and rigorous in managing his society, so, too, would he learn from his trustees, associated architects, and fellow antiquaries in the slowly emerging science of landmark preservation.

One of SPNEA's significant contributions to the American profession was the scientific regimen that it gradually developed. Yet, largely because Appleton learned on his feet, SPNEA's methodology stood second to that of SPAB, though more recent writers have tended to conflate the two organizations.[5] Appleton's work actually combined the well-established tradition of antiquarianism, so keenly followed by his father, with the

emerging field of historical archaeology. While most professional archaeologists were focusing on the ruins of Old World civilizations, and slighting the prehistoric vestiges of Native Americans, particularly in the East,
the study of historical archaeology was slowly taking form. It was in many
ways a stepchild of historians, anthropologists, and antiquaries such as
Isham and Appleton who studied the written record as they explored the
often overlooked material culture of their forebears.[6]

True to the scientific precepts of progressivism, Appleton wanted to
order historical archaeology as a discipline. Like the methods of a laboratory, preservationists first needed information. In the generation before
SPNEA's founding, Isham called for "the collection of scientific data" and
the taking of "accurate measured drawings," as did Porter in his *Rambles
in Old Boston*. Dow, in fact, told SPNEA's first annual meeting that one
of its main tasks was "collecting authoritative facts" on the construction
of buildings, the development of crafts, and the patterns of living.[7]

Indicative of its early focus on the structural makeup of buildings,
SPNEA accepted the taking of measured drawings as a form of preservation. That policy compromised the movement, did nothing to enhance
the landscape, but illustrated a scientific principle that quantitative description was a valid form of evidence. These measured drawings would
little resemble the sketches that antiquaries had earlier published. For
example, Edwin Whitefield issued at his own expense in the 1880s a half-
dozen or more books in which he sketched, often with a romantic bent
and some adaptation, what he called "the homes of our forefathers."
SPNEA wanted instead exact structural plans. It undertook this rather
tedious task because most architects regarded ancient houses as unsightly
and insignificant. When the Shumway house in Fiskdale, Massachusetts,
faced destruction in 1914, for instance, Appleton was "perfectly certain
the Boston Society of Architects would have scorned the idea of being
asked to measure it." By the 1920s, however, SPNEA did reach an accord
with some in the BSA.[8]

Appleton's search for measured drawings brought Donald Millar to
his attention. One year after his ordination as an Episcopal clergyman in
1910, Millar met Appleton and began the study of old buildings. Having
earlier learned drafting in an architect's office, Millar would contribute a
handful of articles to *Architectural Record* and author two books on
buildings and furniture. By the time of Appleton's death in 1947, he had
made detailed drawings of some twenty-five houses, room by room, for
the society. Appleton pushed Millar, not always successfully, to include
minor details that the draftsman thought "relatively unimportant" so as,
Millar said, to have "a complete record" of the building.[9]

Apparently, measuring a building was not always a simple proposition.
In 1916 Millar wanted to measure the elegant Craigie-Longfellow house
in Cambridge, owned by Appleton's cousin Alice. She refused, and Millar,
believing that only the written record stood permanent, claimed it would

have been a "loss to posterity." Her thinking about home and privacy
was shared by many in her generation. It would have been "indelicate,"
she thought, "to print the whole of ones private home for the public to
see." She worried that it "might be copied exactly" by a builder "and
thus take away the uniqueness of her home." She ultimately relented, and
eleven detailed plates on the house appeared in his *Measured Drawings
of Some Colonial and Georgian Houses* (1916).[10]

The collection of measured drawings represented one aspect of
SPNEA's eventual role as a major clearinghouse for historical information
on New England. Appleton collected tens of thousands of photographs
and postcards—some 50,000 in the first decade alone—as well as books
and pamphlets that depicted the built and natural landscapes. He also
used the pages of SPNEA's *Bulletin* and *Old-Time New England* to dis-
seminate information on history, material culture, and craftsmanship. No
other contemporary journal better illustrated a region's heritage than did
Old-Time New England. In the 1920s, for example, Dr. Henry Chapman
Mercer contributed numerous, highly detailed articles on the tools of preindustrial carpenters.[11]

In the course of collecting data, Appleton constantly ran into one stum-
bling block—the lack of an inventory of extant historical buildings. In
Connecticut, he was apt to pull out Isham's book or unpublished materials, but he lacked any such guide to the Bay State. While he searched,
he kept a detailed record of his findings, often going into dilapidated
buildings. He and Kelly visited one ruin, for example, and "found some
good panelling and many flea-bitten cats." Fortunately, recounted a colleague, "there were no visitors around" to see them later "in a neighboring pasture, stripped down as much as the law would allow, delousing
themselves."[12]

Appleton praised the *Commission des Monuments Historiques* for beginning an inventory of French antiquities. So, too, did SPAB propose a
survey of ancient buildings—a written, drawn-to-scale, and photographic
document of the environment. Hoping to spur Yankees, SPNEA noted
that the survey of London had led to "a profound change in the attitude
of the English public toward the historic monuments of the country."
New England did follow suit, but in a very limited way with the Historic
American Buildings Survey (HABS).[13]

Appleton tried to apply these principles elsewhere, as in the case of the
APVA. Working with Kimball, he proposed that Virginia create an art
commission to survey the state, inventory worthwhile buildings, and prevent harmful alterations. However, the female-led APVA would have only
one seat on this board which, Appleton hoped, would be dominated by
preservation-minded architects and professionals. He worried that his
ideas might be taken as "purposeless criticism," but told the APVA's president that "the architectural and historical heritage of Virginia is so wonderful that it seems a pity any of it should be lost." As the Virginia move-

ment evolved, those ladies did lose ground, figuratively and literally, to northern-trained gentlemen in the National Park Service and Colonial Williamsburg Foundation.[14]

Just what to do with a building in ruins or disrepair was perhaps the most hazardous decision in setting a methodology. Like most Americans, Appleton tripped on this step. SPAB had warned prospective restorers that a structure was "like a house of cards; as soon as you interfere with the construction of one part, it is almost certain to set other parts moving." Being one who learned on his feet, Appleton sought local counsel. He asked Chandler for advice, and he addressed the annual meeting in 1912. Yet Chandler was surely fallible. Not only had he been criticized for overrestoring such seventeenth-century dwellings as the Revere and Nurse houses, but he later made known his opinion that the preservation movement had gotten out of hand. "There is much misplaced ectasy indulged in . . . old houses," he said mincing few words. "Many are saved which are not worth the cost of the match which might fire them. Of no particular interest, detail or other saving feature, they are rotten, dirty, ill-planned, and worthless." Just as architects felt their creativity (and commissions) dampened by such recycling, he urged many clients instead to build Colonial Revival homes because they showed artistry and good planning.[15]

Appleton scheduled another address for SPNEA's meeting in 1914 on the question, "How far should the work of restoration be carried?" When the invited speaker cancelled, Appleton turned to board member Cram. Known for his artistry in the Gothic Revival, he spoke on work in England and France. Mixing their conflicting philosophies, "he said that substitution of facsimile work was cold & dead, & not to be tolerated so long as any fragments of the original remained. . . . He said also that good taste is often more important than antiquarian fidelity." The relevance of Carcassonne to the Boardman house was problematic, but Cram was anything but an expert on Yankee vernacular architecture. He, in fact, cared little for its "barren" meeting houses or primitive dwellings. Four years later, SPNEA still showed a much-divided mind. A meeting of the trustees produced a "hot" discussion over what Bolton called "restoration of bad work vs. restoration in good taste which does not follow the original slavishly."[16] SPNEA's president sympathized with Cram's "good taste" school, and most early twentieth-century architects remade old-time buildings according to their sense of aesthetics.

Appleton's soul must have been worrisome because he turned to a clergyman for advice. Millar had criticized Dow's excessive hand in restoring the Parson Capen house in Topsfield, Massachusetts, in 1913. Lacking evidence for some details, Dow had turned to guesswork. He copied the chimney stack from the old Hunt house in Salem, reproduced the latch on the front door of the "Old Indian House" in Deerfield, and introduced conjectural fenestration. As a result, the good reverend accused him of "rank heresy and sacrilege" because he made the house fit his "ideas of what it should have been" in the seventeenth century. Millar had already quarreled with Dow who "firmly [held] his views."[17]

Appleton asked Millar, apparently without result, to write a pamphlet for general distribution "on 'what to do and what not to do'" in such work. He wanted him to cite "without mercy for individuals' feelings the ins and outs of what has already been done elsewhere." Appleton could not write the pamphlet himself, because he feared alienating friends and had a limited familiarity with the issue. He confessed to Father Millar one of his failings—the lexicon of architecture. When they disagreed over the name of one feature of a building, Appleton admitted: "Doubtless you have the technical name whereas I picked up any name that seemed to suit my purpose."[18]

Just as Appleton sometimes lacked the expertise to describe these buildings as precisely as a professionally trained architect, so, too, did he lack knowledge of restoration technique. Yet, this ostensibly was the raison d'être for SPNEA, which he had formed after becoming "so roused" by "the practical destruction through over-restoration" of the Harrington house. As he remembered, "architects felt at liberty to alter the old work to suit their requirements and felt they were improving it almost in direct proportion as they removed the old and replaced it with the new." He admitted that at the time, however, he knew "little enough" about these old houses.[19]

Soon after, SPNEA acquired its first two colonial buildings, the Swett-Ilsley house, built about 1670 in Newbury, and the Cooper-Frost-Austin house, constructed about 1689 in Cambridge. In both houses, SPNEA removed work that did not reflect the colonial period. Four years after acquiring the Newbury house, he regretted that it "has superficially always lacked the element of picturesqueness, which is so great a drawing card." As it restored the house, which was "in totally good condition," SPNEA had "to spend twice its value over again in removing good modern work to uncover the old." For instance, he explained, "there may still be perfectly good plaster ceilings to destroy and remove, [or] fine plastered walls to remove from laths nailed to old panelling." That policy continued when SPNEA acquired the Otis house where "the standard of condition to which it seemed wise to bring it constantly rose" as workers removed newer work.[20]

This type of work raised controversy on both ends of the spectrum. In retrospect, it can be said that SPNEA suffered the curse of moderation. At a time when preservation along the lines of SPAB was not accepted and total restoration was still in vogue in the United States, SPNEA's middle-of-the-road solution won few friends. Some criticized Appleton for being too conservative and saving too much of what Bolton called "bad work." Although SPNEA had partially restored the Cooper-Frost-Austin house to uncover what was later described as "an almost unbelievable density of surviving original trim," Appleton initially confined Chandler's work to the first floor. That was not enough for those Yankees

who wanted an unvarnished image of the colonial. During the tercentenary, for example, an official guidebook apologetically warned sightseers
that "the house as it stands represents no one period but rather a seventeenth-century house with eighteenth-century modifications and nineteenth-century conveniences."[21]

Despite the claim of scientific accuracy, those restorations involved
some degree of conjecture. Dow conceded that "in most instances time
has so carefully removed or disguised the original lines that it is possible
to obtain a correct restoration only by drawing deductions from obscure
scraps of evidence and a comparison of similar types of buildings." Ironically, he also complained about the lack of data for such comparisons.
Appleton admitted as much to an English preservationist. In the process
of restoring early houses, he discovered that only one type of sliding sash
frame had survived. Antiquaries were "pretty much driven to reproducing
the existing sample in all cases and then inventing some adaptation of it
to suit the requirements of some particular case." He rebuffed potential
critics by saying that "the damage done [was] . . . slight" because "everyone knows that these windows are wholly new."[22]

SPNEA's work along these lines revealed at least two precepts governing its work. First, cut-off dates were not rigidly set, as they would be in
the reconstruction of Carcassonne and Williamsburg. But when preservationists tried to distinguish between "good" and "bad" workmanship
and materials, they commonly thought that the seventeenth century reflected the "good" work, the nineteenth century the "bad," and the eighteenth century the nebulous middle ground. Of course, those terms were
subjective.

Appleton rhetorically asked his members in 1921, "What is the object
of a restoration?" He replied with certainty: "There can be but one answer. It is to restore a given object to the appearances it had at the beginning or at some other selected time or times of its existence." Such a
"selected time" was a cut-off date, but a related problem was establishing
the beginning. Antiquaries of the day were notorious for dating the construction of a building to an earlier time. Appleton showed skepticism
toward some dates found in tradition, but still frequently erred. Only after
research in court records, as Dow suggested, would more accurate dates
be established. Even today, just when many of these dwellings were constructed cannot be determined. Whatever the case, the push to find the
first-period buildings revealed the widespread belief of Anglophiles that
the settling of New England was its most important era.[23]

Second, there were different standards used to measure the worthiness
of seventeenth- and eighteenth-century buildings and those of later years.
Preservationists such as Dow and Millar may have differed over speculative work, but they shared the perspective of Sellers who so objected to
the machine-made materials and eclectic styles of the nineteenth century
that he drew the cut-off date there. Almost in the same breath that he
praised SPAB, the man who was supervising the American Institute of

Architect's restoration of Independence Hall departed from SPAB's sentiments and said: "We have not, therefore, the same occasion to deplore the destruction of modern details where changes made in the nineteenth century are in the way of the restoration of an ancient building." Architect Murray Corse gave Appleton the same advice about the Browne house. Equating preindustrial work with creativity, he urged Appleton to employ Chandler because he combined an appreciation of such artistry with a knowledge of archaeology. "After all," Corse thought, "to revive the old feeling, the atmosphere of the old is the most important; and as the old was especially artistic it stands to reason that only an artist can do so. If we simply turn out a dry litteral [sic] reconstruction (as the Germans do) the result is worse than useless, for people think: 'How ugly those old things were. Why spend money preserving them?'"[24] As far as he was concerned, artistic taste and preservation work had to coincide.

If Wells and Corse represented the widespread belief that the imprint of the Industrial Revolution had to be erased from preindustrial buildings, what policies would be developed for other buildings? SPNEA mulled over that question with its Otis house. A relatively little known architect, Henry Charles Dean would supervise most of its work there, having earlier superintended restorations for Nutting's chain and SPNEA's Swett-Ilsley and Boardman houses. He told Appleton that he wanted the restoration of such a refined home to reveal the mastery of its architect and "to blot out every addition and alteration, and to present them in their original form."[25]

Appleton was deliberately ambiguous about this restoration work because he privately recognized the real differences between the methods of SPNEA and SPAB. He admitted to English preservationist John Swarbrick, founder of the Ancient Monuments Society, that he preferred to call the removal of newer materials "repair." "I don't like to use the word 'restoration' for I believe that in Great Britain that has a sinister meaning not given it over here," he wrote. "As a general rule it is quite difficult for us to raise money for the purchase and preservation of the old houses unless it is understood that the building is to be put back as nearly as possible into the condition it originally presented."[26]

Although SPNEA was willing to erase the hand of machine-tending workers or later occupants who altered ancient houses, Appleton echoed SPAB's philosophy when he told Swarbrick that "the best principles" of the field demanded "the preservation of every scrap of the old that can possibly be preserved." Unlike much of the era's work, Dean added that "all restoration of ancient New England houses must be impersonal" because "the great value of a relick is its testimony, and therefore it must ring true." Even Chandler thought that "it is not only safer but infinitely more satisfactory later—from the standpoint both of authenticity and artistic quality—to err on the conservative side."[27] That wisdom was surely easier said than done, however.

Just when to cut off later modifications was a decision that troubled

Appleton. Chandler's work on the Turner house (House of the Seven Gables) raised the issue. Again, Appleton's question should be asked, "What is the object of a restoration?" Emmerton had purchased the seventeenth-century house for use as a settlement, but she also wanted to show the 1840s scene of the novel (Figs. 7-1, 7-2). Appleton did not object, but wondered how such romanticism, personalism, and social welfare would work with a restoration to its ancient appearances. Emmerton admitted that "a blending of periods" was inevitable if she was to establish the "homelikeness" of Hawthorne's atmosphere and avoid "the deadness of a museum."[28]

The restoration was complicated by the fact that the house represented more than one era. With his focus on architectural aesthetics, Appleton regarded its southern ell as "one of the finest examples of 17th century work in New England." It was "very unfortunate" that the house also contained "such superb 18th century work." As a result, he thought that a complete restoration would "have been an unpardonable act of vandalism." Moreover, the house's roof had been simplified, and Chandler, as he reconstructed much of the garret, searched for its long-lost gables to reach the number seven. He even rebuilt its mythical secret staircase. Appleton objected to not only the garret but the recreated chimney; its water table, for example, was "too terrible for words." Over all, the new woodwork, garret, and chimney showed that "the restoration and repairs

FIG. 7-1 House of the Seven Gables (Turner House), Salem, Mass. before restoration (Photograph from the Mary Northend Collection, Courtesy, Society for the Preservation of New England Antiquities)

FIG. 7-2   House of the Seven Gables (Turner House), restored (Photograph by
The Halliday Historic Photograph Co., Courtesy, Society for the Preservation of
New England)

have not been made with the sole object of archaeological accuracy."
Later students would have further difficulty separating authentic and
newer materials because Chandler did not document his alterations. Such
a predicament lent credence to SPAB's warning.[29]

In fact, SPAB advised that any repairs should be "unobtrusive," and
"an imitation of the ancient style should be avoided rather than pursued."
At first, however, Appleton expressly wanted new materials to imitate the
old, as with the Boardman house. "In putting in new sills," he wrote, "the
old sills were taken out and laid on the ground beside the new one, which
had been made exactly like the old, so that the continuity of the work
will be perfect, every new piece being made exactly like the old taken out
to make way for it." He tried to use old materials where possible, going
so far as to purchase a "doomed" dwelling in Beverly and use its old
bricks on the house. He soon recognized the dilemma. Just how would
archaeological accuracy and the scientific protection of these documents
be ensured when new materials could easily pass for authentic ones? By
1914 he admitted that "in many of the older restorations it is already
becoming difficult to distinguish the new from the old." Like the excavations at Herculaneum, he urged preservationists to photograph their
work thoroughly. "In no other way," he said, "can the authenticity of

the old work be positively identified or the architectural history of the structure be accurately written."[30]

Photographs and measured drawings would be used to document the process, as would the introduction of markers or signals to show new work. While he worked on the Otis house restoration, Appleton experimented with the placement of tacks in new painted wood, or later a small impression stamped into unpainted new wood, to differentiate it from the old. The practice caught on, and visitors were unable to tell any difference. He compromised the principle of archaeological exactitude when it came to old wood that had once been painted. There was no need to paint it again, he said, because "the appearance of new paint throughout is fatal to that appearance of antiquity that is so pleasing to the eye." Isham sensed Appleton's inconsistency. He thought, for example, that Appleton's use of tacks was "a trifle inconspicuous," and told him that he had already been painting his new wood a different color. SPAB also wanted new materials different from the old. Catering to antimodern tastes, Appleton's foremost priority was the appearance of antiquity, authenticity, and continuity. Kelly shared that belief. As in the case of unpainted interiors, he said, "age, wood, smoke, and sunlight have combined to produce a mellow richness that is far more lovely than any effect of paint could be."[31]

Although SPNEA's work on old houses was intrusive when compared with that of SPAB, it was still conservative when contrasted with that of Nutting. Throwing the principle of archaeological accuracy to the wind, he even encouraged "the acquisition of old paneling and its installation in rooms which perhaps never had any." Contradictions never ended: He criticized Virginians who dressed up their old plantation houses and asked, "Well, what are we to do? The offenders cannot be sent to jail, and ostracism is out of date. That is why we let the bad work go on." He also established workshops that cranked out ersatz antiques and hardware to satisfy the consumer's craving for 100-percent-American forms. Fakes were not new in furniture making, and Erving found ones that were "executed so skillfully that they challenge the best judgment of the expert." Appleton similarly worried about Nutting's new work. He urged him "very strongly to mark every piece" that he produced "in such a way that it can never be confused with the old." Inevitably it was, and his reproductions became instant antiques.[32]

As Appleton matured, he increasingly recognized the complexity and controversy associated with restoration. He first dealt with the quandary of cut-off dates. As early as 1918, he advised the DAR that because the Baury house (1750) in Newton Lower Falls, Massachusetts, showed such "a mixture of styles," it should "leav[e] the structure pretty much as found, in order to show the evolution of styles." Soon after he felt confident enough to take on the French school and thought that it was "not always advisable to go back to the original appearance of a building. Some of them show such an interesting lot of evidence of evolution of styles and periods as to justify the retention of these alterations." He faced that issue with the lean-to addition on the Jackson house, which was "wholly uninteresting" but added to "the quaint appearance of the old house." He admitted his own uncertainty "whether it is always wise to scrap second period work in order to go back to our idea of what first period work looked like." Mixing the aesthetics of antimodernism and the exactitude of archaeology, he kept the lean-to and accepted such an evolution.[33]

Appleton warned that such work "should be put in the hands of none but the most careful, trusted and tried mechanics." The problem generally was finding those workers. Just as architects had been trained to create, not preserve, so, too, were carpenters and masons. While the Lee house was being restored, Appleton cautioned Bush to keep a constant eye on the carpenters who had "a most annoying way of ripping out [and discarding] the particular bits which carry the evidence of what old work was." Similarly, Isham's work on the Arnold house was delayed because it was "practically impossible to get any competent person" to repair the chimney. Those workers required the constant supervision of "an architect of great experience." As restoration was underway on the Lee house, Appleton told Seymour: "You see in this sort of thing it is impossible to tell what is ahead of one, and it becomes necessary to do the work by the day, and take it as it is found." Even those architects were not always to be completely trusted. The Boardman house, for example, was "far too good to express the opinion on restoration of any one man," and Appleton wanted Isham, Chandler, and Dow to consult with Dean on its restoration. He still wanted all the evidence retained to document just what had been taken out from where.[34]

In both old England and New, preservationists faced another difficult question: What modern conveniences could be put into those old buildings? Isham had once lamented that old houses in Rhode Island which showed "all the care the ancient craftsman could bestow" were being destroyed by such devises as modern stoves and fireplaces. Appleton's fascination with the construction of postmedieval dwellings led him at first to hold those comforts at arm's length. After the purchase of the Boardman house, he told Millar: "We don't want to put any modern improvements in the house if we can possibly avoid it. We don't want a telephone, or running water, a toilet room, or gas, or electric lights, or furnace, or in fact anything at all." Such a conservative policy could be followed only if a caretaker's cottage was built nearby. Appleton, in fact, estimated that a cottage, an underground passage connecting the two buildings, and an unclimbable steel fence to deter the Calabrian neighbors would cost much more than the restoration itself, and he never went through with the plan. SPNEA left the house unfurnished.[35]

Appleton did see the financial necessity of introducing those comforts into a seventeenth-century house that was to be occupied and commercially used. In fact, when he founded SPNEA he recognized that there was already a surfeit of house museums and stressed that the society would make modern use of its buildings. He allowed the introduction of modern plumbing, lighting, and heating at the Swett-Ilsley house because the tenants planned to establish an antique shop and tearoom. The Arnold house, on the other hand, lent "itself with great difficulty to modern uses," and he resisted. Like the Boardman and Browne houses, it eventually became a study property. SPAB also accepted the introduction of such conveniences as steam heating and electric wiring into medieval buildings if the structure and appearance were not compromised.[36]

Pressed by circumstances, Appleton justified other changes. The Shirley-Eustis house, for instance, was endangered by its location "in the middle of such a vast sea of wooden buildings" in Roxbury. He reluctantly accepted the idea of placing metal sheathing on the house to delay a fire and give firefighters time to respond. After a half-dozen coats of paint had been applied, he thought that "our members would [not] be able to detect the difference at the distance of ten or fifteen feet." That threat prompted the fireproofing of other historic buildings, as in the earlier cases of Faneuil Hall and the Old South Meeting House, where structural steel supports and a metal-girded roof replaced original materials. Even more radical, but more common, was moving an entire building to widen the streets. Whether it affected Bulfinch's Otis house or Peter Harrison's Old City Hall in Newport, Americans wanted broad streets for their cars. Historic buildings had to be moved, and preservationists relented.[37]

Just what changes were acceptable in restoration was addressed by Dean before he put his hand to the Otis house. Picturing a continuum in landmark restoration, it went from good (impersonal, scientific, and conservative) to bad (personal, speculative, and severe). "Some methods result in hinting at their ancient charm and distinction," he wrote, "while other methods caricature their vanquished antiquity, or grandeur and nobility." Two case studies—Appleton's restoration of the Browne house and Isham's work on the Old Stone House—will illustrate this.[38]

In 1903 Isham restored the Whitfield house in Guilford. Built in 1639–40 as a fortified house for Rev. Henry Whitfield, the Old Stone House was later damaged in a fire, renovated many times, and left with its interior gutted. A preservation coalition then purchased it to open a state museum. All that was left of the original building, said Appleton, was the front and west walls, but Isham was given "the hopeless job" of restoration. Essentially, "there were two courses open" to him:

> One, to make a perfectly frank idealization of what he thought an artistic interior of that old stone shell might possibly have been like in the old days . . . but without a shadow of authenticity behind it. The other possibility—and the one which he deemed wisest to adopt in view of the future use to which the building was to be put—was simply to make a big exhibition hall for museum purposes, and it seems to me that what he has done is well adapted to that use without any pretenses at keeping much of any old work in the process.[39]

Appleton's opinion was challenged by his colleagues. Dean called Isham's work a "sombre spectacle" that "caricature[d]" the dwelling's original "grandeur and nobility." Seymour objected because "the house in its present form is misleading, is not beautiful, is not at all adapted to museum purposes and presents no picture of Whitfield's time." He complained so strenuously that he later refused to trust Isham with the Lee house. Erving predicted correctly that it would have to be re-restored, and Kelly did undertake that task rather imaginatively for the Works Progress Administration (WPA) in 1936. Appleton conceded that the Old Stone House should have been left "openly and frankly a ruin," a course consistent with the philosophy of SPAB. "Altogether the whole thing is just the kind of proposition that I personally fight shy of," he told Seymour, "and prefer leaving it to somebody else to bother with."[40]

Unlike the Whitfield house, the Browne house appealed to SPNEA's founder in a powerful way. Originally a one-room cottage of two stories with a garret when built sometime between 1694–1701, it stood in ruins in 1917. The town's mayor actually told him that "there was not enough to the Brown house to warrant its being preserved." Yet Appleton was interested "just because there is so little there that it is worth saving. That is to say, it is a house practically in its original condition, unspoiled by later changes of the old work." Because it was in an "extremely ruinous condition," he knew that any restoration would "involve the discarding of a considerable portion of the old work" and replacing it with new materials "made exactly like the old so that the continuity of the structure is unimpaired."[41]

Located on a suburban lot earmarked for development, the Browne house faced demolition. Unwilling to pay $3,000 for the lot, he negotiated to buy the ruin and told Isham that the owner "would be a Jew if he asked $50 for it." In October 1917, he reported to Isham and Chandler his plan to buy the house, disassemble it, and reconstruct it elsewhere. Isham and Chandler disagreed and gave him crucial advice. "Keep the old building in situ," Isham wrote from Providence.

> It has too many secrets to reveal. It has more to tell us than a little, not particularly about framing, which is really about all you could preserve if you took it down and stored it, but about windows and stairs. All these little bits of extremely important detail will be lost unless you work slowly along with the house as it stands and ask your questions of it as you go *and have the house to go back to* if you don't understand the answer to some query and want to ask it over. *Do not tear it down*, it is too important. And don't work without some architect at your elbow. If you have Chandler get him to stay there as much as he can. "DO NOT TEAR THE HOUSE DOWN!!"[42]

Chandler agreed. Dismantling it would not simply damage the chimney, which notwithstanding measurements and photographs could never be exactly rebuilt, but sever it from the landscape. So unlike the spirit that would animate Ford at Greenfield Village, Chandler reminded Appleton that the house was "connected with the history of the neighborhood and should remain where it is." In the interim, "the weather must be kept out of the old ruin," and he suggested using old sail cloths for the roof's gaping holes. Appleton subsequently advised those who wanted to protect unkempt buildings to keep "the roof tight and the windows whole" until funds and friends were available (Figs. 7-3, 7-4, 7-5).[43]

This good advice did not qualify as collateral for a purchase, however. Appleton could not find an interested party to buy and preserve the house, nor was he able to persuade his board to acquire it. A frustrated Isham told him to give up, but as of December 1918 Appleton still planned to buy the hulk, dismantle its oldest section, and move it to Saugus. Evidently his interest still revolved around its framing, but Isham's description of the house as a laboratory to study a wide range of details wore on him and he bought it himself. As he said, "Doubtless no building in New England was ever rescued from a condition of decay approximating that of the Browne house." He proved that no house was "beyond redemption."[44]

Appleton personally restored the Browne house in 1919–20. True to form, he removed an antebellum ell of two stories and concentrated his

FIG. 7-3   Abraham Browne House, Watertown, Mass., before restoration (Photograph by The Halliday Historic Photograph Co., Courtesy, Society for the Preservation of New England Antiquities)

Fig. 7-4   Abraham Browne House, during restoration (Photograph by F. P. Le-mont, Courtesy, Society for the Preservation of New England Antiquities)

Fig. 7-5   Abraham Browne House, restored, 1924 (Photograph by George Bray-ton, Courtesy, Society for the Preservation of New England Antiquities)

work on what he believed to be the colonial house. While he restored it, he showed a budding scientific methodology. Not only did he meticulously photograph and record what he found and did, he picked through the scrap piles and saved the evidence. He hired "careful workers" who were "trained to do this very sort of restoration work" and daily supervised the process. When he came across mysteries, he asked Isham and Chandler for advice. At times, their failure to agree humored him. But when Appleton removed what he thought was later work and without Isham's purview, the architect was likely to throw "forty fits." Sometimes he followed their advice, as in the removal of furring around a window, and later regretted it after thinking that it was original. Over all, the Browne house was his major work in restoration. Appleton passed it on to SPNEA, which outfitted the house as a museum. By the 1930s tourists paid a mere fifteen cents for what a guidebook called "one of the best restorations in New England." As Isham had warned, the building proved to be unique not for its framing, but its fenestration. The house had the best preserved triple casement window frame in New England, and museums in Boston and New York used it as a model for their displays. It also held unique wrought iron hinges and a Norfolk latch on the chamber door.[45]

Despite the evident differences, both Isham and Appleton remade the past. While the situation of the Whitfield house forced Isham into conjecture and some artistry, that of the Browne house allowed Appleton to exercise a method that was more archaeologically and historically accurate. His work typified much of what would come for SPNEA and establish its lofty reputation in the field. It was not preservation in the sense of SPAB, but it was usually rigorous, methodical, and a model for the profession.[46]

By the late 1920s, Appleton expressed great interest in another project that similarly committed itself to scientific method, architectural aesthetics, and corporate structure. In 1926 the Williamsburg Holding Corporation (WHC) began to acquire select sites in the Old Dominion's second capital and quickly outpaced SPNEA as the nation's largest preservation corporation. Not only did the WHC differ dramatically from the APVA, but John D. Rockefeller Jr.'s largess in Williamsburg—to the tune of almost $100,000,000—created an aura that lured Appleton. What the magnate was accomplishing, he said in 1933, was "so closely along the lines of what we are doing in scattered units that the results are of greater interest to us, perhaps, than to any other single group in the country."[47]

That fascination wore thin as Appleton realized the scale of this remaking of history. Over the years, the WHC (and its successor, the Colonial Williamsburg Foundation) would demolish or move over 700 buildings from the district, reconstruct some 350, and restore 88. Not willing to take on the magnate or his Boston architectural firm, Appleton privately dissented from that emphasis on reconstruction. "By all means," Appleton later advised a preservationist in North Carolina, "concentrate on things which are actually remaining to be preserved and don't build over again on the old foundations a building that has disappeared." Appleton's advice was not heeded and North Carolinians followed the Williamsburg model in 1952 when they began to reconstruct Tryon Palace in New Bern, which had burned to the ground in 1798.[48]

If North Carolinians turned a deaf ear, what influence did SPNEA have from these beginnings? For one, its promotion of tourism, advocacy of restoration, and identity with the male worlds of architecture and science laid the groundwork for the New Deal's involvement in preservation through the WPA and HABS. With those agencies, as well as the Civilian Conservation Corps, the U.S. Government significantly, but at first tentatively, entered the preservation movement. To the dismay of Virginia preservationists, Leicester B. Holland, who had helped organize HABS in 1933 under the National Park Service, even credited SPNEA "with priority in the work of preservation of historic spots" in the nation. Holland served at the time also as chairman of the Committee on Preservation of Historic Buildings of the American Institute of Architects. Steeped in that male world, he slighted the APVA because it allegedy spent too much time laying monuments and too little time preserving buildings. Most pointedly, he misidentified its female personalism as a distracting "social function" of women. In the vein of SPNEA, he oriented the federal program to its scientific method, architectural focus, and male standards.[49]

HABS heeded SPNEA's call for a scientific inventory of America's antiquities and recorded almost 700 buildings through drawings and photographs by 1941. That process did too little, however, to protect the historic landscape because over one-third of those sites would be destroyed by the 1960s. HABS also played a role in the era's cultural politics. In the Depression, Holland regarded landmarks as symbols of the necessary values to rebuild America. Those buildings expressed, he said, "the sturdiness and the heroic spirit of the hardy early pioneers who had such great confidence in themselves and in the land which they loved, toiled for and peopled, and in which they laid the enduring foundations of the greater America of today."[50]

The work of the U.S. Government and SPNEA would dovetail during the 1930s. Despite his belief in states' rights and localism, Appleton worked with federal authorities, transferring the Derby house to the National Park Service, and unsuccessfully persuading it to assume control of the Shirley-Eustis house. The federal government helped publicize Yankee antiquities as well. Heading HABS in New England was Frank Chouteau Brown, a progressive who not only had earlier assumed the role of informal censor in Boston but sanctioned SPNEA, edited *The White Pine Series*, and contributed to and later edited *Old-Time New England*. The WPA's Federal Writers' Project also published a cultural history for each state that examined its economy, society, and historic architecture. Listed town by town and geared to automobile travel, the WPA's guide, as in *Massachusetts: A Guide to Its Places and People* (1937), offered a detailed list of many buildings that attracted the interest of preservationists. When it set those landmarks as a vital element in a community's memory, it heeded Appleton's call by defining heritage to include the historic landscape. That publication still generated controversy within the ranks of traditionalists, however. The Writers' Project, for example, gave more attention to the Sacco-Vanzetti case than to the Boston Tea Party. Some prominent Brahmins wanted the books thrown into a heap and burned.[51]

Historic preservation during the 1930s, whether in Williamsburg, Guilford, or Boston, revealed the tremendous changes that had been implemented in a generation. The string that connected 1910 and 1940 was obviously SPNEA. Surely it differed from SPAB and reflected prevailing American practices—it was a private, elite-led society that accepted the policy of returning New England's dwellings to ancient appearances. Well before SPNEA's day, a standard had been set from which it was difficult to diverge; traditionalists who funded and supported the movement wanted old buildings to be antiqued through restoration.

The work of SPNEA during the progressive era was transitional, therefore, as preservationists gradually began to differentiate between reconstruction, restoration, and preservation. The battle between those who artistically, if not whimsically, restored old buildings and those who advocated historical archaeology was one of the forces shaping SPNEA during the early twentieth century. Appleton bridged the two, but increasingly voiced his belief in archaeology. SPNEA's methods would embody progressivism with its stress on scientific technique, professional expertise, and archaeological accuracy. As preservationists remade historic New England, they used the know-how of modern science to reestablish what was ostensibly the authentic look of old-time Yankee life.

8

"Reminders of the Dignified Life of Our Forefathers"

Presenting History Through Material Culture

"Authenticity" and "continuity" were words frequently mentioned by preservationists not simply to define the desired qualities of historic sites but implicitly to show their dissatisfaction with modernity. As a result, Appleton and his colleagues wanted to develop museums that would illustrate the early lives of Yankees and show their relevance to modern New England. While SPNEA principally focused on preserving threatened buildings, it also worked to recreate the earlier environment by establishing an arts-and-crafts museum, developing period rooms, and building a folk park such as Skansen. Ironically, these efforts were both helped and hampered by a newer interest in antiques. More Americans were indeed finding solace in an imagined past through its material vestiges, but as art museums, speculators, and homeowners increasingly absorbed the nostalgia of the Colonial Revival, they began to ransack old buildings. By the 1920s preservation was readjusting to the contours of consumerism.

What pushed SPNEA into the museum movement was the realization that there were glaring holes in the historical picture. For too long scholars had almost solely relied on the written records of once-famous Yankee men, thus slighting the more numerous settlers who left little or no written record. That omission was aggravated by the fact that many antiquaries, nurtured by a heady brew of Victorian domesticity, were interested in early homelife. Dow wrote in *Old-Time New England*:

> It is a lamentable fact that the present generation possesses little accurate information on the every day life and surroundings of the early settlers in New England. . . . The newly settled country had no artists to paint pictures of household interiors in the manner of the Dutch painters and the diarists and letter writers of that time when they used a quill pen devoted little thought to the homely happenings of the household or to the costume and furniture with which every one was familiar.

Whereas Dow wanted to integrate written and material records, Nutting voiced a forthright antiintellectualism. "Men's thoughts," he asserted, "are often best expressed by the creation of their hands."[1] Whatever their intent, the collections of these antiquaries helped to remake the image of the old-time Yankee.

Unlike the holdings of other museums, SPNEA wanted to stress the authentic, everyday life of the past. Earlier galleries had displayed relics of past Americans, but presented them either in a lifeless way or as bizarre curiosities. More traditional museums, on the other hand, rarely exhibited either architecture or the folk arts and crafts. Preservationists such as Appleton, Isham, and Dow were cultural nationalists, however, and they used the scientific methods of progressivism to kindle their nostalgia for the preindustrial world. Through archaeology and preservation, their museum pieces would recapture a spirit that had been lost in the machine age. Too few Americans cherished those "beautiful bits of human work," said Isham, but he regarded them "as reminders of the order and dignified life of our forefathers." Appleton admitted, however, that he was "grass green" on such materials as furniture and relied on Erving, Nutting, Dow, and other collectors for advice.[2]

George Francis Dow (1868–1936) descended from Puritans who settled Massachusetts in 1637 and later moved to New Hampshire (Fig. 8-1). After attending a Boston commercial school, he entered business, rose to the top of his company, but increasingly spent his time studying colonial New England. In 1898 he was elected secretary of the Essex Institute, the nation's oldest local historical society. He spent the next twenty years running its museum, editing local records, and learning first-hand about buildings.

Dow was not only one of the first in the nation to use the period room and outdoor museum to exhibit historical materials but one who strove to present them authentically. In 1907 he illustrated the typical interior of a New England kitchen (1750), bedroom (1800), and parlor (1800). Only a glass wall separated the visitor from the fully furnished room, and he predicted that it *"cannot fail to serve as object lessons* and convey an historical illustration far more effective and impressive than could be secured by any text book." Dow also imitated the European practice of building outdoor museums. In 1910 he acquired the John Ward house (c. 1684) and moved it behind the museum. He opened it to the public two years later with furnished rooms, "hostesses" outfitted in homespun period costumes, and a garden outside.[3]

The turn toward period rooms represented a major shift in the preservation movement. In the nineteenth century, and the trend endured well into the twentieth, preservationists most valued historic sites for the heroic deeds and inspirational values associated with them. As curators and preservationists tried to make those forebears seem more human and influential in the present, they increasingly used material objects to reinforce the interpretation. Subsequently, it was demanded that those objects be scientifically restored and professionally displayed. Gradually, the aesthetics of design became a principal focus of the movement and a primary

FIG. 8-1   George Francis Dow (Photograph by A. O. Elwell, Courtesy, Peabody Essex Museum)

concern of curators. Over and above the merits of accurately restored artifacts, that turn showed the confluence of men and progressivism, the quest for authenticity in the machine age, and the material and scientific precepts defining Western civilization.

Whether the case concerned a period room or a piece of antique furniture, preservationists thought that the sight of those forms would prompt Americans—newcomer and native alike—to accept their aesthetics, work harder, live more humbly, and appreciate Yankee traditions. That Ruskinian premise revealed a reductionist environmentalism that inspired a wide range of reformers who promoted crafts, built parks, or exhibited artifacts. This Colonial Revival was directed partly at the curriculum because, as one Massachusetts official conceded in 1917, little consensus existed among educators on "generally accepted standards of what should be taught to non-English speaking people." Yankees imple-

menting a civics program for youth accordingly used artifacts and concluded that without those "historic collections" it would have been "almost impossible to teach the children intelligently."[4]

Appleton picked up Dow's interest in everyday life but, while looking
for early artifacts, they faced two very different obstacles. For one, many
Yankees were simply trashing old things in the dustbin of history. "The
American temperament usually esteems lightly anything that is old or not
'up to date,' " Dow explained, and most, as a result, discarded those
everyday items that were not new and useful. In 1914, for example, Robinson discovered that the old milestone that stood between Salem and
Danvers (and was inscribed "June ye 11, 1707") had been jettisoned by
city workers. At the dump he had to fight to get it back. "One has to be
pretty autocratic to preserve things you know," he told Appleton.[5]

As great a problem was posed by the budding cult of antique collectors
who drove up costs and demand. With the flourishing of the Colonial
Revival, many old-stock Americans were acquiring early art, silver, furniture, and domestic goods. Yankees of Norton's stripe had a sense of
personalism, prized their ancestors' belongings as mementos to which
affection could cling, and squirreled them away in attics and barns. This
newer phase of collecting was more motivated by a rejection of mass
manufacturing, a quest for higher status, and a nativistic appreciation of
truly American artistry. It repudiated what an old-blooded Yankee like
Erving called the European "decadence" of the High Victorian and Second Empire styles. Equating these colonial vestiges with the imagined
order and peacefulness of their forebears, most collectors preferred the
Georgian, but later buyers opened their wallets for the simple wares of
the founding period after the emergence of the arts-and-crafts movement
and the inflation of prices for Georgian artwork. Museums followed suit,
as did exhibitions and the Walpole Society.[6]

Henry Wood Erving worked in the Walpole Society and SPNEA to
redefine the canons of culture. This affluent Connecticut banker was the
foremost expert of his day on colonial furniture. During the xenophobia
of the 1920s, he admitted his appreciation for pieces such as the Connecticut chest in that they "followed no European model but were one
hundred per cent American." Only sixty chests remained, however; "like
many other pieces of furniture, these were considered hopelessly out of
fashion by many housekeepers of later generations" and trashed. Refuting
those who slighted the pioneers and ballyhooed progress, Erving claimed
that "few pieces of modern household furniture, be they ever so grand or
ornate, present so dignified and distinguished an appearance as the Connecticut chest." He emphasized that the chest, and many other furnishings, not only proved that the early colonists had "comforts and luxuries"
but showed an "originality of design" unlike anything in England at the
time. Like Appleton and Nutting, he redefined aesthetics to include the
practicality of the simple life and oppose the pretense of the Gilded Age.[7]

Yet no mere aestheticism moved Erving. His antiques also became time machines through which he could feel the presence of his forebears. The collector who "best enjoys his valued pieces," he said, could "see reflected in his mirrors the faces of former possessors, and can recreate the people of olden time sitting in his chairs, at his desks, and before his andirons." Imbued with that personalism, he hoped to regain his ancestors' spirit through collecting and preservation.[8]

No more admiring a student of Erving could be found than Nutting, who dedicated the first two volumes of his *Furniture Treasury* (1928) to him. He had founded museums and workshops, which failed financially, but did find success by publishing books and hand-tinted photographs of old-time scenes. During his day, he was the preeminent salesman for the cult of collecting. Expressing a commonly held sentiment, Nutting asked Yankees to return to tradition. "We are learning," he wrote, "that we have dragged in material from afar which was not so good as that which lay around us." His nativism dovetailed with the Colonial Revival, moreover. "There is enshrined in the forms of furniture used by our ancestors," he preached, "a spirit absent from the exotic shapes that come from Italy and France." Regarding these antiques as "the only tangible relics of our ancestors," he demanded that curator and collector emulate their forms. "Not to copy these approved types is a crime," he pronounced, "because the only alternative is the making of mongrel mixed shapes."[9]

Appleton admired his tastes for sure. After visiting his Wentworth-Gardner house, he cautioned: "If I ever found your caretaker away and had an automobile of my own at the house, you would miss the furniture." So disillusioned by the upheavals set off by the French Revolution, Nutting romanticized old New England. So disturbed by the Industrial Revolution, he dismissed any piece of furniture that was machine made. "It entirely lacks individuality, the touch of the hand and the feeling of the artificer," he warned Appleton. "There never was a piece of it worth saving and the time will never come when it will be of value." He conceded Appleton's expertise in architecture, but warned that it would be "unfortunate" if SPNEA promoted the preservation of machine-made artifacts or buildings. Nutting's advice wore on Appleton in 1921 when SPNEA was offered the Enoch Robinson Round House (1854) in Somerville, Massachusetts. "In many ways this would make an ideal period house for the display of mid-Victorian black walnut," he told his members, "but the present is probably fifty years too early for anything of the kind, since to most people that period represents the very quintessence of the ugly."[10]

Dow, Nutting, and countless antiquaries experimented with period rooms, but SPNEA was slow to join the bandwagon. It turned down the chance to buy the Shirley-Eustis house in 1911, largely because Appleton was "badly equipped" to manage "a show house." It acquired the Fowler house in 1912 and slowly developed plans for "a combination period house, appropriately furnished, and a museum." Yet neither Appleton nor Dow took much interest in showing the nineteenth-century house.

Thirty years later, its condition was such that "the furnishing is neither outstanding nor complete." What kept SPNEA from establishing a show house was not only Appleton's fiscal conservatism but his rapid acquisition of real estate. By 1933 the American Association of Museums listed SPNEA as the organization that had the most historic house museums for public exhibition—twenty-two—but most had limited furnishings or displays.[11]

More so than period-room displays, Appleton wanted SPNEA to establish an arts-and-crafts museum in Boston. Since the Museum of Fine Arts had opened in Boston in 1876, it had defined "fine arts" in the Old World's elite tradition of painting and sculpture and largely ignored the vernacular Yankee heritage. Like the Louvre, the MFA also displayed its artwork in cold, formal galleries. Shortly before founding SPNEA, Appleton complained that such "picture galleries are awful rooms." He said in his debut *Bulletin* that SPNEA wanted a historical museum whose collection "shall be to New England what the Germanic Museum at Nuremberg and the Bavarian National Museum at Munich are to Bavaria," the latter of which had seventy-six period rooms and galleries by 1900. SPNEA's museum director said later that it wanted "a folk museum" that would appeal to both "the casual visitor" and "the expert collector." His museum "would teach Americanism not only to the children coming from New England stock but to the children of other traditions and other races who have come to live here."[12]

Appleton was further motivated by a strong regional pride. "It is a strange and unaccountable fact," he reported in 1919, "that Boston, the most historic city in America and the natural center for the antiquarian and ethnographic culture of all New England should not possess a great historical museum." The lack of a museum had forced New Englanders to sell their antiquities elsewhere. In 1909, for example, Eugene Bolles was preparing to loan his collection of seventeenth-century furniture to the MFA. Owning no American furniture, the Metropolitan Museum of New York wanted it instead, and its assistant secretary Henry Watson Kent, who was most impressed by Dow's work in Salem, traveled to his native Boston to dine with Bolles. As Appleton watched, the Metropolitan bought his 600-piece collection and it became the core for its American Wing. Seeking the best money could buy, the museum hired the consulting services of Isham and the technical skills of Dow, who assembled two period rooms; the wing's much-publicized debut in 1924 "brought the subject of antiquities more to the fore than ever previously."[13]

Had the Hub had its own arts-and-crafts museum, Appleton claimed, the Bolles collection would have stayed in Boston. The same pattern unfolded in numismatics. Boston had about ninety percent of the nation's historic coins in the 1880s, but lost them to outside sales, and he doubted that "Boston leadership in this line of antiquities will ever return." Even with Native American artifacts, he worried that "New England pride" would be hurt if New Yorkers came in, excavated sites, and took the artifacts back to Gotham, as they did after Archer Huntington founded his Museum of the American Indian in 1916.[14]

Appleton wanted a philanthropist to establish an endowment of $400,000 so that SPNEA could display its acquisitions—everything from interiors taken from demolished houses to "the old doorway, [which] at last accounts was stored in a barn, awaiting the axe and the wood pile." New England was rich in antiques, and collectors scavenged everywhere. He complained in 1920, for example, that "every abandoned cellar hole and tumble down old house [in Essex County] gets ransacked several times a day by passing automobiles." Appleton regularly reconnoitered the scene and, after visiting one friend's house, told her that he was so impressed by her curios that he woke up having "vivid dreams" about them. They were "much too good to be knocking around a suburban house and should go into our collection." As prices skyrocketed, he conceded: "I hate to buy anything"! SPNEA also developed a library, but the trustees refused to allocate money for its purchases. Rather than compete with established archives and those New York collectors who had pushed the price of rare books and manuscripts "to unbelievable market values," SPNEA instead sought those items that were commonly discarded, such as postcards, photographs, negatives, and architectural drawings.[15]

Some controversy followed, however, over SPNEA's acquisitions policy. Just as preservationists split between the grand house and simple house schools, so, too, did they differ over the museum. Curator Dwight Prouty wanted to emulate the German museums, but stressed a traditional approach. "What we must look for in Boston," he said in 1913, "is the local prototype of the Great Elector," and acquire materials associated with the likes of Hancock and Winthrop. He in fact wanted a collection of clothes representing the governors of New England's states. Such a focus on the great men of history shifted considerably when Dow joined SPNEA in 1919, serving first as the editor of *Old-Time New England* and then as curator until his death in 1936. Carrying on what he began at the Essex Institute, he searched for the ordinary materials of everyday life. The museum would reflect his tastes and hold strong collections in such familiar items as baskets and jugs, as well as children's toys and dolls.[16]

Another point of controversy followed from the museum's attempt to show, as did the Scandinavian folk parks, "a natural pride of race" in its holdings. In 1917, for example, a well-intentioned Beacon Hill resident wanted to donate a piece from Wales that had once been a fixture in a house owned by Harrison Gary Otis. Appleton told her in a rather undiplomatic outburst, perhaps impassioned by the U.S. Senate's decision that day to enter the war, that "It would be a wholly inappropriate mantelpiece to incorporate in any one of the houses we now own, and as a piece of *foreign* workmanship could have no possible place in our museum." Though he sounded much like Nutting, his passions cooled, his tastes widened, and he later said that SPNEA was collecting "everything on England, Scotland and Ireland that happens to come our way, for the simple reason that every bit of it must be the ancestral home of some Americans."[17]

As it turned out, SPNEA's acquisitions greatly outpaced its abilities, partly because Appleton raced to "beat the Essex Institute" in its holdings. That contest forced him to store things "in barrels and cases, wholly inaccessible to our members and the public." The new headquarters at the Otis house failed to provide sufficient space, and even then he wanted more secure, fireproof facilities. After the police strike in 1919 and during what he called "these times of wide-spread criminality," he feared that SPNEA's collections were threatened by burglars and arsonists. "We are constantly being told," he informed his readers, "what we have received is the second best, the choicest things having gone elsewhere on account of our fire risk."[18]

Financially strapped and overcommitted, that predicament made obvious SPNEA's limited abilities and Appleton's unwillingness to set priorities. Just as he preached "a gospel of further acquisitions" for historic sites, so, too, did his museum grow. By 1917 he realized as well that there were substantial differences between a historic house and a historical museum for the display of artifacts. "An old house is not the ideal place for a museum," he admitted; instead it was most "useful when fitted up in the style of the period." A historical museum was particularly needed because most of the society's properties did not exhibit collections. The Boardman house, for example, was left unfurnished, while the Swett-Ilsley house was leased as a tearoom. Appleton eyed four large dwellings behind the Otis house to convert into a museum, but kept his hopes from his board "for fear of ridicule, as the project is so absolutely beyond our present means." He finally put the question to the trustees in 1921, and they nixed his plan.[19]

Undeterred, Appleton lined up his supporters, including Browne and Nutting. Eliot also spoke to the annual meeting in 1921 specifically about the museum. They concurred with Appleton that "any effort to separate the old house work from Museum work is bound to end disastrously." In many ways, he had realized that, despite SPNEA's success, a museum was necessary to reeducate the populace more effectively. Only after a consequent regeneration of traditionalism would more houses actually be saved. A complementary relationship existed between the influence of the preservation movement and traditionalism.[20]

Appleton desperately wanted a museum, and threatened to resign unless the trustees reversed their course. They relented. SPNEA acquired the four buildings, but not solely for a museum. Mayor Curley jarred SPNEA and its friends when he proposed widening Cambridge Street; he told SPNEA in 1924 it would lose the Otis house if it was not moved. On a site forty feet to its rear, SPNEA moved the Otis house in 1925, demolished two of those structures, and then established the New England museum in the remaining Lynde Street buildings (Figs. 8-2, 8-3). The Otis house meanwhile focused its displays on upper-class life during the Federal era, and drew its largest crowd during an eleven-day period in 1932, the depth of the Depression, for an exhibit commemorating Washington's birth. Those 6,000 visitors represented about ten times the annual norm, however.[21]

Those period rooms proved also to be quite a curse for preservationists. Although Dow was willing to use new, but antiqued, woodwork as a background for his artifacts, that compromise was unacceptable to many collectors, such as Henry Davis Sleeper who lent a hand to the destruction of New England's oldest house and even served as SPNEA's first museum director.[22] Major museums followed suit, including the MFA and the

FIG. 8-2 Harrison Gray Otis House, removal, 1925 (Photograph by William Sumner Appleton, Courtesy, Society for the Preservation of New England Antiquities)

FIG. 8-3   Interior view of the Harrison Gray Otis House, showing original dining room used as an exhibition space, 1926 (Photograph by George Brayton, Courtesy, Society for the Preservation of New England Antiquities)

Metropolitan, when they began to display early American art and furnishings. Their conservation of antiques threatened the preservation of buildings as they began to acquire old houses, or more commonly their desirable rooms, and dismantle the woodwork—paneled walls, mantelpieces, cabinets, and old flooring—for reerection in the museum.

Appleton developed a love-hate relationship with those curators. He admitted privately in 1918 that he prized the Short house (c. 1732) in Newbury, Massachusetts, which SPNEA would eventually acquire in 1927, and asked Millar to measure it sub rosa. It was "so good" an antiquity that he only mentioned it to his "best friends for fear the Brooklyn or New York museums would hear of it and want to tear it to pieces." The failure of Nutting's museums in 1918 heightened his worries. Pressed for cash, Nutting sold most of his furniture and put his houses on the market. Appleton most worried about Portsmouth's refined Wentworth-Gardner house (Fig. 8-4). Once hearing of its sale, he warned that "it would be an act of vandalism to take it apart for reerection as period rooms." Nutting replied: "Needs must where the devil drives."[23]

Appleton urged Kent "to take the whole" house, rather than its pieces, even if it had to be reerected "under a glass roof" at the museum or in Central Park. He did complain in his *Bulletin*, but mostly held his punches

FIG. 8-4 Wentworth-Gardner House, Portsmouth, N.H. (Courtesy, Society for the Preservation of New England Antiquities)

because he was hoping to use the museum's auspices to lure a Gotham philanthropist. Appleton tried to cut his losses, and warned New Englanders that the assault had only begun. Those museums sometimes asked SPNEA for help in finding suitable rooms to dismantle, but Appleton said that his response had "always been a decided negative." He favored *it situ* preservation and only when a building stood before the wrecking ball would he approve such work.[24]

The episode did not lead to a "war" between curators and antiquaries, as one historian has described it. The Metropolitan eventually relented because of constrained finances, left the house largely intact (taking only the paneling and furniture from an upstairs bedroom), and later allowed SPNEA to administer the site. The publicity heightened interest in American antiques, often to the detriment of preservation. Apparently, the heat was turned on SPNEA as well. Appleton responded to an irate Israel Sack, the renowned collector who later purchased The Lindens and sold it for removal to Washington, D.C., that he was "far from disapproving unconditionally of the purchase of old houses for museum purposes." It depended on the circumstances. Believing that New England museums had long neglected vernacular forms, he had actually encouraged one museum to acquire "a very simple room of unpainted white pine beautifully colored by time." His proposal bore no fruit because the material was ostensibly "beneath the museum's standard."[25]

The case of the George Jaffrey house (c. 1725) in Portsmouth in 1920 was even more revealing. It was bought at a public auction by an antiques dealer who in turn sold it to the MFA. The museum intended to strip its woodwork and, as it reported, "after that removal to sell the house and land." At the time, the museum had no American period rooms and gave short shrift to American arts and crafts. According to one historian, the MFA's new interest in Americana revealed a loss of influence for the aristocrats and a gain for professional curators. In this case, however, J. Templeman Coolidge III, a Brahmin artist and collector, had apparently heeded SPNEA's call to acquire the vernacular.[26]

Long desiring that shift, Appleton rejected any cry of vandalism over the MFA's plan for the Jaffrey house. He misrepresented its fate to his readers and reported that the MFA had acted only because the building could not have remained on the site. He instead blamed the residents of Portsmouth. "If the people of a given locality are unable or unwilling themselves to protect its meritorious old work," he warned, "then they must expect to lose it to outside buyers who so keenly appreciate it as to be willing to secure it for removal." He was not willing to alienate the MFA, whose curators were undeterred. What it did not use from the house incidentally ended up in SPNEA's collection.[27]

At the same time, SPNEA's president served on the MFA's Board of Trustees, as he would through 1933. While the museum continued its assault on these buildings, Bolton turned a blind eye and deferred to the perceived necessity of Brahmin solidarity. By 1937 the MFA's American rooms held some "memorable" interiors. Most notable were three rooms it acquired in 1922 that were designed by Samuel McIntire for Oak Hill in Peabody. "Despoiled of its trim," historian Walter Muir Whitehill said, Oak Hill was later razed for a shopping center.[28]

Appleton complained that such vandalism seemed all too common in the United States. "In Europe," he claimed in 1919, "this probably would be inconceivable." His rosy picture misstated the case. One historian estimated that in the period from 1890–1920 Americans spent more money acquiring art, principally from Europe, than ever was the case for any people in history. It occurred even while war was destroying much of that land, perhaps leading to the failure of SPNEA's 1914 resolution. Recognizing that in 1916, Bolton was amazed "how Europe is being stripped to carry taste over the seas to us!"[29]

Whether affluent individuals or respected institutions, conspicuous consumption encouraged Americans to purchase not only the works of Rembrandt and Rodin but historic buildings, or their rooms, to transplant to the New World. Before the war Americans had bought paintings, sculpture, and other easily transportable commodities, but afterwards they turned their eyes on architecture. Americans particularly explored England, hoping to find some antiquity at a good price. England's courts opened the door wide by undercutting the Ancient Monuments Act (1913) and allowing the sale of a London staircase—wrongly attributed to William Hogarth—to the Art Institute of Chicago. English preservationists, as well as Appleton, were outraged, but the spoils had only begun.[30]

No better example occurred to Appleton than that of Agecroft Hall, a fifteenth-century manor house that had fallen into decay. In 1926 Appleton heard that "a very wealthy" American was negotiating to buy the Lancashire estate for removal to the United States. He warned Swarbrick, but wanted SPNEA's name left out of the publicity because of "the possibility that the individual having this particular bit of destruction in mind may be one of our friends and helpers." Voices of protest were raised in the House of Commons, but to no avail.[31] Other Americans had already purchased Warwick Priory, originally built in the twelfth century.

Actually the culprits were not Yankees, but Virginians who, like many elite in the Old Dominion, had a strong affection for the country life. Worse yet, Appleton heard that both buildings were to be modified considerably to meet their owners' tastes. The massing and lines of Warwick Priory, for example, were changed to resemble Sulgrave Manor, the ancestral home of Washington. Swarbrick emphasized, however, that such buildings were tied intimately to their locale. "To sever them from their original soil and merely re-construct a few fragments on a remote continent," he told Appleton, was robbing them of their place and time.[32]

Appleton worried that the example set by Agecroft Hall would snowball. "The amount of money available for such things here," he warned, "is absolutely unlimited, and the number of people having large fortunes is extremely great. All of them will feel that if they don't take what they want the next person will get it." Unwilling to blame either the seller or buyer, he faulted England's preservation movement and government. "Your Ancient Monuments Board is not as courageous as it should be," he told Swarbrick. So unlike Ashbee who earlier wanted to centralize American work, Appleton urged Swarbrick to decentralize English efforts, require in situ preservation, and, as a last resort, use eminent domain. Powys and SPAB rejoined, however, that such legislation ran counter to his country's "deep-rooted" principles. The roll of vandalism finally prompted the American Institute of Architects to denounce the "craze," but only the austerity of the Depression abated the destruction. Even then, affluent institutions and individuals could still bankroll their plunder, as in 1936 when the Metropolitan and Henry Francis du Pont despoiled Ye Olde Burnham Inn (c. 1675–1700) in Ipswich.[33]

For over twenty years Appleton had anticipated the dilemma. He had seen developers run roughshod over fragile buildings, as well as the public readily escape the troubled present through touristic jaunts into the past. These factors, together with his bent for remaking history, prompted him to urge Yankees to create their own Skansen with buildings threatened by demolition. Ethnographer Arthur Hazelius had expanded his Nordiska Museet (1872) by opening Skansen near Stockholm in 1891. There he amassed folk buildings from across Sweden, employed artisans to display their crafts, and focused on the country life that was fast disappearing. His deradicalized depiction did not show, however, the other side of peasants' lives, whether their rebellions against the privileged or their daily privation. Morris extolled this "newly-invented study of living history," and others imitated it elsewhere, as did Anders Sandvig in 1904 at Maihaugen in Lillehammer, Norway.[34]

Like Morris, some Yankees used Skansen to educate the public about the ills of industrialism and commercialism. Mary Bronson Hartt, a popular writer and later editor of *Museum News*, pictured those living museums as "a revolt against the uniforming effect of civilization, which goes about to reduce the diverse children of men to the likeness of bullets cast in one mold." Unlike "the cheap falsity of the Midway" that "degraded" folk cultures at the world's fairs, Skansen not only showed the worth of that tradition but served as "a perpetual protest against the American way of 'doing' things." As she saw the situation, America's promotion of modern industry and commerce threatened the heritage of distant lands as well as its own. She warned that "Old New England is passing away."[35]

As early as 1914, Appleton repeated her call for a "Skansen Open Air Museum" in New England, but omitted her polemic against American capitalism. Preservationist and curator alike were laboring to put more life into their artifacts as the public became entranced by the razzle-dazzle of Model-T's, moving pictures, and Sears's catalog. Before a national audience in 1919, he called for the creation of a Yankee folk museum. "In its ultimate consummation," he wrote citing Sandvig's philosophy, "it shall be a collection of *homes* where one, as it were, can walk straight into the homes of the people who have lived there, learn to know their mode of living, their tastes, their work. For the home and its equipment are a picture of the people themselves, and in the old hereditary homesteads it is not only the single individual who is mirrored, but it is the whole race, generation after generation." Sandvig wanted, as did Appleton, "to place the entire village, as a complete whole, in this big picturebook." The manor house, the craftsman's cottage, and the peasant's hut would be there, "and from the top of the hill the old village church shall send forth the peel of its bells over these relics of bygone days."[36]

Appleton wanted to replicate Sandvig's scheme, but only use buildings threatened by demolition. As a result, the park would have few first-rank buildings because he wanted them kept on their original sites. Rather than create a park by happenstance, he wanted "a series of closely connected villages, each representing a fifty-year period in New England history." Like Maihaugen with its church on the hill, Appleton's village would have "its meeting-house situated on the village green or facing the village square and surrounded by the typical buildings of its period." It would show the everyday patterns of the village and employ artisans in period costume who preserved their crafts. As it insulated antiquities from modern, corrupting surroundings, it would allow visitors to immerse themselves in the site's mystical aura.[37]

Appleton's picture of the colonial landscape was certainly more myth than fact. The comforting image of a meeting house on the green surrounded by dignified homes did not reflect the colonial period at all, but instead a growing urbanism and an accommodation to industrialism that occurred in the late eighteenth and early nineteenth centuries. That landscape developed because of a traumatic change in the subsistence economy of the countryside and the emergence of a market economy in the town. Nineteenth-century Yankees perceived the significant shift, and romanticists embraced the village as a means to order their fast-changing society and create an image of a better (and lost) community. They passed on that image, and it became an icon.[38]

Appleton never built his own folk park, but his plan did bear some fruit. In varying degree, Ford, Riddle, and Dow were affiliated with SPNEA and established their own Skansens, but showed the paradox of progressivism. During the era the quest for scientific documents, authentic experience, and physical verisimilitude had surely been heightened, yet these three showed that it was easier to invent a past than to preserve one. Imagination replaced historical fidelity as they remade history. The reasons for their success, and his failure, illustrate the changes within American preservation.

If SPNEA objected to wealthy parvenus buying a heritage in distant lands, this habit was best shown by its vice-president for Michigan. Many antiquaries shared his deep streak of antiintellectualism and belief that everyday artifacts could "keep history fresh and alive for the children of this country." He began his roll of acquisitions with Wayside Inn (1686) in Sudbury, Massachusetts. So much associated with Longfellow's poem, it went on the sale block in 1922 and Appleton worried about its fate. Some Yankees, including Charles Francis Adams, wanted to buy it, but failed. Then, "our fellow member" bought it, Appleton said, and "the enterprise could not have ended more fortunately." By the end of the decade, he spent over two million dollars, in his lifetime closer to five, as he created a colonial preserve at Sudbury. *Old-Time New England* declared that his work showed "the fitting kind of piety" that Yankees expected. Ford further cultivated their friendship, as when he invited the Boltons to his "Neighbor's Night" in 1924.[39]

So, too, did Appleton hope that Ford would build a folk park for SPNEA. His big check never materialized, however, and his work ran counter to Appleton's philosophy of in situ, archaeologically minded preservation. One Longfellow descendant visited the inn, for example, and said that the floor seemed a bit stiff. Ford promised to fix the problem with American know-how by concealing springs under the floor to give it more elasticity. His assistant also scoured the New England countryside, and acquired old buildings that were stripped to furnish the inn or moved intact to its grounds. Befitting his love of school primers, Ford even moved to his grounds the schoolhouse on Redstone Hill of "Mary had a little lamb" fame.[40]

For another, he invented an even larger village in Michigan. Dedicated in 1929, Greenfield Village was a posthumous tribute to the values and landscape that his flivver helped to destroy. Ambivalent about modernity, he lamented the waning of old-time traditions, but still worshiped machinery. As a result, he centered his park around the mythical New England green and added everything from a seventeenth-century cottage from England to a Cape Cod windmill built by the Pilgrims.[41] Unlike Skansen which glorified the world that was lost, Ford used his old-time props to revive earlier values for modern industry.

Not one, but two SPNEA officers fabricated communities that mimicked history. Connecticut vice-president Theodate Pope Riddle invested her fortune in a school. As was the case with Olmsted and an untold number of social planners, Riddle, who was the state's first registered female architect, designed a controlled environment to foster acceptable behavior and attitudes. With upwards of five million dollars, she replicated the preindustrial architecture of old England and New at Avon Old Farms, which she opened in 1927 on 3,000 acres of Connecticut farmland. She predicated the school on the virtue of manual labor and the simple life. It became an old-fashioned community guided by the medieval spirit and untouched by mechanization. Ironically, Ford and Riddle had won their wealth through the industrial age. What he embraced in mechanized progress, she rejected.[42] Obviously their villages were utter fabrications. While the flivver king bought and transformed the buildings of diverse lands, the medievalist architect cloned a lost era.

Appleton instead preached the importance of in situ archaeology. Failing to find a benefactor, he spurred English preservationists to create an open-air park, hoping that Yankees would then copy their Anglo-Saxon cousins. In 1926 he asked the Ancient Monuments Society to create a Skansen from doomed buildings, and predicted that American tourists "would more than pay the interest on the expense." At the same time, he recognized that some ancient villages warranted absolute protection. With his bent for money-making, Appleton recommended that such a village "be put under glass and kept unchanged, and then the whole place 'worked' . . . for all it is worth in the way of attracting scores of thousands of visitors every year." Appleton predicted that increased tourism would entice public authorities to act, and a government commission and the AMS did soon recommend creating such village museums.[43]

It was not Appleton but Dow who created an outdoor colonial park. His interpretive and inventive bent became apparent as he suggested in *Old-Time New England* in 1930 just how the folk buildings should appear. So unlike the circumstances of the early colonies, but so typical for modern times, each room would have its specialized function and be appropriately furnished so that "the coverlet is on the bed and the kettle is in the fireplace." Moreover, the harmony and constancy that he ascribed to village life would be ensured by a controlled landscape. "There must also be space and cover," he thought, "so that one building does not clash with its neighbor."[44]

As at Skansen, the folk park "would show the roots of customs buried in the past" and how they were expressed in the crafts and community. Its shops would be "filled with life" as busy, happy artisans worked in the vein of the Protestant ethic. He expected this living history to so contrast with "the monotony of an ordered museum" that it would "foster the best kind of national feeling." He admitted that he held no "purely sentimental aim" but strove "to increase the knowledge and love of one's native land." Paradoxically, Dow's work in court records had disclosed that this had hardly been an idyllic world. Knowing well their profanity, loose living, drunkenness, and petty crime, he had admitted five years earlier that there were "as many sinners as saints" in the Bay Colony. Like so many Colonial Revivalists, however, his longing for an imagined community proved stronger than belaboring such unfortunate facts.[45]

His thinking further revealed some troubling assumptions about the creativity and vitality of the folk culture. Picturing an evolutionary development, he thought that "there is a tendency for new customs and objects of daily use, whether introduced from abroad or originating within the country, to come in at the top of the social strata, to spread downward, and eventually to be preserved in the lower strata and in the remote districts."[46] Perhaps that top-to-bottom movement was the case in the industrial economy with its more costly and controlled means of production. Yet it was not necessarily the pattern in preindustrial times or even with more recent vernacular culture. Dow's "top-down" perspective clashed paradoxically with his idealism about the vernacular.

Dow's chance came in 1930 when Salem commissioned him to build a colonial hamlet for its tercentennial celebrations. A bequest of $300,000 had been earmarked for a city park, but Appleton instead urged authorities to create a local Skansen with ancient, but endangered, buildings. He readily offered his society's services. Pioneer Village proved to be a pale reflection, however, not only of Skansen but Appleton's proposal. Commemorating the arrival of Winthrop and his Puritans in 1630, Salem recreated his ship *Arbella* and settlement. Lacking extant remnants or drawings, and relying on a very sketchy written record, Dow modelled the "Governor's Fayre House" on the Fairbanks' home. He surmised that the other dwellings had been built with wattle-and-daub and thatched roofs. Chandler supervised the conjectural reconstruction. Though far-fetched, Dow reported: "Seldom has reproduction of the past been carried out with such fidelity and with such success."[47]

Although Pioneer Village was conceived as a temporary attraction, authorities decided to make it permanent as a means to Americanize the newcomers. Local school children from peasant cultures came in throngs and ironically saw Yankees pay homage not only to the preindustrial past but to folk traditions they themselves were sacrificing in the name of progress. The museum educated others as well. Calvin Coolidge told the nation, for example, to see its depiction of "the bare necessities" of that day in order to "reduce complaint and increase contentment" during the Depression. Pioneer Village was well received. According to the Writers' Project, it represented "village life in epitome." Its buildings showed not only the social and economic hierarchy but the means through which the region was developed and disciplined. It included "a blacksmith's forge, a saw-pit, a brick kiln, as well as the grim whipping posts and stocks."[48]

SPNEA never built its own Skansen, mostly because its funds were scarce, Appleton's standards too demanding, and the imaginative work of the likes of Ford and Dow too appealing. Pioneer Village and Wayside Inn did set a pattern in New England, however. In the late 1930s, Albert B. Wells, a wealthy businessman, founded Old Sturbridge Village in western Massachusetts. With blueprints from Chandler, he placed his buildings, which had been moved from other sites or built on the scene, at first with little sense of archaeological or historical fidelity. Like Salem's Americanization campaign, Old Sturbridge Village attempted to remake the industrial worker. Employing over 3,000 laborers, Wells was hard pressed to preserve his Anglo-American culture because most of the community were Canadians who spoke French, practiced Catholicism, and held on to their traditional ways. He resultantly used the museum to teach his workers to "appreciate how the early New Englander's ingenuity and thrift and self-reliance paved the way for some of man's greatest material achievements." Determined to reinforce the economy after its collapse, he wanted to show the young worker "how modern industry assures a life far more abundant than what existed under a handicraft system."[49]

Old Sturbridge and Greenfield Village, as a result, represented the other side of Skansen's coin. If Wells and Ford wanted to show that modern industry had created a better material life for workers, Sandvig and Hazelius pictured the appealing life that was lost through such industrialization. Pioneer Village and Avon Old Farms meanwhile taught appropriate values through remade medieval environments. None matched Appleton's proposal for a folk park, but he kept on trying to find a patron until his death.[50] SPNEA's demand for in situ preservation, archaeological method, and historical fidelity simply could not match the innovative nostalgia practiced by Dow, Riddle, and others. Their outdoor parks, moreover, were much more effective than house museums and period rooms in carrying a message to the populace. Rivalling the creativity of the moving picture, they were based on the belief that history could be remade, regardless of the known facts, as long as it had an authentic look and ambience.

EPILOGUE

Whether it was the campaign to remake the Revere house in 1905 or Pioneer Village in 1930, preservationists were consciously linking past and present to underscore their belief that New Englanders must learn from their colonial forebears. Change had accelerated so swiftly that cultural vertigo seemed to be setting in. As preservationists remade their regional image and traditions, they equated their needs with those of an increasingly diverse society. Yet their gospel had distinct permutations. Some such as Titus, Bush, and Edith Wendell prized domesticity and personalism. More weighty in defining the profession and society's concept of preservation were the views of Appleton, Isham, and Chandler. Appleton's belief in private initiative and architectural aesthetics, as well as his lifelong devotion to the cause, shaped not only SPNEA but the region's movement. He learned from many colleagues in Brahmin and professional circles, but, as he matured, he reciprocated and tutored more than a generation of preservationists. SPNEA taught them to appreciate New England's antiquities as symbols of Yankee values, to use them as documents to study earlier societies, and to market them as means to boom the economy. Such conflicting usages often created inconsistency and paradox.

Tradition-minded Yankees knew that New England had been transformed by immigration and industrialization. Yet preservationists did not retreat amid the flurry of change. Instead they regrouped. Inspired by a fiery brew of noblesse oblige, filiopietism, and real fear, Yankee preservationists broadcast a message to New Englanders, old blood and new, to protect these Anglo-Saxon antiquities. Through private organizations, and public ones that they could influence, tradition-minded Yankees further used the preserved past to sanction their culture as the region's official creed and to Americanize the immigrants. As the Colonial Revival waxed, traditionalists called their work one of uplift and enlightenment, but the other side of the coin, of course, revealed an attempt to order the populace and protect their own standing.

Older values seemed out of touch with newer realities, however. As New England's large cities elected charismatic immigrant politicians, old-time Yankees reasserted their control over the region's identity. Most Yankees cared little for the historic landscape, but more nostalgic ones saw its remade form as a symbolic representation of traditionalism. Once those buildings became encrypted with ideology, they became part of the accepted heritage. Similarly, as New England's workers fought the factory's exploitation, progressives pictured a past where hard work, personal virtue, and obedience to law had guaranteed a man's success. The

Scots' work at Saugus, Revere's willingness to Americanize, and Fowler's rags-to-riches mobility, it was said, offered lessons for immigrant and Yankee alike. What relevance those traditions had to factory workers was problematic, however. On the same note, Brahmins idealized rural life; most could escape to their country cottage or suburban home to enjoy its rewards. SPNEA's many country dwellings reinforced those beliefs, but contrasted strangely with the tensions and disorder of cities.

Troubled by their own era's untold complexity, preservationists remade the past as homogeneous, virtuous, and simple. They saw the buildings of the seventeenth century, for example, as symbols of a community whose leaders were moral and responsible, whose people were hard working and family-oriented, and whose customs and laws ensured peace and order. That world, preservationists believed, was more personal and meaningful than their own. The shock of the new so troubled some preservationists, including Appleton, Nutting, and Sears, that they suffered a nervous collapse; their therapy was an immersion of antiquarian studies. Ambivalent about "progress," they used the mythical past not simply as a foil to critique the present but to solve their own personal crisis.

Students of the region's literature, geography, and history have shown how Yankee writers had been redefining their history and traditions in light of the economic changes of the nineteenth and early twentieth centuries. The preservation movement continued that pattern and, as the contest for power became more heated, it adapted to an evolving traditionalism. That process could entail one or more of the following steps: elevating obscure Yankees to heroic dimensions, selectively interpreting the historical record, picturing undocumented lore as accepted fact, fabricating legends, or, most evident of all, restoring a site to cleanse a building of modern corruption and recreate the appearance of authenticity. A cyclical relationship existed between traditionalism, preservation, and the remaking of history and culture; the first led to the second, the second to the third, the third reinforced the first, and the process repeated itself. These preservationists encrusted their favored traditions in material forms for practical reasons. Artifacts served as credible props for ideology.

That invented image had immediate repercussions. Even before the founding of SPNEA, Appleton and the SR were recasting Harrington and the Minutemen as role models whose courage and sacrifice deserved emulation against the much-exaggerated threat of socialism. SPNEA acquired the Fowler house in 1912, and that similarly prompted Appleton to raise Fowler from obscurity to icon. Fowler's industry, self-help philanthropy, and rural habits reinforced those Yankees who were accommodating their customs to the new corporation. The purchase of the Boardman house two years later led Appleton to recast it as a memorial to those "Scotch" immigrants who had adopted Yankee ways. That model led Yankees to question the worth of newer immigrants and demand that they abandon older ways.

Even in Appleton's image of a folk park with its community around a green there was much invention. Preservationists' bucolic picture of the country village lent credibility to those who wondered about the viability of the modern metropolis. Those villages outside the nineteenth-century city had actually been borderland communities whose residents juxtaposed rural and urban living and tried to brake industrialism's effects on the New England landscape. By the early twentieth century those villages were often preserved and anchored by the comforting sight of restored colonial houses and churches on the green.[1] Ironically, Appleton came across many dwellings, such as the Norton house at Guilford, whose remoteness from the village, primitive construction, and occupancy by ne'er-do-well settlers should have dashed that mythical image. Yet he could not break loose from the nostalgia of his day; the focus of preservationists on the small town and their disregard for the city only tended to universalize those myths.

What impact did that remade past have? Not only had Yankees carried their invented landscape to the West and made them national myths, but those inventions shaped the remaking of twentieth-century New England. What happened in Boston was a natural result of that reverence for village life. Guided by such nostalgia and cultural politics, Boston's town fathers never did accept the West End's diversity or control what they deemed to be its chaos (Fig. Ep.-1). Leaving the Otis house and West End Church intact, they erased fifty acres of its buildings in 1958–60 in what was perversely called "urban renewal." SPNEA recognized the travesty. Writing in *Old-Time New England*, Abbott Lowell Cummings, who subsequently served as SPNEA's third director, deplored the destruction and wondered if "later generations who examine our twentieth-century protestations of interest in an American heritage will find such raids on cultural capital totally incomprehensible." Today the Otis house seems lost in the hodgepodge that remains. In fact, its very meaning is questioned. A popular Boston journalist and architect recently contrasted the building's use in the 1890s and 1990s, and implicitly challenged Appleton's notion of preservation. Whereas the rooming house with storefront shops had "participated fully in the life of the street," it now appears "chilly and withdrawn behind its granite wall and front lawn" and "offers little interest or pleasure to the passerby."[2]

If the West End's demise was rooted in the drive of progressives to reshape the city, the case of the North End had a different outcome. The West End fell because of its proximity to Beacon Hill and the commercial district, but the North End was saved by its seclusion. Its crowded tenements and foreign tongues scared most Yankees who, like Appleton, prized Old North Church and the Revere home, but were willing to see much of the rest fall. Bostonians ignored Ashbee's advice to link the work of preservation, settlements, and city planning in such neighborhoods. By the late 1920s almost 800 people per acre still lived there, and such continuing neglect led a student of Boston's history to claim that as late as 1929 the city had no preservation movement. A later generation of urban

FIG. EP.-1   Harrison Gray Otis House and West End Church, 1940 (*Old-Time New England* 30 [April 1940]: 119)

reformers, most notably Jane Jacobs in 1961, saw the North End differently. Though in the minority of architectural planners, she described the North End as the type of healthy and friendly community that warranted protection.[3]

Evidently there was a chasm separating the interests of Appleton and Jacobs. Her hopes for reviving human bonds through the architecture of old neighborhoods not only resembled the personalism of earlier women, but was so dependent on the government funding and city planning that he resisted. In fact, a recent study of Boston's landscape blamed SPNEA's narrow and "purist" work for creating a schism between planners and preservationists. Because Appleton dealt with individual houses, not neighborhoods, the efforts of the planning, parks, and preservation movements were uncoordinated. That charge has some merit, but it assumes a commonality of interest that was lacking in Yankee progressivism. As in "Boston-1915," historic preservation was a neglected stepchild of more fashionable movements. Other critics have implicitly challenged Appleton's commercial and aesthetic preoccupation with the look of antiquity. Today, some New England communities are so worried about their touristic image that they have neglected less attractive historic neighborhoods and buildings, including industrial, commercial, and farm structures.[4]

So much a part of the progressive era and so intent on crafting a profession, Appleton wanted order, efficiency, and scientific method in the movement's operations. He was sometimes slow in implementing those qualities in his own organization, however. As in some corporations with a domineering founder, SPNEA revolved much around his orbit. Privileged by his birth and wealth, he wanted it done his way, though he was all the while learning on his feet. Later students would praise his professionalism, partly in reflection on his lifelong accomplishments but also in reaction against the misdirected work of architects and their wealthy benefactors who were literally inventing historic sites across the nation.

Unlike preservationists in Virginia and New York, Appleton single-mindedly focused his work on historic materials, defined by their age and aesthetics, but that did not mean that his preservation society had no role to play in parallel movements, such as the promotion of the civil religion and good government. It instead meant that while SPNEA preserved antiquities, traditions, and "good taste," its allies in government, journalism, education, and landscape and architectural design would apply those measures to their reform interests. Much like the arts-and-crafts architecture of Gustav Stickley, who emphasized country life, a middle-class appeal, and masculine values, the net effect of preservation was one where the rural, manly built cottages of simple farmers became the regional symbol. Like the mother wine, the picture of modern New England would resemble the old as the region continued to embrace endless Colonial Revivals.

SPNEA's links with the corporate model of progressivism became further evident in its business-minded use of old buildings. Whether used as shrines, tearooms, or tourist attractions, these buildings had a useful purpose, and that was to put money into the economy. The pursuit of growth still defined the region and its preservation movement. Yet Appleton's demands for archaeological accuracy and scientific method often put a crimp on the practical use of these old buildings. Sometimes it was for the better, as in his qualms about the reconstructions underwritten by the likes of Rockefeller and Ford. Other times, he was flying into the wind. He surely lost the debate with Frank Bourne and Susan Frost over their mutual policy of buying endangered properties, renovating their interiors, and reselling them to private buyers. Most preservationists would sub-sequently accommodate the market by encouraging interior renovation and facade preservation.[5]

Appleton even tried to export his market-oriented brand of preserva-tion to the British Isles. First organized by socialists such as Morris and Ashbee, the English movement had used preservation to challenge indus-trial capitalism. The Medieval era and its communitarian guild became an alternative to the exploitive factory. This romantic vision of the past, and its implicit remedy for the present, waned as the English preservation movement was likewise pulled by architectural aesthetics, professional-ism, and a market orientation.[6]

As SPNEA pushed tourism to aid its cause, it groomed New England's image for the flivver-driving wayfarer. The problem with tourism, then and now, however, is that tourists see what they want to see. As in a hall of mirrors, the artifacts and meaning of history, as well as the continuity from past to future, are distorted when the past is indeed that foreign country. Bending to public tastes, and resultantly shaping the next gen-eration's concept of history, this tourism often remakes the past as a dime-novel, a Harlequin romance, or a Disneyesque theme park. Such fantasy particularly caters to nostalgia and a reactionary response to the inevi-table future. Such a heritage industry in Britain, said historian Robert Hewison, has misallocated resources, intensified the feeling of decline, and impeded the necessary creativity for change.[7] Although Appleton had cor-rectly sensed that a reciprocal relationship existed between educating the people and preserving the past, he depended on the marketplace to solve his problem. He did not conceive a means of educating tourists to see the past in a light other than the bright and distorting glow of progress.

Instead of Morris, Yankee preservationists followed the program of progressivism. Appleton found an outlet in the drives to implement "Bos-ton-1915," revise the Massachusetts constitution, and Americanize the immigrant, but the nitty-gritty work of preservation always came first. He clashed frequently with the newcomers, as did most preservationists on the East Coast. In a few cases, some tried to accommodate the de-mographic and cultural shift. In Salem, the Seven Gables became a settle-ment, while in an African-American neighborhood of Richmond, the APVA turned a historic house into a Negro Art Center. SPNEA never considered an urban venture along those lines. All the while, a battle ensued over the future of Boston. In 1925 Mayor Curley told Bostonians to avoid the road set by Puritan and Yankee, one leading to "parochial-ism" and economic decline, and instead to find a community "regardful of the true meaning of Americanism." Never willing to accept an Amer-icanism where second-generation immigrants held such influence, Apple-ton sang "praise be" upon hearing of Curley's defeat in 1936.[8]

Like progressivism, the preservation movement became enchanted by professional experts, scientific method, and quantifiable data. Its profes-sionalism was defined by not only the business world but the academy of architecture. Under Appleton's tutelage, the movement became more focused, specialized, and tightly run. Distrustful of public involvement and confident about his own approach, Appleton demanded that others emulate his work. Perhaps his question about the goal of restoration should again be asked. If the goal of the movement was to heighten the interest of the populace in its heritage, this model based on corporate structure and architectural aesthetics often chilled popular participation and indeed strove to keep the public at arm's length. Building a profession exacted quite a cost when it came to community involvement and popular education. SPNEA implicitly acknowledged the fact years later. Whether it was the Cooper-Frost-Austin house in bustling Cambridge or the Browne house in suburban Watertown, those architectural gems failed to pull the community into the preservationist fold. Residents of Cambridge apparently ignored that antique because it was owned by aloof outsiders. In Watertown, SPNEA worried about the fate of the Browne house, and its director lamented in 1980, "there has been no record of local interest or involvement, and the Browne House is a fairly invisible SPNEA property."[9]

As the profession evolved from the tenets of corporate progressivism, and instead of sinking its pilings deeper into the community, its leaders turned for help more ambitiously and successfully to larger bureaucratic agencies. As in SPNEA's petition to protect the monuments of Europe in 1914, preservationists gradually assumed an internationalist perspective, one that would be reiterated by the International Council on Monuments and Sites. Similarly, progressives amended the Massachusetts constitution in 1918 to protect historic landmarks. Appleton did fear that preservation would become the football of politics, but he inadvertently set the field for another generation of preservationists who would carry the ball through public agencies. His call was amplified particularly by Cummings and finally heeded by such agencies as the Boston Landmarks Commission and the Massachusetts Historical Commission. Contrary to Appleton's gameplan, SPNEA today does not even consider itself "a preservation agency" because that charge has been assumed by others.[10]

Another result of this shift to architectural and corporate models was the displacement of women in the preservation movement. It is important not only to remember that women had played a significant role saving the Old South Meeting House in the 1870s but to recognize that women's leadership was gradually being undercut elsewhere by male architects and developers. As the DAR restored Independence Hall in Philadelphia in 1899, its work was challenged by architects who questioned the women's oversight. The same pattern followed in New England, whether it involved Boston's Old State House, the Howland and Shirley-Eustis houses, or a graveyard in East Lyme. Women's sense of personalism, as well as their obligations to home and community, were being subordinated to male aesthetics, the promotion of tourism and commerce, and corporate-minded professionalism. Women were quickly losing their custodial influence in this cultural arena. Fanny C. Stone expressed her fear in 1910, for example, that SPNEA would act "like the big corporations" and "swallow up all the local societies that are poor and struggling." A later student of the movement dismissed her worry as "ludicrous," but the larger movement did increasingly reflect the male world and its standards.[11] Women still had clout in female societies, such as the Colonial Dames, or in local ones, as in the Piscataqua Region, where their work and identities more neatly revolved in the traditional orbit of patriotism and personalism.[12]

Women found less room in those newer groups that shaped the movement into the 1930s and beyond, particularly after the Depression decimated the ranks and resources of those private organizations. As in the cases of the National Park Service and Colonial Williamsburg Foundation, those newer models drew from the scientific disciplines of architecture and archaeology, organized along hierarchical and bureaucratic lines, practiced a tradition-minded boosterism, and preached a professionalism that was male in orientation. In the vein of their training, class, and gender, their largely male staffs defined history, preserved its vestiges, but still played an important hand in the cultural politics of their day. Their model of activity became so dominant that others, such as Jacobs with her interest in personalism and neighborhoods, were inhibited. For some time, women were commonly relegated the tasks of all-purpose volunteer, "hostess," and fund raiser.[13] Only recently has the pattern begun to change, and SPNEA, for one, has been headed by women for almost the past decade. Unlike the architectural focus of Appleton and Cummings, Jane C. Nylander, its fifth director, centers her own professional work on the domestic world of women.[14]

In the field as a whole, however, there is considerable discussion about how to extend the definition of historic preservation to include not only the conservation of porticoes, spinning wheels, and battlefields but the cultivation of those life-giving relationships that provide meaning and continuity to communities. If the modern preservation movement is rooted in a reaction to immigration and urbanization, an accommodation to corporate capitalism, and an attempt to order work through professionalism and progressivism, as I have shown, what meaning is there for a nation whose ethnicity, economy, and society continue to change so fundamentally in a postmodern age? What role does historic preservation play in making sense of this newer America? Do preservationists have an obligation to link the historical past and changing present in a way that would both inform and guide the people well into the twenty-first century? To be sure, the lure of old-time New England does have commercial and psychological appeal, but such marketplace, antimodern values have distracted preservationists from presenting—indeed sometimes accepting—an unvarnished image of the everyday life of diverse New Englanders past and present.[15]

Those timely questions become even more pertinent as we face the ironies and paradoxes of the preservation movement during these watershed years in the early twentieth century. Appleton and like-minded colleagues explored the seventeenth-century world, absorbed the purported values of its vernacular materials, and returned to influence their own times. Trying to bridge the elite and mass cultures of modern New England, SPNEA repackaged this remade folk tradition for the aspiring middle-class consumer, as well as for more upper-crust audiences. Unlike Colonial Williamsburg, which extolled the aesthetics of elite planters, SPNEA devoted much attention to redefining the folk as a tradition for rich and poor alike. Brahminism did absorb bits and pieces of the vernacular through the Colonial Revival, thus diluting what was once a distinct upper-class tradition. Moreover, the mass culture also assimilated the preserved past, whether through the lessons taught at the Revere home, the crafts revival, or the public-school classroom.

But, for all of Appleton's interest in the folk, the New England that he and his colleagues remade was one generally recast within an elite context, whether the Puritanism of John Cooper, the Federalism of Otis, the Brahminism of Norton, or the progressivism of "Boston-1915." Not only would later preservationists reopen the record in search of women, African-Americans, Native Americans, and the more humble European settlers, they would also reclassify some of those buildings Isham and Appleton regarded as those of common men as actually those of a lesser elite.

Those modern Yankees spoke approvingly of the folklife of preindustrial times—its tight-knit family, home production, localistic character, and reluctance to change. Not only was that construct a myth often at odds with historical reality, but in the early 1900s these Yankees dismissed those same characteristics of the peasants who emigrated from Italy, Poland, and other Eastern European lands. Generally, preservationists rejected pluralism and demanded an Americanization of the newcomers. The ultimate paradox by the early twentieth century, however, was that tradition-minded progressives had embraced so much of the modern corporate order that it was difficult to define a Yankee tradition amid the flurry of change.

SPNEA encouraged New Englanders to see themselves as Yankees rooted in small communities mindful of established traditions. Herein lies another paradox. As the modern economy homogenized more and more local communities, progressive and preservationist alike led movements that championed their values, but they, too, fostered a monotheistic country ideal, a stereotypical New England, and a mythical image that surely had touristic appeal but less and less relevance. America's future could instead be glimpsed in the metropolis, with its diversity and complexity, but the past that progressives idealized and preservationists conserved was, much like the Norton house in rural Guilford, in flux.

While Appleton and his colleagues equated their desired life with that of the colonial period, his own sense of aesthetics and domesticity would

lead him eventually to value the best of the Victorian era and disregard
Nutting's warning to steer clear of those mongrel, machined forms. By
the late 1930s, for example, SPNEA came close to acquiring the Morse-
Libby house (1863) in Portland, Maine. Showing how far he had traveled
since his first days as an Anglo-Saxon-minded preservationist, Appleton
called the Italian Villa "the finest mid-Victorian house in New England,
perhaps in America, one that should be made our most sumptuous and
outstanding Victorian landmark." By that time, many Yankees thought
that family values had still been strong in the Victorian era. Antimodernism influenced this nostalgia, as did the aging of Appleton's own generation and the ceaseless assault on that era's architecture.[16] His interest in
Victoriana, albeit its elite artistry, represented a shift, therefore, from his
own Colonial Revival roots to a more eclectic aesthetics.

SPNEA's importance in preserving those material forms should not be
understated. Historians who study colonial society repeatedly refer to the
homes, landscapes, and artifacts that early twentieth-century preservationists struggled to save. Such buildings as the seventeenth-century
Boardman, Cooper-Frost-Austin, Arnold, and Browne houses are still recognized as first-rate antiquities. Students have equally learned from preservationists that a more complete picture of early life can be seen by
integrating buildings, household goods, and court records into traditional
source materials.[17] SPNEA's acquisition of two dozen buildings in its first
twenty years, however, pales in number to those that were actually preserved by its friends and allies. As a result, modern historians have increased opportunity to study a society that was certainly more complex
than pictured by early twentieth-century antiquaries.

Preservationists bequeathed many buildings to study, but the integrity
of those artifacts has been clouded by the effects of restoration and the
assumptions that guided it. Whether it was the case of Appleton trying
to recover the medievalisms of craftsmen or the artistry of Bulfinch, that
process of antiquing a building, sometimes on the flimsiest of evidence or
mere wishful thinking, was a form of remaking history. Today, the restoration work of Chandler, Dean, and others so easily passes for the real
thing that questions are raised (but answered only tentatively) about genuine colonial work. Lines have been blurred between authentic and con-
trived, as Appleton had predicted. Only the fallible, often cryptic, records
of early restorers enables modern students to separate one from the other.

The work of surveying the landscape and preserving a historic site was
further flawed when antiquaries transposed their modern world into the
past. They assumed, incorrectly, that the buildings most typical of early
construction were those of Essex County. The county was unique in New
England, however, for at least two reasons. Its two-story homes of the
seventeenth and eighteenth centuries were the rule for its building stock,
not the exception; most of the New England landscape had instead been
dotted with one-story homes. Essex County also had the greatest number

of surviving seventeenth-century buildings. What was unique about Essex, however, became the imagined past of New England.[18]

Moreover, the East Anglian tradition that shaped the building patterns of Essex County, as well as that of the nearby counties of Suffolk and Norfolk to the south, was surely important, but the early settlements of New England had actually been more diverse. There were at least thirteen different beachheads of colonial settlement, representing a half-dozen distinct English regions. Each possessed its own discrete subculture and, by the eighteenth century, had formed at least six subregions different from Puritan Boston. What early antiquaries did not recognize, moreover, was that a building's features depended particularly on those different regional customs. Those settlers who founded Plymouth, for example, brought a different building tradition. The archaeological discovery there of what had been a three-room long house, for instance, has no counterpart in the legacy passed on by earlier preservationists.[19]

Other assumptions misled these preservationists. For one, Isham and Kelly had believed that these patterns of construction could be ordered according to modern state boundaries. For another, they shared a Darwinian preconception that the earliest buildings had been one-room cottages and that settlers subsequently erected larger structures. Kelly went so far as to draw six precise steps in the evolution of the plan of colonial houses. In fact, as Cummings has more recently shown, early colonists had introduced a variety of forms, befitting their distinct backgrounds, but their successors gradually reduced the variety to a more select few.[20] As a result, what had been diverse became uniform; the Yankee custom became, ironically, one not of individualism but convention. Moreover, that convention became even more uniform as early antiquaries, who depicted the founding period as a more homogeneous fabric, restored what they assumed to have been the common pattern. The abundance of hall-parlor dwellings leaves the false impression of a homogeneous cultural fabric in earlier times. Students of vernacular architecture are now slowly unravelling those threads and reweaving it to show more varied, complex strands.

While a majority of the extant homes derive from those Yankees of conspicuous wealth or at least some affluence, and thus form the image of colonial New England, what is missing from the landscape are not only the simplest tumble-down shelters of the lowest ranks of society but often the once-prevalent, modest, one-story home of the middling farmer. Appleton pictured the "Scotch" house as one of those modest homes built for simple immigrants, for example, but his successor at SPNEA described it instead as one revealing a "lavish display" of interior woodwork.[21]

Another paradox resulted from the antiindustrialism that moved the likes of Appleton and Nutting. They so regretted the changes wrought by the modern machine that they not only used restoration to remove their corrupting touches from old buildings but celebrated the handwork of craftsmen. It has been subsequently revealed, however, that machine technology entered New England through water-powered sawmills much earlier than they had thought. At the Jackson house, New Hampshire's oldest dwelling, for example, a power-driven saw produced not only its floor boards but plank walls. What antiquaries revered as traditional forms of construction could have instead showed change brought by new technology.[22] Though Appleton lived on a trust established by a manufacturer and remade another industrialist into an icon at the Fowler home, he was surely more than ambivalent about industrialism.

Moreover, Appleton first suggested that such dwellings as the Browne and Boardman houses had been built within the first generation after the Puritans' arrival. Later students reevaluated those construction dates and pushed them back, sometimes as much as a half century. That revisionism is slow to change the legend behind such houses as that of Rebecca Nurse, however. For another, forty years after acquiring the Boardman house SPNEA abandoned the "Scotch" attribution, but more recent tourist guides still attribute it to the Scots.[23]

This remaking of history was buttressed by architectural restoration. Yet by the 1930s SPNEA informed its members that restoration was not the only course to be considered while preserving old buildings. Earlier preservationists had unquestionably accepted the practice, but a generation after its founding SPNEA advised that the first question to be asked was "Shall the house be restored as originally built? Or shall the additions from time to time over a century or more of occupancy be allowed to stand?" Despite SPNEA's acknowledged ambivalence, and with Williamsburg's successful reconstruction much touted, this policy of restoration was the professional rule until a later generation began to adopt the contrary philosophy of Morris. After Appleton's death, SPNEA continued to restore its buildings and perhaps compromise their integrity, as in the case of the Arnold house in 1951 where inaccurate fenestration was introduced. SPNEA felt pressed to reexamine its approach by the 1970s and decided that newly obtained properties would be kept as acquired, with the primary goal being repair, not restoration.[24] Semantic differences between preservation, restoration, and reconstruction, as well as the falsity of that remaking of history that restoration and reconstruction entailed, could no longer be glossed over. The historical circle is apparently completing itself, returning preservation to the philosophy, but not the politics, of Morris.[25]

SPNEA has recently tried to make sense of Appleton's legacy. It still mostly holds colonial- or Federal-era dwellings, but has acquired everything from the Bowen house (1846), a Gothic Revival cottage, to Henry Davis Sleeper's eclectic "Beauport" (1907), to the Gropius house (1938). The acquisition of that Bauhaus dwelling of Walter Gropius, complete with its art and furnishings, was a stunning accomplishment for an antiquarian society. Its modernist design rejected the past, but it has since become an antiquity to be prized! "The landmark takes its place as part of the history that it has spurned," wrote Ada Louise Huxtable, "and the movement that rewrote history becomes history. Always, history wins."[26]

Appleton discarded but one property, the Derby house. As a result of his "gospel of further acquisitions," the society's funds became overextended, its staff overcommitted, and its properties underinterpreted. The society jettisoned a few more houses immediately after his death, but by the mid-1970s SPNEA had some sixty properties, with half of them in the Bay State. His successors have been forced to trim and reorder the society's holdings. With crimped finances in 1979 SPNEA decided to sell fourteen of those that lacked an endowment and defied either effective exhibition or lease, including the Fowler, Nurse, and Short houses. With a change in Massachusetts law, they were sold with easements, whereby the society's Stewardship Department protects designated architectural and decorative elements. The case of the Fowler house illustrated the problem. Appleton's acquisition was questioned from the start, and by the 1980s SPNEA concluded that it "cannot be said to have any other value than that of representing a characteristic house of an aspiring mercantile figure of the period." It was "an isolated artifact" in an uninteresting neighborhood and failed to draw public interest.[27] When it was acquired, it served a very practical purpose of refurbishing the image of a proper Yankee. That having been accomplished, a later generation pursued other interests.

Today, the holdings of SPNEA fall roughly into three groups: study houses illustrating mostly seventeenth-century architecture; showhouses representing a particular period; and houses exhibiting decorative arts collections. What was lost in the shuffle was Appleton's arts-and-crafts museum. SPNEA instead has focused on artifacts in context. As a collector, Appleton literally wanted more, but his successors have focused on sites that are rich in artifacts and lend themselves more to interpreting New England's past. According to Nylander, SPNEA is "a museum of cultural history." It has trimmed its holdings to forty-four, half of which are open to the public as historic house museums, and another eleven as unfurnished study houses. Slightly less than 50,000 visitors see those properties each year.[28]

All in all, those artifacts preserved during the progressive era made sense most particularly in the context of traditionalism's bid to Yankees who had drifted from the fold. Preservationists recast and restored these buildings as historical environments through which those Yankees could be taught notions of community and leadership, as well as the simpler values of rural living. SPNEA partly directed its appeal to a Yankee upper class that was assimilating newer elements. Although this elite largely identified with those who held wealth and power, it was anything but united in behalf of historic preservation. As was the case for many years before and after, the region's elite often saw old buildings and neighborhoods not simply as castaways from the past but as breeding grounds for alien peoples and cultures.

Appleton and SPNEA significantly pushed architects and historians to scrutinize more ordinary buildings. Entranced by the aura of the seventeenth century, Appleton, much like the medieval craftsmen, was so troubled by the shock of the new order that he tried to use those houses to control the chaos beyond the threshold. Fearing social discontinuity and the loss of tradition, he admitted shortly before World War Two that "the very purpose of our Society's existence is to restrain the ceaseless law of change with reference to certain antiquities of the past considered worthy of as prolonged a life as it is humanly possible to give them."[29]

During the progressive era, preservationists encrusted their hopes and beliefs in these material forms. True to Ruskin, aesthetics became a moralistic crusade. They spoke to receptive Yankees who could influence the image of the past and vision of the future purveyed in schools, newspapers, and other fountains of culture. Preservationists such as Appleton and Chandler were every bit the progressive reformer as were Emmerton and Woods. Not only did their image of New England become dominant, their movement, together with its strengths and weaknesses, caught on. To be sure, later preservationists would develop newer interests in diversity and community and examine those preserved sites with a perspective different from Appleton's intent. The interpretation of symbols and documents is obviously never a static process. But what is significant is that the old-time New England so favored by the likes of Appleton and Isham with its premodern air of timber-framed dwellings has become the central image of a region with so many immigrants, cities, and skyscrapers.

Appendix A

Buildings Acquired by SPNEA 1910–1930

Swett-Ilsley house (c. 1670), Newbury, Mass. (gift, 1911)

Samuel Fowler house (1809), Danversport, Mass. (gift, 1912; deaccessioned in 1980)

Cooper-Frost-Austin house (c. 1689), Cambridge, Mass. (gift, 1912)

"Scotch"-Bennett-Boardman house (c. 1687), Saugus, Mass. (purchase, 1913–14)

Laws house (c. 1800), Sharon, N.H. (gift, 1915; deaccessioned in 1948)

Harrison Gray Otis house (1796), Boston (gift, 1916)

Eleazer Arnold house (c. 1687), Lincoln, R.I. (gift, 1918)

Quincy Memorial house (1904), Litchfield, Conn. (bequest, 1922; deaccessioned in 1951)

Conant house (c. 1738), Townsend Harbor, Mass. (bequest, 1922; deaccessioned in 1976)

Abraham Browne house (c. 1694–1701), Watertown, Mass. (gift, 1923)

Jackson house (c. 1664), Portsmouth, N.H. (gift, 1924)

Richard Derby's barn, Watertown, Mass. (purchase, 1924–25; demolished in 1988)

Chaplin-Clarke-Williams house (c. 1671), Rowley, Mass. (gift, 1925; deaccessioned in 1975)

Richard Derby house (1762), Salem, Mass. (purchase, 1927; deaccessioned in 1936)

Crocker Tavern (1754), Barnstable, Mass. (bequest, 1927; deaccessioned in 1974)

Short house (1733), Newbury, Mass. (gift, 1927; deaccessioned in 1980)

Rebecca Nurse house (c. 1678), Danvers, Mass. (gift, 1927; deaccessioned in 1981)

"Drummer" Stetson house (c. 1700), Hanover, Mass. (gift, 1928; deaccessioned in 1978)

Tristam Coffin house (c. 1654), Newbury, Mass. (gift, 1929)

Colonel John Thatcher house (1680), Yarmouthport, Mass. (gift, 1929)

Emerson-Howard house (c. 1680), Ipswich, Mass. (gift, 1929; deaccessioned in 1981)

Peter Tufts house (c. 1675), Medford, Mass. (gift, 1930; deaccessioned
     in 1982)
Croade house (18th c.), Lincoln, R.I. (gift, 1930)
Spaulding Grist Mill (1840), Townsend Harbor, Mass. (gift, 1930; deac-
     cessioned in 1981)

Sources: "Report of the Corresponding Secretary," *Old-Time New England* 32 (April
1942): 107–11; Carol S. Ritt (comp.), Property List, 24 March 1992, Stewardship Dept.,
SPNEA.

Appendix B

Amendment to the Massachusetts Constitution

As introduced in 1917, the amendment read:

> Full power and authority is hereby granted to the General Court to authorize the Commonwealth or any city or town to make such complete or partial taking of, or to impose such restrictions on, any property of historical or antiquarian interest, belonging to any individual, corporation, or association, as will maintain it in its condition, appearance or location, or restore it to, approximately or wholly, its ancient condition, appearance or location: *provided, however*, that whenever any property is completely or partially taken, or is restricted, hereunder, the owner shall receive reasonable compensation therefor.

As passed by the convention and ratified by the populace in 1918, the amendment read:

> The preservation and maintenance of ancient landmarks and other property of historical or antiquarian interest is a public use, and the Commonwealth and the cities and towns therein may, upon payment of just compensation, take such property or any interest therein under such regulations as the General Court may prescribe.

Source: Debates in the Massachusetts Constitutional Convention, 1917–1918, Vol. III (Boston: Wright & Potter, 1920), 741; Commonwealth of Massachusetts, *Amendments Passed by the Constitutional Convention* (Boston: Wright & Potter, 1918), 10.

Appendix C

Votes Passed by the Board of Trustees of the Society for the Preservation of New England Antiquities on Wednesday, 14 October 1914

Whereas, the present unfortunate state of war in Europe is causing such widespread destruction of buildings of the greatest artistic, architectural and historic importance, which, with their contents, are not only irreplaceable but represent also our most precious heritage from the past, and

Whereas, it is the duty and privilege of each generation to safeguard the world's artistic heritage and to hand it on uninjured to succeeding generations in order that their inheritance be not impaired, be it

Voted, that the Board of Trustees of this Society for the Preservation of New England Antiquities hereby respectfully petitions the President of the United States to use his influence with each warring nation to the end that famous buildings and all other objects of artistic, architectural and historic importance be in so far as may be kept apart from the sphere of active hostilities, and where this is impossible that they be in no way used for purposes of attack or defense, or for military observation, since such use must invariably tend to attract the fire of the opposing forces, and be it further

Voted, that the President be respectfully petitioned to urge the combatants to send to America for temporary safe keeping, and always subject to such final disposition as the treaties of peace shall require, such moveable art objects of great value to all humanity as may best warrant such precaution either by reason of their own merit or because of their present exposure to damage, as, for instance, from aerial bombs, and be it further

Voted, that copies of these votes be sent other patriotic, historical and learned societies, with the request that they strengthen the position here taken by passing votes similar to these.

Source: Circular Letter, 14 October 1914, SPNEA.

NOTES

Abbreviations

Archival materials are used by permission of the respective institution.

AAS   American Antiquarian Society, Worcester, Massachusetts

AQ   *American Quarterly*

APVA   Association for the Preservation of Virginia Antiquities, Richmond, Virginia

Bull.   *Bulletin of the Society for the Preservation of New England Antiquities*

JAC   *Journal of American Culture*

JAH   *Journal of American History*

JASAH *Journal of the American Society of Architectural Historians*

JHG   *Journal of Historical Geography*

MHS   Massachusetts Historical Society, Boston

MHSP   *Massachusetts Historical Society Proceedings*

NEQ   *New England Quarterly*

OTNE   *Old-Time New England*

PL   Pulley Library, Harvard University Archives

SPNEA   Society for the Preservation of New England Antiquities, Boston

WP   *Winterthur Portfolio*

Prologue

1. DeMarco, *Ethnics and Enclaves*, xiv, 2; Drake, *Our Colonial Homes*, 19.

2. Appleton quoted in "Paul Revere Memorial," uniden. newspaper, n.d., Revere Scrapbook, SPNEA.

3. "Paul Revere's House Saved," uniden. newspaper, n.d. [1905], Revere Scrapbook; Chandler, "Notes on Revere House," 15.

4. "Holland Article on Preservation Causes Comment," uniden. newspaper, n.d. [1933], Organizations file, APVA; Hosmer, *Presence*, 258.

5. W. Brown Morton III, "What Do We Preserve and Why?" in *American Mosaic*, ed. Stipe and Lee, 153; Murtagh, *Keeping Time*, 34, 80–82; Gillette, "Appleton's Legacy," 34.

6. Kay and Chase-Harrell, *Preserving New England*, 46–47.

7. See, for example, Eric Gable and Richard Handler, "The Authority of Documents at Some American History Museums," *JAH* 81 (June 1994): 119–36,

and Cary Carson, "Lost in the Fun House: A Commentary on Anthropologists' First Contact with History Museums," ibid., 137–50.

8. Morton, "What Do We Preserve," 153.

9. Michel Foucault, *Power/Knowledge*, ed. Colin Gordon (New York: Pantheon Books, 1980), 114; Mumford, *Culture of Cities*, 454.

10. Hofstadter, *Age of Reform*, 138–39; Mann, *Yankee Reformers*, 237.

11. Higham, *Strangers*; Baltzell, *Protestant Establishment*; Lears, *No Place of Grace*; Boris, *Art and Labor*; Bodnar, *Remaking America*; Glassberg, *American Historical Pageantry*; Lowenthal, *Past Is a Foreign Country*; Kammen, *Mystic Chords*; Leon and Rosenzweig, *History Museums*; T. H. Breen, *Imagining the Past: East Hampton Histories* (Reading, Mass.: Addison-Wesley, 1989).

12. Abrams, *Conservatism*; Jack Tager, "Reaction and Reform in Boston: The Gilded Age and the Progressive Era," in *Massachusetts*, ed. Tager and Ifkovic, 232–46; Sproat, *Best Men*; Rodgers, "Progressivism," 113–32.

13. McCormick, "Public Life," 106–14; Wiebe, *Search for Order*; Crunden, *Ministers of Reform*.

14. See, for example, Giffen and Murphy, *"A Noble and Dignified Stream"*; Axelrod, *Colonial Revival*.

15. Robert Blair St. George, " 'Set Thine House in Order': The Domestication of the Yeomanry in Seventeenth-Century New England," in *New England Begins*, II: 186; Rodgers, *Work Ethic*; Bender, *Toward an Urban Vision*.

16. Jaher, "Businessman," 17–39; Aldrich, *Old Money*; Baltzell, *Puritan Boston*; Thorstein Veblen, *The Theory of the Leisure Class* (1899; rept.: New York: Modern Library, 1934).

17. Buell, *New England*, particularly Chap. 13, "The Village as Icon"; Bowden, "Invention of American Tradition," 3–26, "Invented Tradition and Academic Convention in Geographical Thought about New England," *GeoJournal* 26 (1992): 187–94, and "Culture and Place," 68–146.

18. Lucy Stone, "The Old South Saved by Women," *The Woman's Journal* 6 (1875): 236; Holleran, " 'Changeful Times,' " 141–61.

19. Morison, *One Boy's Boston*, 63; Baltzell, *Puritan Boston*, 162, 163. By 1870 the term Brahmin "meant the rich and well-born as well as the cultivated; was used interchangeably with 'upper class'; and was a sign, accordingly, of distinctiveness as well as attainment, the achievement of a degree of security, cultivation, and arrogance that struck observers as noteworthy, if not unique" (Story, *Forging of an Aristocracy*, xiii).

20. Gabriel Kolko, "Brahmins and Business, 1870–1914: A Hypothesis on the Social Basis of Success in American History," in *The Critical Spirit: Essays in Honor of Herbert Marcuse*, ed. Kurt H. Wolff and Barrington Moore, Jr. (Boston: Beacon Press, 1967), 352; Farrell, *Elite Families*, 153–62; Story, *Forging of an Aristocracy*, 173; Hall, *Nonprofit Sector*, 170–87.

21. Morison, *Intellectual Life*, 6; Baltzell, *Puritan Boston*.

22. Lodge quoted in Rhoads, "Colonial Revival and American Nationalism," 252; Chandler, *Colonial House*, 16; Emile Durkheim, *The Elementary Forms of Religious Life* (London, 1915), 219, 230–31; Quantrill, *Environmental Memory*, 3–19.

23. Story, *Forging of an Aristocracy*, 178–79; Paul DiMaggio, "Cultural Entrepreneurship in Nineteenth-Century Boston: The Creation of an Organizational Base for High Culture in America," *Media, Culture and Society* 4 (1982): 33–50.

24. Geertz, "Thick Description: Toward an Interpretive Theory of Culture," in *Interpretation of Cultures*, 17; Jan Cohn, *The Palace or the Poorhouse: The American House as a Cultural Symbol* (East Lansing: Michigan State Univ. Press, 1979), 175–244.

25. Horne, *Great Museum*, 56–65; Lowenthal, *Past Is a Foreign Country*; Bowden, "Invention of American Tradition," 3–26; West, "Historic House Museum Movement."

26. George Orwell, *Nineteen Eighty-Four* (New York: Penguin Books, 1954), 31.

27. Trachtenberg, *Incorporation of America*; Kloppenberg, *Uncertain Victory*.

28. Lindgren, "From Personalism to Professionalism"; Karen A. Franck, "A Feminist Approach to Architecture: Acknowledging Women's Ways of Knowing," in *Architecture*, ed. Berkeley, 201–16.

29. See, Robert Paynter, "Afro-Americans in the Massachusetts Historical Landscape," in *Politics of the Past*, ed. Gathercole and Lowenthal, 49–62; Michael L. Blakey, "American Nationality and Ethnicity in the Depicted Past," ibid., 38–48.

1. The Makings of a Preservationist

1. Pamela Fox, "Nathan Appleton's Beacon Street Houses," *OTNE* 70 (1980): 111–24.

2. Bruce Laurie, *Artisans into Workers: Labor in Ninetenth-Century America* (New York: Farrar, Straus and Giroux, 1989); Jaher, *Urban Establishment*, Chap. 2.

3. Carl Siracusa, *A Mechanical People: Perceptions of the Industrial Order in Massachusetts, 1815–1850* (Middletown, Conn.: Wesleyan Univ. Press, 1979), 116–17; Jaher, "Businessman," 18–20; William H. and Jane H. Pease, *The Web of Progress: Private Values and Public Styles in Boston and Charleston, 1828–1843* (New York: Oxford Univ. Press, 1985), 219; Paul Goodman, "Ethics and Enterprise: The Values of a Boston Elite, 1800–1860," *AQ* 18 (Fall 1966): 438–39.

4. Jaher, "Businessman," 34; Tharp, *Appletons*, 304.

5. Appleton quoted in Jaher, "Businessman," 23–24.

6. Tharp, *Appletons*, 315; Charles C. Smith, *Memoir of William Sumner Appleton, A.M.* (Cambridge: John Wilson and Son, 1903), 10.

7. A. McVoy McIntyre, *Beacon Hill: A Walking Tour* (Boston: Little, Brown, 1975), 18–19.

8. James, *American Scene*, 243; Appleton to Myron A. Munson, 27 March 1914, Appleton Scrapbook, SPNEA.

9. Firey, *Land Use*, table IV; Warner, *Streetcar Suburbs*, 144; Mona Domosh, "Controlling Urban Form: The Development of Boston's Back Bay," *JHG* 18 (1992): 288–306; Warner, *Living and the Dead*, 49; Abram English Brown, "Beacon Hill," *New England Magazine*, n.s. 28 (August 1903): 631–50.

10. Baltzell, *Protestant Establishment*, 127–29; Jaher, *Urban Establishment*, 103; Bertram K. Little, "William Sumner Appleton," *MHSP* 69 (1947–50): 422.

11. Story, *Forging of an Aristocracy*, 163–64; Seymour Martin Lipset, "The Golden Age of Eliot," in *Education and Politics at Harvard*, ed. Lipset and David

Riesman (New York: McGraw-Hill, 1975), 91–131; Blodgett, *Gentle Reformers*, 20–21; Record of William S. Appleton, Jr., A.B., 1896, Harvard Univ. Archives.

12. Wendell to Robert Thomson, 17 December 1893, in *Barrett Wendell*, ed. Howe, 108–9; Eliot quoted in Jay B. Hubbell, *The South in American Literature, 1607–1900* (Durham: Duke Univ. Press, 1954), 548.

13. Norton, "Lack of Old Homes," 640; Wendell to Sir Robert White-Thomson, 16 October 1910, in *Barrett Wendell*, ed. Howe, 190-91, 207; Candee, *Building Portsmouth*, 76–77.

14. Santayana quoted in Tomsich, *Genteel Endeavor*, 1–2.

15. Samuel Eliot Morison, "History," in *Development of Harvard*, ed. Morison, 169; Buell, *New England*; Wood, " 'Build Your Own World,' " 37.

16. Carol F. Baird, "Albert Bushnell Hart: The Rise of the Professional Historian," in *Social Sciences at Harvard 1860–1920: From Inculcation to the Open Mind*, ed. Paul H. Buck (Cambridge: Harvard Univ. Press, 1965), 129–174.

17. Appleton to Nathaniel Jackson, 8 July 1920, Jackson house file, SPNEA; Harry Brown, Notes for Fine Arts, I: 19, PL; Norton, "Address," 1881, 31, 37; Writers' Project, *Massachusetts*, 622.

18. Brown, Notes, I: 19, 63; III: 333, PL.

19. George H. Chase, "The Fine Arts 1874–1919," in *Development of Harvard*, ed. Morison, 130–33; Brown, Notes, III: 439–40, PL; Lears, *No Place of Grace*, 66; Vanderbilt, *Norton*, 205–8.

20. Norton, "American Archaeology," 8; Norton, "Waste," 303.

21. Norton, "Lack of Old Homes," 636; Morton Keller, "The Personality of Cities: Boston, New York, Philadelphia," *MHSP* 97 (1985): 11; Thernstrom, *Other Bostonians*, 221, 227.

22. Norton, "Lack of Old Homes," 638, 640; Cummings, *Framed Houses*, 204; Allen, *In English Ways*.

23. Edward Bellamy, *Looking Backward, 2000–1887* (New York: New American Library, 1960), 34.

24. Ibid., 45, 51, 67, 89, 206, 213.

25. Thompson, *William Morris*; Stansky, *Redesigning the World*.

26. Norton quoted in Vanderbilt, *Norton*, 203; Rydell, *All the World's a Fair*, 38–71; R. Reid Badger, *The Great American Fair: The World's Columbian Exposition and American Culture* (Chicago: Nelson Hall, 1979), 119–23.

27. Norton, "It's Dogged," 226; Lears, *No Place of Grace*, 62, 65, 76; Boris, *Art and Labor*, 44–45; David Lowenthal, "Age and Artifact: Dilemmas of Appreciation," in *Interpretation*, ed. Meinig, 103–28.

28. Nathan Shiverick, "The Social Reorganization of Boston," in *A Social History of the Greater Boston Clubs*, ed. Alexander Williams (Barre, Mass., 1970); Baltzell, *Protestant Establishment*, 135–36.

29. George Dudley Seymour to Appleton, 7 March 1914, Seymour file, SPNEA; Appleton, Autobiographical sketch, ms., draft copy, n.d., Appleton file; author's conversation with Abbott Cummings, 27 January 1992; Farrell, *Elite Families*, 35–36.

30. Lears, *No Place of Grace*, 243–47; Green, *Fit for America*, 137–66.

31. Woodward D. Openo, "The Summer Colony at Little Harbor in Portsmouth, New Hampshire, and Its Relation to the Colonial Revival Movement" (Ph.D. thesis, Univ. of Michigan, 1990), 25.

32. Appleton, Diary, 13 February, 2 March, 25 September, 4 October 1906, SPNEA; Katherine H. Rich, "Beacon," *OTNE* 66 (Winter-Spring 1976): 42–60.

33. Ross, *Theory of Pure Design*, 1; Ross, *On Drawing*, 4, 204.

34. Edward W. Forbes, "Denman Waldo Ross," *Harvard Alumni Bulletin* (n.d.): 55–57, Ross file, PL; "Denman Waldo Ross," *Harvard University Gazette*, 15 February 1936; Appleton, Diary, 5 November 1906, 16, 18, 24 January, 8 March, 3, 16, 17, 18 April 1907.

2.   Progressivism and the Remaking of Memory

1. Appleton, "New England's Antiquarian Heritage," ms. of an article that appeared in the *Boston Transcript*, 15 April 1939, SPNEA.

2. Bolton, "Small Town," 94–96; Crunden, *Ministers of Reform*, x.

3. McCormick, "Public Life," 107; Rodgers, "Progressivism," 113–32.

4. Crunden, *Ministers of Reform*.

5. Abrams, *Conservatism*; Lears, *No Place of Grace*; Constance K. Burns, "The Irony of Progressive Reform, 1898–1910," in *Boston 1700–1980*, ed. Formisano and Burns, 133–164.

6. Hofstadter, *Age of Reform*, 163–64; Abrams, *Conservatism*, 143; Blodgett, *Gentle Reformers*, 31–32; Aldrich, "Unguarded Gates," in Albert J. Beveridge, *Address Delivered by Ex-Senator Albert J. Beveridge of Indiana on Washington's Birthday, February 22, 1921* (New York: Sons of the Revolution, 1921), 29–30; Philip Edward Sherman, "Immigration from Abroad into Massachusetts," *New England Magazine*, n.s. 29 (February 1904): 671–81.

7. Norton, "Intellectual Life," 312; Kennedy, *Planning the City*, 137; Boyer, *Urban Masses*.

8. Rosenzweig, *Eight Hours*; Green and Donahue, *Boston's Workers*.

9. Bolton, Note-Book, 29 June 1914, Bolton Papers, MHS; Len De Caux, *The Living Spirit of the Wobblies* (New York: International Publishers, 1978), 71–76.

10. Nutting, *Biography*, 261; Nutting, *Massachusetts Beautiful*, 278.

11. Cram quoted in Bolton, Note-Book, 12 March 1914, Bolton Papers; Bolton, Note-Book, 21 May 1914, 11 August 1919, ibid.; Boris, *Art and Labor*, 151; Green and Donahue, *Boston's Workers*, 69; Chandler, *Colonial House*, 18.

12. Russell Conway quoted in Kay, *Lost Boston*, 217; Rosen, *Limits of Power*, 212–26.

13. Jack Tager, "Massachusetts and the Age of Economic Revolution," in *Massachusetts*, ed. Tager and Ifkovic, 9. The census of 1915 set Boston's population at 745,439, of which 268,154 were foreign born, and 257,403 were natives whose father was foreign born (Boston Committee, *A Little Book*, 56).

14. Wolfe, *Lodging House*, 17–18; Warner, *Streetcar Suburbs*; Lankevich, *Boston*, 54, 57.

15. Lankevich, *Boston*, 52; Jackson, *Crabgrass Frontier*, 51; Domosh, "Controlling Urban Form," 288–306.

16. Appleton to Clarence Gilbert Hoag, 16 February 1915, Appleton Scrapbook; French, *New England*, 224; Wolfe, *Lodging House*, 23, 67.

17. French, *New England*, 223; Flower, *Civilization's Inferno*, 13–14; Horatio Brooks Hersey, "The Old West End," *OTNE* 20 (1929–30): 162–77; Trout, *Boston*, 14–15; Donald K. Gorrell, *The Age of Social Responsibility: The Social Gospel in the Progressive Era, 1900–1920* (Macon, Geo.: Mercer Univ. Press, 1988).

18. Wolfe, *Lodging House*, 25; Peel, "On the Margins," 813–34; Woods, *Americans in Process*, maps IV and VI.

19. James, *American Scene*, 231–32; Abrams, *Conservatism*, 289.

20. Drake, *Our Colonial Homes*, 17, and *Old Landmarks*, v.

21. James, *American Scene*, 228–29.

22. Ibid., 233–41; Sullivan, *Boston*, 31–32; Firey, *Land Use*, 161–65; Holleran, " 'Changeful Times,' " 191–204. Today, little remains of that Park Street scene other than the unaltered church (Lyndon, *City Observed*, 22–24).

23. Woods, *Americans in Process*, v; Fitzgerald quoted in Cutler, *"Honey Fitz,"* 32, 213; French, *New England*, 221, 226.

24. Aldrich quoted in Solomon, *Ancestors and Immigrants*, 88; Fitzgerald quoted in Cutler, *"Honey Fitz,"* 83; Geoffrey Blodgett, "Yankee Leadership in a Divided City, 1860–1910," in *Boston 1700–1980*, ed. Formisano and Burns, 87–110.

25. Quoted in Abrams, *Conservatism*, 146, 147; Cutler, *"Honey Fitz,"* 128–31; Kennedy, *Planning the City*, 119–27; Paul Kleppner, "From Party to Factions: The Dissolution of Boston's Majority Party, 1876–1908," and Burns, "The Irony of Progressive Reform, 1898–1910," in *Boston 1700–1980*, ed. Formisano and Burns, 126–27, 150–51.

26. Fitzgerald quoted in Cutler, *"Honey Fitz,"* 32, 213; Abrams, *Conservatism*, 147; Frank Chouteau Brown, "Boston's Growing Pains," *Our Boston* 1 (November 1926): 12; Warner, *Living and the Dead*, 48–49. Ironically, the Yankee-led Metropolitan Improvement Commission endorsed the idea of building a new city hall on the Common (Kennedy, *Planning the City*, 143).

27. Cutler, *"Honey Fitz,"* 65, 100, 154.

28. Curley quoted in Cutler, *"Honey Fitz,"* 11, 30–33; Kennedy, *Planning the City*, 129–55; Charles H. Trout, "Curley of Boston: The Search for Irish Legitimacy," in *Boston 1700–1980*, ed. Formisano and Burns, 165–195.

29. Curley, *I'd Do It Again*, 3, 11, 30–32; Bolton, Note-Book, 23 February 1914, Bolton Papers; Robert Mullen, "Poor Old Boston," *Forum* 103 (May 1940): 233; Beatty, *Rascal King*, 166.

30. Robert A. Woods, "Traffic in Citizenship"; William I. Cole and Rufus E. Miles, "Community of Interest"; and Woods, "Assimilation: A Two-Edged Sword," in *Americans in Process*, 189, 332, 358, 360, 363–64; Bushee, *Ethnic Factors*, 150; Kleppner, "From Party to Factions," 122.

31. Woods, "Assimilation," in *Americans in Process*, 368; Appleton to William W. Rucker, 16 February 1915, Appleton Scrapbook; Appleton to Harrison Gray Otis, 14 April 1924, Otis house files, SPNEA. Appleton supported the Hare System of the Single Transferrable Vote, proposed by the American Proportional Representation League, in which ward-based aldermen would have been replaced by a Board of Directors that was elected at large and would have selected the mayor. If enacted, the plan would have redistributed votes to Yankee candidates and blocked the winner-take-all system that enabled ethnics to control Boston's government.

32. Porter, *Rambles*, vii–viii.

33. Flower, *Civilization's Inferno*, 67, 215, 235–37; Gorrell, *Age of Social Responsibility*.

34. Woods, "Livelihood," in *Americans in Process*, 146; Sam Bass Warner, Jr., "Preface," in Kennedy and Woods, *Zone of Emergence*; Woods, "Notes on the Italians," 452.

35. Bolton, Note-Book, 27 April 1913, Bolton Papers; Caroline S. Atherton and Elizabeth Y. Rutyan, "The Child of the Stranger," in *Americans in Process*, ed. Woods, 316; Rhoads, "Colonial Revival and Americanization," 341–61.

36. Bushce, *Ethnic Factors*, 158.

37. Abbott Lowell Cummings, "Massachusetts and Its First Period Houses: A Statistical Survey," in *Architecture*, 113-121; Drake, *Our Colonial Homes*, 19. Edward Thompson Taylor of the Seamen's Bethel Church inspired Melville's depiction of Father Mapple in *Moby Dick*. Emerson ranked him with Demosthenes and Shakespeare.

38. Drake, *Our Colonial Homes*, 18; "Paul Revere Memorial," uniden. newspaper, n.d., Revere Scrapbook. The officers of PRMA came from the ranks of *The Social Register* and included Mayor Henry Higginson as treasurer. Its permanent executive committee held delegates from virtually every patriotic society, the principal of the immigrant-attended Paul Revere School, and highly placed politicians. A tally of the largest contributors ($100 or more) revealed that the overwhelming majority were listed in *The Social Register*.

39. W. Sumner Appleton to the editor, "Ask Aid to Patriotism," *Boston Post*, 16 June 1905; Appleton, Diary, 6 June 1906; Appleton quoted in "Paul Revere Memorial," uniden. newspaper, n.d., Revere Scrapbook; "By-Laws of the Paul Revere Memorial Association," Article II, Revere house file.

40. Guild, Circular Letter, 29 November 1907, Revere Scrapbook; "The 225-Year-Old Landmark that Boston Soon May Know No More," *Boston Globe*, 11 April 1905.

41. Woods, "Notes on the Italians," 452; Guild, Circular Letter, 29 November 1907, Revere Scrapbook. Violent crime, in fact, was declining sharply (Tager, "Age of Economic Revolution," in *Massachusetts*, ed. Tager and Ifkovic, 22).

42. "Paul Revere the Business Man," *Boston Herald*, 15 April 1906; Wiebe, *Businessmen and Reform*.

43. Quoted in Cutler, *"Honey Fitz,"* 27.

44. Mrs. Nathaniel Thayer, "The Immigrants," in *Nineteenth Century Massachusetts*, Vol. IV in *Commonwealth History of Massachusetts*, ed. Albert B. Hart (1930; rept.: New York: Russell & Russell, 1966), 142–200; Appleton to Sir, 25 February 1907, Revere Scrapbook; PRMA, *Handbook of the Paul Revere Memorial Association* (Boston: PRMA, 1950).

45. "Paul Revere's House Saved," uniden. newspaper, n.d. [1905], Revere Scrapbook; Chandler, "Notes on the Revere House," 15; Campbell, *Cityscapes*, 4–5.

46. Shackleton, *Boston*, 171; Appleton, "Destruction and Preservation," 144; Sullivan, *Boston*, 36; Mass. Comm., *Pathways*, 26.

47. Bolton, Note-Book, 6 February 1914, Bolton Papers; various cartoon clippings, Appleton Scrapbook #24, SPNEA; Solomon, *Ancestors and Immigrants*, 201; Higham, *Strangers*, 155–57; Green, "Popular Science," 10.

48. Mary Antin, *The Promised Land* (Boston: Houghton Mifflin, 1912), 204–5, 224–25; Bolton, Note-Book, 1 April 1914, 27 April 1913, Bolton Papers; Appleton to Clarence Gilbert Hoag, 16 February 1915, Appleton Scrapbook.

49. Appleton, "Two Interesting Restorations of Old New England Churches," *Bull.* 3 (February 1913): 2; "R. Clipston Sturgis," in *Boston Society of Architects: The First Hundred Years, 1867–1967*, ed. Marvin E. Goody and Robert P. Walsh (Boston: Boston Society of Architects, 1967), 79–80; Openo, "Summer Colony at Little Harbor," 8.

50. Trout, *Boston*, 10; Bolton, Note-Book, 21 May 1914, Bolton Papers; Shackleton, *Boston*, 164–65.

51. Sartorio, *Life of Italians*, 49, 56–57; Bodnar, *Remaking America*, 41–77; see Woods, *Americans in Process*, Map III and Map IV.

52. Dennis P. Ryan, "The Crispus Attucks Monument Controversy of 1887," *Negro History Bulletin* 40 (January–February 1977): 656–57. Governor Oliver Ames, who spoke at the monument's dedication before a crowd of 25,000, conceded that "every man who opposed the monument would have been opposed to the Revolution" (ibid., 657).

53. Sons of the Revolution, untitled pamphlet, 12 December 1905, SPNEA; Appleton to Frank Carruthers, 12 December 1905, Appleton Scrapbook.

54. Appleton, Diary, 18 April 1906, SPNEA; Boston Transit Commission to the Various Patriotic Societies, 1 May 1906, Appleton Scrapbook; Appleton to George G. Crocker, 1 May 1906, ibid.; Crocker, "The Passenger Traffic of Boston and the Subway," *New England Magazine*, n.s. 19 (January 1899): 523–41; "Rights in Old State House: W. S. Appleton Takes Issue," *Boston Transcript*, 5 May 1906.

55. Appleton, Diary, 29 May, 15 June 1906; Fitzgerald to Appleton, 16 June 1906, Guild to Appleton, 29 June 1906, Appleton Scrapbook; "Old State House Saved," *Boston Transcript*, 16 June 1906; Cheape, *Moving the Masses*, 103–53.

56. Mass. General Court, *Report of Hearings* (1907), 4–5, 7–9.

57. Mrs. Charles H. Masury in ibid., 15–16.

58. Lyndon, *City Observed*, 4-6; Sullivan, *Boston*, 33–34.

59. Arthur A. Shurtleff, "The Practice of Replanning," *Charities and the Commons* 19 (1 February 1908): 1529–32; *Report Made to the Boston Society of Architects by Its Committee on Municipal Improvements* (Boston, 1907); Krieger and Green, *Past Futures*.

60. Appleton, Diary, 16, 30 January 1906; Whitehill, *Boston*, 188; Lewis Mumford, "The Significance of Back Bay Boston," in *Back Bay Boston*, ed. Boston Museum of Fine Arts, 18–35; Boyer, *Moral Order*.

61. Appleton, Diary, 29 October 1908; Hosmer, *Preservation*, 152; Lyndon, *City Observed*, 79, 182.

62. "Boston-1915 Leaders Tell What the Movement Is," *Boston Herald*, n.d. [1910], in Boston-1915 Scrapbook, SPNEA; Kennedy, *Planning the City*, 123–27; James Weinstein, *The Corporate Ideal in the Liberal State, 1900–1918* (Boston: Beacon Press, 1968). "Boston-1915" invited most of the city's unions to join, setting the tack for the corporatist movement of the 1930s. Not surprisingly, the Executive Committee did not invite the city's immigrant associations. It wanted only those "organizations which properly belong to an intelligent co-operative movement" (*What Boston-1915 Is* [Boston, 1910]).

63. "Boston-1915 Leaders Tell What the Movement Is," *Boston Herald*, in Boston-1915 Scrapbook; *What Boston-1915 Is* (Boston, 1910); Kellogg, "Boston's Level Best," 390.

64. Appleton, Diary, 11, 12 October 1909; *"1915" Boston Exposition: Official Catalog* Part I (Boston: "1915" Boston Exposition, 1909), 33; Marguerite S. Dickson, "Parks and Parkways in Boston," *Our Boston* 1 (July 1926): 11.

65. Kellogg, "Boston's Level Best," 383; Gilman to Appleton, 19, 21 February 1910, Boston-1915 Scrapbook; Appleton to Robert Bottomley, 2 May 1910, ibid.; Civic Conference agenda, 7 May 1910, ibid.

66. "Billboard Legislation," *New Boston* 1 (June 1910): 80–81; Edward T.

Hartman, "Boston's Housing Laws," *New Boston* 1 (February 1911): 445; "Civic Conference," *What Boston-1915 Is* (Boston, 1910), 19; Rosenzweig, *Eight Hours*, Chap. 3.

67. Appleton's handwritten comments on Charles F. Lovejoy to Appleton, 10 November 1910, Boston-1915 Scrapbook; James P. Munroe to Appleton, 21 November 1910, ibid.

68. Rev. Francis E. Clark in "A Few Comments," *What Boston-1915 Is* (Boston, 1910), 38; "Boston's Housing Problem," *New Boston* 1 (May 1910): 10, 12.

69. Kennedy, *Planning the City*, 125; Stanley K. Schultz, *Constructing Urban Culture: American Cities and City Planning, 1800–1920* (Philadelphia: Temple Univ. Press, 1989).

70. Appleton, Diary, 22 October 1906, 10 January 1907, 6 January 1909, 8 March 1910.

71. Appleton, Diary, 16, 18, 24, 26 March 1909.

72. James, *American Scene*, 257; Appleton to Secretary, Lexington Historical Society, 6 January 1910, Lexington file, SPNEA; Appleton, Diary, 18, 22 December 1909. The Harrington house must have been relatively insignificant to Fred Smith Piper because he did not include it in his survey of the town ("Architectural Yesterdays in Lexington," *Lexington Historical Society Proceedings* 4 [1905–1910]: 114–26).

73. Appleton, Diary, 22 December 1909; Appleton to Caroline P. Heath, 5 May 1910, DAR file, SPNEA.

74. Appleton, *Bull.* 1 (May 1910), 4; Arthur Benson Tourtellot, *Lexington and Concord: The Beginning of the War of the American Revolution* (New York: W. W. Norton, 1959), 128, 135, 268; Robert A. Gross, *The Minutemen and Their World* (New York: Hill and Wang, 1976); Richard Shenkman, *Legends, Lies, and Cherished Myths of American History* (New York: William Morrow, 1988), 155.

75. Linenthal, *Sacred Ground*, 14–25; "Jonathan Harrington," *National Cyclopaedia of American Biography*, I:367; George B. Forgie, *Patricide in the House Divided: A Psychological Interpretation of Lincoln and His Age* (New York: W. W. Norton, 1979), Chap. 5; Writers' Project, *Massachusetts*, 257.

76. Appleton to Charles Francis Adams, 14 November 1912, Buckman Tavern file, SPNEA; Appleton to A. E. Locke, 10 January 1913, ibid.; Mass. Constitutional Convention, *Debates*, III: 741–44.

77. Appleton to Heath, 5 May 1910, DAR file; Appleton, Diary, 28 December 1909; Appleton, *Bull.* 1 (May 1910): 4.

3. The Founding of SPNEA

1. Appleton, "Destruction and Preservation," 143; Appleton to Henry C. Mercer, 19 June 1922, Mercer file, SPNEA; Drake, *Our Colonial Homes*, 1–2.

2. Appleton, "The Home of John Hancock, Beacon Street, Boston," *Bull.* 1 (May 1910): 1; Carl Greenleafe Beede, "Has a Dozen Houses, Wants More," *Christian Science Monitor*, 27 November 1926; Drake, *Our Colonial Homes*, 5.

3. Drake, *Old Landmarks*, vi.

4. ASHPS, *Seventeenth Annual Report* (Albany: Argus, 1912), 15, 18; Schuyler, *New Urban Landscape*, 143–46; Hosmer, *Presence*, 261–62. By the late

1970s the Trustees of Reservations owned 64 sites in 46 communities, totalling 14,286 acres (Mass. Hist. Comm., *Cultural Resources*, 52).

5. Mrs. J. Taylor Ellyson, "Extracts from the Report of 4 January 1908," *Year Book of the APVA* (Richmond: Wm. Ellis Jones, 1908), 21; Appleton, Diary, 20 January 1910; Appleton to Mrs. C. A. Gosney, 6 July 1939, N.C. Preservation Society file, SPNEA; Appleton to Donald Millar, 21 October 1915, Millar file, SPNEA.

6. Appleton, "Society for the Protection of Ancient Buildings," *Bull.* 5 (December 1914): 18–19; Horace Wells Sellers, "Protection of Historic Buildings," *Journal of the American Institute of Architects* 8 (February 1920): 63.

7. Morris quoted in Nikolaus Pevsner, "Scrape and Anti-Scrape," in *Future of the Past*, ed. Fawcett, 50; Thompson, *William Morris*, Chap. 6; Charles Dellheim, *The Face of the Past: The Preservation of the Medieval Inheritance in Victorian England* (Cambridge and New York: Cambridge Univ. Press, 1982), 85–92; Stansky, *Redesigning the World*.

8. Morris quoted in Nicholas Boulting, "The Law's Delays," in *Future of the Past*, ed. Fawcett, 16; Tschudi-Madsen, *Restoration*; SPAB, "Principles of 1877," broadside rept. 1906, SPAB file, SPNEA.

9. Basil Oliver, "Country Buildings," in *The National Trust: A Record of Fifty Years' Achievement*, ed. James Lees Milne (London: B. T. Batsford, 1945), 86; A. R. Powys to W. S. Appleton, 4 February 1924, cited in "A Method of Cooperation," *OTNE* 15 (October 1924): 91–92; Appleton, "Preserving the Antiquities of New England," typescript, n.d., Appleton file; Boris, *Art and Labor*, 44.

10. Ashbee, *Report*, 5–7; Robert Winter, "American Sheaves from 'C.R.A.' and Janet Ashbee," *Journal of the Society of Architectural Historians* 30 (December 1971): 317–22; Wright, *Moralism*, 127–28; Boris, *Art and Labor*, 15, 16, 33; Murtagh, *Keeping Time*, 34; see also Ashbee, *American Sheaves and English Seed Corn* (London, 1908).

11. Quoted in Hosmer, *Presence*, 257; Kloppenberg, *Uncertain Victory*.

12. Bledstein, *Culture of Professionalism*.

13. Appleton, "Destruction and Preservation," 179.

14. [Appleton], "The Society for the Preservation of New England Antiquities," *Bull.* 1 (May 1910): 4; Appleton, "Destruction and Preservation," 132–33.

15. Appleton to Judge Samuel H. Fisher, 29 January 1926, SPNEA; Steinitz, "Rethinking," 16–26.

16. Charles K. Bolton, "Tribute to William Sumner Appleton," *OTNE* 30 (April 1940): 109; Appleton, Diary, 4 January 1909 (sic—should be 1910), SPNEA.

17. Appleton, Diary, 4 January 1910, 11, 14 February 1910; House No. 206, Senate No. 281, Massachusetts General Court (1910); "For the Care of Antiquities," *Boston Globe*, 21 April 1912.

18. Kennedy, *Planning the City*, 116.

19. "Tribute to William Sumner Appleton," *OTNE* 38 (April 1948): 78; Dorothy Appleton Weld to Bertram K. Little, 2 April (1948?), Appleton file; Appleton to Frances E. D. Porteous, 14 February 1919, SPNEA.

20. Appleton, Diary, 19 April 1910; Annual Meeting Report, 3 March 1913, Advisory Committee file, SPNEA.

21. Record of Charles Knowles Bolton, A.B. 1890, Harvard Univ. Archives; Bolton, Note-Book, 5 April 1890, 17 January 1907, Bolton Papers; John D. Rockefeller to Sarah K. Bolton, 10 October 1905, Bolton Family Papers III-22, AAS.

22. Bolton, "Small Town," 94–96.

23. James, *American Scene*, 232; Bolton, Note-Book, 13 March, 23 May 1911, 12 January 1912, Bolton Papers.

24. Bolton, *Scotch Irish*, 301, 303, 306; Margaret Marsh, "Suburban Men and Masculine Domesticity, 1870–1915," in *Meanings for Manhood*, ed. Carnes and Griffen, 111–27; Green, *Fit for America*.

25. Bolton, *Private Soldier*; Bolton, *Real Founders*, 57; Morison quoted in Kammen, *Selvages & Biases*, 84; James Truslow Adams, "Review of *The Real Founders of New England*," *NEQ* 3 (January 1930): 179–82.

26. Bolton to Appleton, 20 March 1919, Bolton file, SPNEA; Charles Knowles Bolton, *Portraits of the Founders* (Boston, 1919); among other things, Bolton wrote the "Introduction" in W.P.A., Historical Records Survey (Mass.), *American Portraits (1645–1850) Found in the State of Maine* (Boston, 1941) and *American Portraits 1620–1825 Found in Massachusetts* (Boston, 1939). Besides serving as treasurer of NEHGS from 1908–13, Bolton was a trustee of the Museum of Fine Arts from 1916–33. He was also a member of the MHS, AAS, and the Colonial Society of Massachusetts.

27. Bolton, Note-Book, 18 September 1915, Bolton Papers.

28. "William Crowninshield Endicott," *OTNE* 27 (January 1937): 116.

29. Appleton to Bolton, 27 June 1917, Bolton file. The society's charter required that a majority of trustees were citizens of Massachusetts (Section 6, "An Act to Incorporate the Society for the Preservation of New England Antiquities," 1910).

30. In 1916, for example, SPNEA held eight meetings, none of which occurred during the four summer months. Out of thirty trustees, the average attendance was between seven and eight (Lawrence Park, "Annual Report of the Board of Trustees," *Bull.* 7 [May 1916]: 3).

31. Appleton to Frances E. D. Porteous, 4 February 1919, Appleton file; Alexander, "Sixty Years," 19.

32. Appleton to George A. Plimpton, 19 July 1922, Plimpton file, SPNEA; Appleton to Henry Wood Erving, 14 February 1919, Erving file, SPNEA.

33. Henry W. Erving to Appleton, 24 February 1923, Erving file; Aldrich, *Old Money*, 30.

34. Lindgren, *Preserving the Old Dominion*, Chap. 10; Appleton, "Annual Report," *OTNE* 11 (July 1920): 41; Greenleaf, *From These Beginnings*, Chap. 3.

35. Sears, *Gleanings*; Sears, *Fruitlands*, xiii–xvii; Writers' Project, *Massachusetts*, 512–13; Barton, *History's Daughter*, 7, 48.

36. Stillinger, *Antiquers*, 105, 166.

37. Appleton to Seymour, 9 March 1914, Seymour file; Seymour to Appleton, 25 September 1915, ibid.; Donald Lines Jacobus, *A History of the Seymour Family* (New Haven, p.p., 1939), 407–21, 575; Stillinger, *Antiquers*, 88–90; Seymour, "Ithiel Town—Architect," *Art and Progress* (September 1912): 714–16.

38. Seymour quoted in Stillinger, *Antiquers*, 93; Seymour to Appleton, 22 April 1915, Seymour file; Taft quoted in Jacobus, *Seymour Family*, 542.

39. Jacobus, *Seymour Family*, 411–12.

40. Norton, "Lack of Old Homes," 640; Bolton, Note-Book, 16 August 1898, Bolton Papers; Appleton to Donald Millar, 16 April 1918, Millar file; Appleton, "Annual Report," *Bull.* 5 (April 1914): 12.

41. Arthur Little, *Early New England Interiors: Sketches in Salem, Marblehead, Portsmouth and Kittery* (Boston: A. Williams, 1877); Theodate Pope to Appleton, 28 June 1916, Wildman house file, SPNEA.

42. Cram, *My Life*, 30; Cram, "Architecture," in *Fifty Years*, 340; Wilson, "Ralph Adams Cram," 193–214; Beebe, *Boston*, 231, 259; Robert Muccigrosso, *American Gothic: The Mind and Art of Ralph Adams Cram* (Washington, D.C.: Univ. Press of America, 1979).

43. Cram, *Convictions*, 80, 81; Cram, *My Life*, 218, 273; Cram, *Ministry of Art*, 60–61; Nutting, *Biography*, 269; Lears, *No Place of Grace*, 203–8.

44. Appleton to Mrs. C. A. Gosney, 6 July 1939, N.C. Preservation Society file.

45. Seventy-five percent of those Bostonians who contributed $50 in the first year to become Life Members were listed in *The Social Register*. Within one year SPNEA was "well established" with over 300 members ([Appleton], *Bull.* 2 [August 1911]: 17–18).

46. Thompson to Appleton, n.d., Appleton Scrapbook; [Appleton], "The Society for the Preservation of New England Antiquities," *Bull.* 1 (May 1910): 5; Appleton, Diary, 19 October 1910; Baltzell, *Puritan Boston*, 29; Jaher, *Urban Establishment*, 112–14; "A Method of Cooperation," *OTNE* 15 (October 1924): 92.

47. Adams quoted in Allen Gutmann, "Images of Value and the Sense of the Past," *NEQ* 35 (March 1962): 9; Sullivan, *Boston*, 53.

4. Preserving Antiquities as Symbols and Documents

1. Erving to Appleton, 14 February 1921, Erving File.

2. Appleton to Erving, 15 February 1921, Erving File.

3. Appleton, "Annual Report," *Bull.* 9 (November 1918): 24; Appleton, *Bull.* 1 (February 1911): 6, 8.

4. Harold D. Eberlein, *The Architecture of Colonial America* (Boston: Little, Brown, 1915), 39–44; Geertz, *Interpretation of Cultures*; Marc, *Psychology of the House*, 67; Boris, *Art and Labor*, 12.

5. Gowans, *Images*, 116–17; Stilgoe, *Common Landscape*, 321–23; Deetz, *In Small Things*, 38–40. See also Darrett B. Rutman, "Assessing the Little Communities of Early America," *William and Mary Quarterly* 43 (1986): 163–78.

6. Kelly, *Connecticut's Old Houses*, 13; Noble, *Wood, Brick, and Stone*, I: 136–37; Amos Rapoport, *House Form and Culture* (Englewood Cliffs, N.J.: Prentice-Hall, 1969), 6–7.

7. Appleton, "Annual Report," *Bull.* 6 (April 1915): 10; Appleton to Murray Corse, 16 March 1918, Brown house file; Appleton, "Harry Dean's Work," n.d., Dean file, SPNEA.

8. Allen, *In English Ways*, 224–231; Cummings, *Framed Houses*, 203.

9. Henry C. Dean to Appleton, n.d. [1914], Dean file.

10. Isham and Brown, *Early Rhode Island Houses*, 83; Appleton to Harry

Dean, 8 April 1914, Dean file; Cummings, *Framed Houses*, 203; Kelly, *Connecticut's Old Houses*, 40–41; Wood, " 'Build Your Own World,' " 32–50.

11. Isham and Brown, *Early Rhode Island Houses*, 88–89; Follett, "Norman Isham," 144–52.

12. Simon J. Bronner, "Object Lessons: The Work of Ethnological Museums and Collections," in *Consuming Visions*, ed. Bronner, 217–54; Stocking, *Objects and Others*.

13. Appleton, Diary, 20 August 1910.

14. James, *American Scene*, 265–67. At the time the Seven Gables had yet to be restored.

15. *Salem News* quoted in Farnam, "George Dow," 82; Leon Whipple, "Hawthorne Gives Alms," *Survey* 55 (October 1925): 45; Rosenzweig, *Eight Hours*, 150; Hornblower quoted in Hartmann, *Movement to Americanize*, 89; Bellah, *Broken Covenant*, 94; Solomon, *Ancestors and Immigrants*.

16. Dow to Appleton, 5 April 1911, Old Bakery file, SPNEA.

17. Appleton, "The Old Bakery," *Bull.* 2 (August 1911): 13–15.

18. Emmerton, *Chronicles*, 47; Nathaniel Hawthorne, *The House of the Seven Gables, A Romance* (Boston: Ticknor, Reed, & Fields, 1851), 9.

19. Chandler, *Colonial House*, 1, 2, 5–6, 18; Cummings, *Framed Houses*, 204.

20. Emmerton, *Chronicles*, 39, 55; Whipple, "Hawthorne Gives Alms," 45–46; Appleton, "Annual Report," *Bull.* 3 (July 1912): 15; Appleton, "A Summer's Record," *Bull.* 7 (December 1916): 13.

21. Appleton, "Annual Report," *Bull.* 3 (July 1912): 17.

22. Ibid., 13; Appleton, Circular Letter, 14 April 1911, Swett-Ilsley Scrapbook, SPNEA; Wm. H. Tweddle to Appleton, 29 May 1911, Swett-Ilsley file; "Old Ilsley House to Be Preserved by Historical Folks," *Newburyport Herald-Leader*, 10 June 1911; City Improvement Society, *Places of Historical Interest within the Limits of "Ould Newbury"* (Newburyport, 1897).

23. Appleton, Circular Letter, 14 April 1911, Swett-Ilsley file. The fireplace is one of the widest on record in New England and was probably built when the house was altered in the second quarter of the eighteenth century (Cummings, *Framed Houses*, 120).

24. Nutting, *Massachusetts Beautiful*, 9; Nutting, *Biography*, 139, 140; Marc, *Psychology of the House*, 98–99; Nutting to Appleton, 7 November 1914, Nutting file; Bellamy, *Looking Backward*, 45; Appleton, undated report, Swett-Ilsley Scrapbook; Mass. Comm., *Pathways*, 129; Marsh, "Suburban Men," in *Meanings for Manhood*, ed. Carnes and Griffen, 111–27.

25. Endicott to Appleton, 9 October 1911, Endicott file, SPNEA; Appleton to John Morgan, 29 December 1913, Morgan file, SPNEA; Samuel Francis Batchelder, "Peter Harrison," *Bull.* 6 (January 1916): 17–18. The Lindens was purchased twenty years later, dismantled, and reconstructed in Washington, D.C.

26. Appleton to David Bonner, Jr., 1 August 1919, Fowler house A&M file, SPNEA; Appleton, "The Samuel Fowler House: Our Second Acquisition," *Bull.* 3 (March 1912): 5, 6.

27. Appleton, "Fowler House," 3–5.

28. Ibid.; Green, *America's Heroes*.

29. Appleton, "Destruction and Preservation," 167; Lowenthal, *Past Is a Foreign Country*; Hobsbawm and Ranger, *Invention of Tradition*.

30. Thornton, *Cultivating Gentlemen*, 208–12; Cram, *My Life*, 230–32.

31. Norton, "Reminiscences," 13; Appleton to Mrs. Chauncey Smith, 27 March 1912, C-F-A house Acq. file, SPNEA. Bolton failed to mention the house in *The Gossiping Guide to Harvard and Places of Interest in Cambridge* 2d ed. (Cambridge: Tribune, 1895).

32. Appleton, "The Movement to Buy the Cooper-Austin House," *Bull.* 3 (March 1912): 9; Mrs. Silvio M. DeGozzaldi, "An Account of the Occupants," ibid, 4. According to recent studies, the house was built by a son of Deacon John Cooper (Myron O. Stachiw, "Cultural Change in Cambridge: The Cooper-Frost-Austin House and Its Occupants," *OTNE* 70 [1980]: 31–44).

33. Josiah Frederick Frost, "Frost Family Association," appeal, July 1913, C-F-A house H&B file, SPNEA; Mass. Comm., *Pathways*, 37–39.

34. Bolton, Note-Book, 1 November 1912, Bolton Papers; another twenty-two supporters gave $50, one $75, and one $150 (Appleton to John G. Long, 4 April 1912, Long file, SPNEA); Abrams, *Conservatism*, 71–72; Leslie Woodcock Tentler, *Wage-Earning Women: Industrial Work and Family Life in the United States, 1900–1930* (New York and Oxford: Oxford Univ. Press, 1979), 17–18.

35. Hawkes, "The Abijah Boardman House," in *Hearths and Homes of Old Lynn* (1907), 12–22, excerpted by SPNEA, Boardman file, SPNEA; Green, *America's Heroes*.

36. Hawkes, *Hearths and Homes*, excerpts, SPNEA; Charles H. Adams to Ida Farr Miller, n.d., Boardman file.

37. Appleton "Destruction and Preservation," 166; Appleton to Annie S. Symonds, 15 December 1916, Boardman file; Appleton, "Annual Report," *OTNE* 12 (April 1922): 168.

38. Appleton to Lynde Sullivan, 6 November 1913, and 1 May 1914, Boardman file; Appleton to Donald Millar, 6 May 1916, Millar file; Appleton to E. B. Newhall, n.d., Boardman file; Appleton, "Annual Report," *OTNE* 12 (April 1922): 167.

39. Appleton to Ida Farr Miller, 3 March 1915, Boardman file; George Howard Cox to Appleton, 26 November 1915, ibid.; "Subcribers to the Special $1,000 fund for the Bennett-Boardman House," n.d., ibid.; "Pageant to Celebrate Centennial of Saugus," *Boston Globe*, 27 June 1915.

40. Appleton to Edward L. Tilton, 22 September 1916, Boardman file; Appleton to Andrew Carnegie, 16 November 1916, ibid.

41. Carnegie to Appleton, 27 November 1916, Boardman file; Lears, *No Place of Grace*.

42. Abbott Lowell Cummings, "The Scotch-Boardman House—A Fresh Appraisal," Parts I and II *OTNE* 43 (Winter & Spring 1953): 57–73, 91–102; Hawkes, *Hearths and Homes*, excerpts, SPNEA; Whitefield, *Homes of Forefathers*, n.p.; Appleton, "Annual Report," *Bull.* 9 (November 1918): 18; Appleton to Edward L. Tilton, 22 September 1916, Boardman file; Mass. Comm., *Pathways*, 174–76.

43. Cummings, *Framed Houses*, 144, 205; Cummings did verify the earlier existence of two facade gables, but could not date their removal ("Narrative Report," 1982, Boardman house file, Stewardship Dept.); Edward N. Hartley, *Ironworks on the Saugus: The Lynn and Braintree Ventures of the Company of Undertakers of the Ironworks in New England* (Norman: Univ. of Oklahoma Press, 1957), vii.

44. Appleton, "Annual Report," *Bull.* 7 (May 1916): 4–5; Bolton, "Tribute

to William Sumner Appleton," *OTNE* 30 (April 1940): 108; Appleton, "Destruction and Preservation," 167.

45. Emily M. Morison to Appleton, 7 May 1916, Otis house Acq. file, SPNEA; Writers' Project, *New Hampshire*, 503.

46. Appleton, "Report," *OTNE* 32 (April 1942): 112; Writers' Project, *New Hampshire*, 220–21. SPNEA deaccessioned the Laws house in 1948 and "Bleakhouse" in 1976.

47. "Save Harrison Gray Otis House," *Boston Globe*, 2 August 1916.

48. Woods, "Assimilation: A Two-Edged Sword," in *Americans in Process*, 380; Appleton to Otis, 16 April 1916, Otis house Acq. file; Baltzell, *Protestant Establishment*, x.

49. Appleton to Mrs. Barrett Wendell, 14 April 1917, Otis house Acq. file; Bolton, Note-Book, 24 May 1916, Bolton Papers; Appleton to George N. Black, 29 June 1916, Otis house Acq. file; Appleton to Miss F. B. Upton, 13 July 1917, Otis house H&B file, SPNEA; "The Harrison Gray Otis House," *Bull.* 8 (March 1917): 7.

50. Morison, "A Brief Account of Harrison Gray Otis," ms., Otis house Acq. file; ibid. as printed text, *Bull.* 8 (March 1917): 3–6; Curley, *I'd Do It Again*, 3; Baltzell, *Puritan Boston*, 23; Warner, *Living and the Dead*, 154–55; Jaher, *Urban Establishment*, Chap. 2; Lyndon, *City Observed*, 25–26, 87, 93, 96, 102; Matthew Edel, et al., *Shaky Palaces: Homeownership and Social Mobility in Boston's Suburbanization* (New York: Columbia Univ. Press, 1984), 198–205.

51. Appleton to Seymour, 28 May 1914, Seymour file; Appleton, "Annual Report," *OTNE* 12 (April 1922): 176, 177; Appleton to Frederick E. Norton, 22 December 1914, Norton house file, SPNEA; Appleton to Rollin S. Woodruff, 11 January 1917, ibid.; Drake, *Our Colonial Homes*, 203–4.

52. Appleton, "Annual Report," *OTNE* 12 (April 1922): 177; Appleton to Erving, 10 August 1921, Erving file; Appleton, "Annual Report," *OTNE* 24 (July 1933): 29–31.

53. Kelly, *Early Domestic Architecture*, 1.

54. Ibid., 1, 2, 14; Nutting, *Massachusetts Beautiful*, 285.

55. Kelly, "The Norton House," *OTNE* 14 (January 1924): 122–30; Appleton to Caroline P. Heath, 5 May 1910, DAR file; Garvan, *Architecture*, 117–18, 128.

56. Appleton, "Society Collects Old Houses," *New York Sun*, 17 May 1930; Appleton, "Annual Report," *Bull.* 10 (October 1919): 5; "Antiquarians Preserve Old House," *Providence Journal*, typescript, Arnold house H&B file, SPNEA; Bowden, "Invention of American Tradition," 3–26.

57. No author, typed history of house, n.d., Arnold house H&B file; Kelly, *Connecticut's Old Houses*, 20–21; Appleton, "Destruction and Preservation," 168; [Appleton], "The Eleazer Arnold House," *Art and Archaeology* 8 (May-June 1919): 191.

58. Appleton to Mary C. Wheelwright, 11 June 1915, Brown house Scrapbook, SPNEA; "Brief Account of the Abraham Browne Estate in Watertown, Massachusetts," October 1924, Brown house H&B, SPNEA.

59. Appleton to Geo. Peabody Wetmore, 11 January 1915, Brown house Scrapbook; Appleton to Mary Wheelwright, 18 December 1918, ibid.; Appleton to Heloise Meyer, 21 April 1919, ibid.; Appleton to Eleanor Standen, 14 December 1937, quoted in Hosmer, *Presence*, 250.

60. "Restore Brown House, Watertown," *Boston Traveler*, 8 July 1920; Allen, *In English Ways*, 122–23, 224.

61. [Appleton], "The Abraham Brown House, Watertown, Massachusetts," *Art and Archaeology* 8 (May-June 1919): 191; Appleton to Mary C. Wheelwright, 15 July 1918, Browne house Scrapboook; Appleton to Heloise Meyer, 17 January 1917, Meyer file, SPNEA; Appleton, Memorandum, 12 April 1919, Browne house Scrapbook; Appleton to Murray Corse, 16 March 1918, Corse file, SPNEA; Appleton, "Annual Report," *Bull.* 7 (May 1916): 16.

62. Appleton to Nathaniel Jackson, 8 July 1920, Jackson house file, SPNEA; Appleton, Notes on the Jackson House, 4 April 1923, Jackson house H&B file; Appleton, Jackson House, n.d., ibid.

63. Wendell to Sir Robert White-Thomson, 7 April 1912, in *Barrett Wendell*, 247; Wendell quoted in Persons, *Decline of Gentility*, 274; Bolton, Note-Book, 7 May 1914, Bolton Papers.

64. Nathaniel Jackson to Appleton, 22 August 1922, Jackson house file; Appleton, Notes on the Jackson House, 4 April 1923, Jackson house H&B file; Harris Walter Reynolds, "Jackson House," typescript, n.d., ibid.

65. Jackson to Appleton, 12 December 1923, 24 May 1924, and Appleton to Jackson, 19 November and 14 December 1923, Jackson house file; John W. Durel, "Historic Portsmouth," *Historical New Hampshire* 41 (Fall-Winter 1986): 107–11; Virginia Tanner, *A Pageant of Portsmouth* (Concord, N.H.: Rumford Press, 1923); Candee, *Building Portsmouth*, 4; Aldrich, "Unguarded Gates," 29–30; Solomon, *Ancestors and Immigrants*, 82.

66. Elizabeth Porter Gould, "The Home of Rebecca Nurse," *The Essex Antiquarian* 4 (September 1900): 135; Charles Sutherland Tapley, *Rebecca Nurse: Saint But Witch Victim* (Boston: Marshall Jones, 1930); Appleton, "The Acquisition of the Rebecca Nurse House," *OTNE* 19 (October 1928): 90; Appleton, "Society Collects Old Houses," *New York Sun*, 17 May 1930; Writers' Project, *Massachusetts*, 431; Mass. Comm., *Pathways*, 57–59. Subsequent researchers have been unable to date the house's construction. It was probably built in the early eighteenth century.

67. Appleton, "New England's Antiquarian Heritage," *Boston Transcript*, 15 April 1939; Appleton, "Annual Report," *OTNE* 11 (April 1921): 188; Appleton to Mrs. Charles K. Bolton, 30 October 1914, Swett-Ilsley file; Swett-Ilsley Binder, Stewardship Dept., SPNEA.

68. Appleton, "Annual Report," *Bull.* 7 (May 1916): 13; "To Let the Cooper-Austin House," *Bull.* 4 (August 1913); "Browne House," *OTNE* 14 (July 1923): iv; Appleton to J. C. Flamand, 14 March 1914, Cooper house H&B file; Jan Whitaker, "Catering to Romantic Hunger: Roadside Tearooms, 1909–1930," *JAC* 15 (Winter 1992): 17–25.

69. "Mrs. Ellyson Reports on Work of Society," *Richmond Times-Dispatch*, 7 January 1917. SPNEA apportioned its dues according to a three-tier scale in 1910: Associate ($2/year), Active ($5), and Life ($50 in one year) (*Bull.* 1 [May 1910]: 7).

70. Appleton, "Annual Report," *Bull.* 3 (July 1912): 21. In that 1921 campaign, thirty donated $100 or more ($3,925), thirty-two gave $50–75 ($1,662), and fifty-two contributed $25 ($1,300), totalling $6,887. Another 332 members gave $2,367. Twenty-five percent of the contributors, therefore, gave almost seventy-five percent of the funds (extracted from "Annual Report of the Treasurer," *OTNE* 12 [October 1921]: 83–87).

5.   Defining a Preservation Movement

1. Rodgers, "Progressivism," 113–32; Wiebe, *Search for Order*; Hall, *Nonprofit Sector*, 36–57.

2. Appleton, "Report," *OTNE* 32 (July 1941): 25.

3. Appleton to Isham, 31 December 1923, Isham file; Writers' Project, *Rhode Island*, 370; Downing, "Historic Preservation," 10–14.

4. Appleton, "Annual Report," *Bull.* 7 (May 1916): 26–27; Appleton, "A Summer's Record," *Bull.* 7 (December 1916): 3–4; Writers' Project, *Connecticut*, 164–65. The house was actually built in the early eighteenth century (Abbott Cummings to author, 14 February 1992).

5. Appleton to Mrs. M. W. Thornburgh, 29 October 1921, Thornburgh file, SPNEA; Downing, "Historic Preservation," 12.

6. Wallis D. Walker to Bolton, 3 April 1916, Trustees Meetings, SPNEA; Appleton to Mrs. C. A. Gosney, 6 July 1939, N.C. Preservation Society file.

7. ASHPS, *Seventeenth Report* (1912), 15, 18; Appleton, "Annual Report," *OTNE* 11 (April 1921): 186, and 12 (April 1922): 188; Appleton, "New England's Antiquarian Heritage," *Boston Transcript*, 15 April 1939. By 1936 SPNEA's membership was 2,380.

8. Appleton to Celeste E. Bush, 16 January 1914, Lee house file; Appleton to Mercer, 19 June 1922, Mercer file, SPNEA; Appleton to E. J. Frothingham, 14 September 1918, Hazen Garrison file, SPNEA.

9. Harris Walter Reynolds, "History Speaks Through Living Things in an Old House on Lynde Street," *Boston Evening Transcript*, 14 March 1923; Appleton, "Annual Report," *Bull.* 4 (August 1913): 28; Appleton, "Annual Report," *OTNE* 13 (April 1923): 192.

10. Appleton, "Destruction and Preservation," 131–83; Appleton to Donald Millar, 18 June 1919, Millar file; Appleton to Mary Northend, 21 September 1918, Northend file, SPNEA.

11. Appleton to Judge Samuel H. Fisher, 29 January and 26 May 1926, SPNEA; Appleton to Donald Millar, 19 September 1919, Browne house file; Appleton to Kimball, 5 November 1928, Kimball file, SPNEA; Kimball to Appleton, 10 November 1921, ibid. Over their lifetimes, John D. Rockefeller, Sr. donated about $600,000,000, Andrew Carnegie about $325,000,000, and Henry Ford $37,500,000. Ford reportedly thought that endowments were "an opiate to imagination, a drug to initiative" (Quoted in Greenleaf, *From These Beginnings*, 5, 7).

12. A. Lawrence Kocher to Appleton, 13 April 1928, and Appleton's reply, 14 April 1928, American Institute of Architects file, SPNEA; Hosmer, *Presence*, 296–97.

13. Appleton to Fannie S. Lee, 29 November 1915, Lawrence file, SPNEA; Writers' Project, *Massachusetts*, 253; Appleton, "Annual Report," *Bull.* 6 (April 1915): 11.

14. Chandler, *Colonial House*, 160; Appleton to Mrs. C. Bolton, 28 March 1914, DR file; Jane R. Wood to Appleton, 11 May 1914, ibid; Appleton to Mrs. C. A. Gosney, 6 July 1939, N.C. Preservation Society file.

15. Gail Lee Dubrow, "Restoring a Female Presence," in *Architecture*, ed. Berkeley, 159–70.

16. J. M. Arms Sheldon, "The 'Old Indian House' at Deerfield, Massachusetts, and the Effort Made in 1847 to Save It from Destruction," *OTNE* 12 (January 1922): 99; Sears, *Fruitlands*, xiii–xvii.

17. Curtis to Appleton, 22 May 1913, Curtis file, SPNEA; Kelly, *Whitfield House*, xix–xx; Arthur W. Leibunguth, "History of Historic Preservation in Connecticut," *Connecticut Antiquarian* 27 (1975): 10–28.

18. Bush to Appleton, 18 June 1914, Lee house file; Appleton to Bush, 17 February 1914, ibid.; Isham to Seymour, 2 March 1914, ibid.; Kelly, *Connecticut's Old Houses*, 47–48; Bush, *Old Lee House*.

19. "Mount Vernon Branch," *Year Book of the APVA* (Richmond: Geo. M. West, 1896), 72; Holmes quoted in Firey, *Land Use*, 167.

20. Appleton to Bush, 13 January 1915, Lee house file; Erich A. O'D. Taylor, "The Slate Gravestones of New England," *OTNE* 15 (October 1924): 59; Appleton, "Annual Report," *OTNE* 30 (April 1940): 130; Lowenthal, "Age and Artifact," in *Interpretation*, ed. Meinig, 123. See also, Peter Benes, ed., *Puritan Gravestone Art I* and *Puritan Gravestone Art II*, Vol. I and III in The Dublin Seminar for New England Folklife (Boston: Boston Univ., 1976, 1978). Even SPNEA took custody of two mid-eighteenth-century burial grounds in the 1930s.

21. Titus to Bolton, 28 April 1912, Howland house file, SPNEA; Writers' Project, *Massachusetts*, 325.

22. John C. Foote to Appleton, 9 March 1915, and his reply, 11 March 1915, Howland house file; McCarthy, *Women's Culture*, 111–45.

23. Appleton, "Destruction and Preservation," 174–75; W. W. Cordingly, "Shirley Place, Roxbury, Massachusetts, and Its Builder Governor William Shirley," *OTNE* 12 (October 1921): 63; Appleton to Annie B. Thiving (sic, Annie H. Thwing, author of *Crooked and Narrow Streets of Boston* [1920]), 2 January 1924, Shirley-Eustis house file; Writers' Project, *Massachusetts*, 170; Frederic C. Detwiller, "The Evolution of the Shirley-Eustis House," *OTNE* 70 (1980): 17–30.

24. Titus to Woodbury Langdon, 28 June 1915, and 24 July 1915, Shirley-Eustis house file; Appleton, Circular Letter, 16 June 1913, ibid.

25. Titus to Langdon, 28 June, 24 July 1915, Shirley-Eustis house file.

26. Titus to Mrs. Paul Hamlen, 6 February 1917, Shirley-Eustis house file; Bledstein, *Culture of Professionalism*. Another student attributes this growing professionalism to the influence of the mugwumps (Geoffrey Blodgett, "The Mugwump Reputation, 1870 to the Present," *JAH* 66 [March 1980]: 880).

27. Appleton to Winifred C. Putnam, 20 February 1924, Shirley-Eustis house file; Appleton, "Annual Report," *OTNE* 29 (April 1939): 145–46; Hosmer, *Preservation*, 175–76, 746–48. The Palladian window at Mount Vernon has been attributed to a pattern book by Batty Langley (Matthew John Mosca, "The House and Its Restoration," *Antiques* 135 [February 1989]: 464).

28. Sumner A. Weld to Ellie Reichlin, 9 July 1984, Appleton file; Dubrow, "Preserving Her Heritage," 87–89; Boris, *Art and Labor*, 99–121.

29. Appleton, "A Summer's Record," *Bull.* 7 (December 1916): 11, 13.

30. Ibid., 11, 12; Sian Jones and Sharon Pay, "The Legacy of Eve," in *Politics of the Past*, ed. Gathercole and Lowenthal, 160–71.

31. Appleton quoted in Hosmer, *Preservation*, 134.

32. Alston Deas, "They Shall See Your Good Works," *Preservation Progress* 7 (May 1962): 1; Hosmer, *Presence*, 300; Lindgren, "From Personalism to Professionalism"; McCarthy, *Women's Culture*, 111–45; Franck, "A Feminist Approach to Architecture," in *Architecture*, ed. Berkeley, 201–16; Howe, "Women in Preservation," 31–61; Howe, "Women and Architecture," in *Reclaiming the*

Past, ed. Miller, 35. Additionally, those women who succeeded in preservation work often accepted the male-defined canon, as did Antoinette Downing, a student of Isham and coauthor of *Architectural History of Newport, Rhode Island,* or worked in the more traditional vein of social reform through preservation, as did Elizabeth Werlein, a New Orleans preservationist who fought her neighborhood's bars and brothels.

33. Carl N. Degler, *In Search of Human Nature: The Decline and Revival of Darwinism in American Thought* (New York and Oxford: Oxford Univ. Press, 1991); Kloppenberg, *Uncertain Victory*; Harris Walter Reynolds, "Saving Old Landmarks," *Current Affairs* (3 March 1924), Clipping file, SPNEA.

34. Appleton to Donald Millar, 5 March 1915, Millar file.

35. Appleton to George S. Bryan, 18 September 1922, Bryan file, SPNEA; Appleton to H. F. Waters, 31 May 1913, Old Bakery file.

36. John Swarbrick to Appleton, 23 November 1925, Ancient Monuments Society file, SPNEA; Stillinger, *Antiquers*, 149–54; Hosmer, *Presence*, 250.

37. Appleton, "Destruction and Preservation," 141, 155, 181; Appleton to Donald Millar, 24 October 1919, Millar file; Writers' Project, *Massachusetts*, 416; Curtis to Appleton, 26 May 1913, Curtis file.

38. Appleton, "Annual Report," *OTNE* 12 (April 1922): 175; Writers' Project, *Massachusetts*, 372; Appleton, "The Threatened Destruction of the John Hicks House in Cambridge," *OTNE* 19 (October 1928): 95–96; Esther Stevens Fraser, "The John Hicks House," *OTNE* 22 (January 1932): 98, 112–13.

39. Nutting, *Biography*; Nutting to Appleton, 30 September 1915, Nutting file; Stillinger, *Antiquers*, 190–91. One student attributed his tension to "a vertigo-producing disturbance of the inner ear" (Joyce P. Barendsen, "Wallace Nutting, An American Tastemaker: The Pictures and Beyond," *WP* 18 [Summer/Autumn 1983]: 187).

40. Nutting to Appleton, 30 September 1915, Nutting file.

41. Nutting to Appleton, 29 December 1914, 26 February, 23 September 1915, and Appleton to Nutting, 25 September 1915, Nutting file.

42. Nutting to Appleton, 7 April 1917, Appleton to Nutting, 4 April 1917, Nutting to Appleton, 18 July 1918, Nutting file; [Appleton], Notes on a Conversation with Wallace Nutting, 8 April 1920, Iron Works file, SPNEA; Appleton to Millar, 20 March 1919, Millar file; Appleton, "Destruction and Preservation," 169.

43. Nutting to Appleton, 15 March 1920, Iron Works file; Appleton to Millar, 20 March 1919, Millar file; Nutting quoted in Dulaney, "Wallace Nutting," 58; Edie Clark, "The Man Who Looked Back and Saw the Future," *Yankee* 50 (September 1986): 175.

44. Appleton to Mrs. Martin W. Littleton, 28 October, 4 November 1912, Monticello file, SPNEA; Appleton to the editor, *Boston Herald*, 13 May 1918.

45. Appleton to Erving, 21 May 1917, Erving file; Shackleton, *Boston*, 146; Lyndon, *City Observed*, 272–73.

46. Appleton, "Annual Report," *Bull.* 7 (May 1916): 24; Appleton to Curtis, 21 October 1913, Curtis file; Writers' Project, *Connecticut*, 184–85, 226.

47. Appleton, "Annual Report," *Bull.* 6 (April 1915): 16; Lyndon, *City Observed*, 24–27.

48. Hosmer, *Preservation*, 474, 564.

49. Appleton, "Destruction and Preservation," 161; Appleton to Seymour, 9

December 1914, Seymour file; Appleton, "Annual Report," *Bull.* 5 (April 1914): 18, and 8 (May 1916): 26; "The Salem Fire," *Bull.* 5 (December 1914): 15–16; Boulting, "The Law's Delay," in *Future of the Past*, 19–20.

50. Appleton to Rev. Glenn Tillery Morse, 21 October 1918, Bay State Historical League file, SPNEA; Appleton to R. P. Bellows, 6 December 1935, Legislation file, SPNEA. Morse would serve as SPNEA's museum director during the 1920s before Dow.

51. Mass. Convention, *Debates*, I: 439; III: 84, 203, 543–49, 674, 739.

52. Ibid., III: 743.

53. Ibid., III: 744–45. A decade later, the "Witch House" was "sadly defaced by a modern drug store which grows out of its side like an excresence" (Mass. Comm., *Pathways*, 166).

54. Mass. Convention, *Debates*, III: 745–47.

55. Ibid., III: 745–46.

56. Ibid., III: 747.

57. The vote in favor of landmark preservation was 183,265 to 81,933; of building zoning, 161,214 to 83,095; of natural conservation, 172,111 to 102,768; and of billboard advertising limitation, 193,925 to 84,127 (Mass. Convention, *Debates*, I: 544; III: 621, 741, 751). The landmarks amendment did not receive, however, a majority of all votes cast.

58. Writers' Project, *Massachusetts*, 174; Bolton, Note-Book, 17 June 1919, Bolton Papers; John L. Bates, "Address," in *Amendments Passed by the Constitutional Convention* (Boston: Wright & Potter, 1918), 16. Bolton and the board members of the Bunker Hill Monument Association voted in 1919 to relinquish control of the shrine to the Metropolitan Parks Commission (Bolton, Note-Book, 17 June 1919, Bolton Papers).

59. E. J. Carpenter to Bolton, 8 March 1919, and Bolton to Appleton, 8 March 1919, Trustees file; Appleton, "Annual Report," *Bull.* 10 (October 1919): 18–19; Writers' Project, *Massachusetts*, 215, 324, 332, 626.

6. Destruction, Development, and SPNEA's Paradox

1. Appleton, "Annual Report," *Bull.* 10 (October 1919): 20–21; Bolton, Note-Book, 22, 25 September 1914, Bolton Papers.

2. Bolton, Note-Book, 17 September 1914, 5 February 1917, Bolton Papers; Cutler, *"Honey Fitz,"* 219; Stillinger, *Antiquers*, 143–48.

3. Appleton to Wendell, 13 January 1915, Wendell file, SPNEA; Appleton to Powys, 14 September 1914, SPAB file, SPNEA.

4. "An Appeal from Europe," *Bull.* 5 (December 1914): 19; Appleton to Wendell, 13 January 1915, Wendell file.

5. Appleton to Lodge, 30 November 1914, Lodge file, SPNEA; Appleton to Wendell, 13 January 1915, Wendell file.

6. Appleton to Wesley Weyman, 18 March 1915, Boardman house file; Bolton, Note-Book, 2 April 1917, Bolton Papers; Mary H. Northend to Appleton, 12 May 1917, and his reply, 16 May 1917, Northend file. Appleton also objected to Northend's promotion of interior renovation of old country homes, as in her *Remodeled Farmhouses* (1915); see Candee, "The New Colonials," in *"A Noble and Dignified Stream,"* ed. Giffen and Murphy, 41.

7. "Mrs. Wendell, Leader in Patriotic Groups," *New York Times*, 4 October

1938, 25; Morison, "A Brief Account of Harrison Gray Otis," *Bull.* 8 (March 1917): 3–6; Creel quoted in David M. Kennedy, *Over Here: The First World War and American Society* (New York and Oxford: Oxford Univ. Press, 1980), 63; Lindgren, *Preserving the Old Dominion*, 196–201.

8. Bolton, Note-Book, 16 March, 6 April 1917, Bolton Papers; "Court House Bomb Kills 2 in Boston," *New York Times*, 17 March 1917, 14.

9. Bolton, Note-Book, 11 August, 10 September, 2 November 1919, Bolton Papers; Appleton, "Annual Report," *OTNE* 11 (July 1920): 41; Beebe, *Boston*, 265–66; Painter, *Standing at Armageddon*, 346–47.

10. Bolton, "A Half-Forgotten Tragedy of 1755," *OTNE* 11 (July 1920): 12, 14; ASHPS, "Prevalence of Crime," *Twenty-Fifth Annual Report* (Albany: J. B. Lyon, 1920): 357; Bolton, Note-Book, 11 August, 4 November 1919, Bolton Papers.

11. Rogers, "Progressivism," 113–32; Lears, *No Place of Grace*; Wright, *Building the Dream*, 164; Marling, *George Washington*; Wallace, "Revitalization Movements," 264–81.

12. Appleton, Circular Letter, 6 December 1923, SPNEA; Boris, *Art and Labor*, 32–52; Wilson, "American Arts and Crafts Architecture," 101–31.

13. George H. Lewis, "The Maine That Never Was: The Construction of Popular Myth in Regional Culture," *JAC* 16 (Summer 1993): 91–99; Green, "Popular Science," 3–24.

14. Wright, *Building the Dream*, 168; Alan Gowans, *The Comfortable House: North American Suburban Architecture, 1890–1930* (Cambridge: MIT Press, 1986); William Butler, "Another City upon a Hill: Litchfield, Connecticut, and the Colonial Revival," in *Colonial Revival*, ed. Axelrod, 15–51; Steinitz, "Rethinking," 16–26.

15. Drake, *Our Colonial Homes*, 2.

16. Cram, "Architecture," in *Fifty Years*, 340; Cram, "A $5,000 Colonial House," *Ladies Home Journal* 13 (February 1896): 17; Isham, "Providence and Its Colonial Houses," *The White Pines Series of Architectural Monographs* 4 (June 1918): 3–12; Shi, *Simple Life*, 186–87.

17. Appleton to Bush, 17 February 1914, Lee house file; Appleton, Memorandum, 12 April 1919, Brown house file; Appleton, "Annual Report," *OTNE* 13 (April 1923): 190; Appleton, "Destruction and Preservation," 131.

18. Kelly, *Early Domestic Architecture*, 2; Chandler, *Colonial House*, 1; "A Year's Work of S.P.N.E.A.," *Boston Evening Transcript*, 12 October 1912; Boris, *Art and Labor*, 44.

19. Sellers, "Preserve the Charm of the New England Village," *OTNE* 20 (July 1929): 46–47.

20. Quoted in ibid. Cram did admit, however, that "living in a rented flat or in a narrow slice of house in a city block" made the resident "no better than a wage-slave, a proletarian" (Cram, *My Life*, 230, 231–32). See also Clark, *American Family Home*, 171–92.

21. Appleton, "The Standish House, Wethersfield, Connecticut," *OTNE* 19 (April 1928): 91, 92; Dow, "Notes and Gleanings," *OTNE* 22 (January 1932): 146.

22. Charles H. Batchelder et al. to John Doe, 14 February 1924, Jackson house file; Wallis D. Walker to Appleton, 16 February 1924, ibid.; Dona L. Brown, "The Tourist's New England: Creating an Industry, 1820–1900" (Ph.D. thesis, Univ. of Massachusetts at Amherst, 1989).

23. French, *New England*, 370; Kay and Chase-Harrell, *Preserving New England*, 45; Whipple, "Hawthorne Gives Alms," 45–46; Lewis, "The Maine That Never Was," 95; Newton C. Brainard, "Main Street, East Hartford, Connecticut, Before and After," *OTNE* 19 (April 1929): 184–85; Isham, "Report on the Old Brick Market or Old City Hall, Newport, Rhode Island," *Bull.* 6 (January 1916): 11.

24. Appleton, "Annual Report," *OTNE* 11 (July 1920): 39; Appleton to Susan B. Willard, 11 March 1913, Advisory Committee file, SPNEA; William B. Rhoads, "Roadside Colonial: Early American Design for the Automobile Age, 1900-1940," *WP* 21 (Summer/Autumn 1986): 133–52.

25. Charles H. Batchelder et al. to John Doe, 14 February 1924, Jackson house file; this letter was actually written by Appleton as a circular; Appleton, "New England's Antiquarian Heritage," *Boston Transcript*, 15 April 1939; for such cases of demolition, see *OTNE* 25 (April 1935): 129–34; Jane Jacobs, *The Death and Life of Great American Cities* (New York: Modern Library, 1969); see also Candee, *Building Portsmouth*. Urban renewal threatened the area in the 1950s, prompting a private corporation in 1960 to create Strawbery Banke, an outdoor museum with restored and moved buildings.

26. George Santayana, *The Middle Span* (New York: Charles Scribner's Sons, 1945), 113; Jaher, *Urban Establishment*, Chap. 2.

27. Robert D. Arner, "Plymouth Rock Revisited: The Landing of the Pilgrim Fathers," *JAC* 6 (Winter 1983): 25–36.

28. Eliot quoted in "Plan 100 Per Cent Pilgrim Memorial," uniden. newspaper (dateline: 17 July 1920), in President's Report of Meetings 1919–1920, APVA.

29. Eliot quoted in ibid.; Kammen, *Mystic Chords*, 64; Walton Advertising Company, ed., *Towns of New England and Old England, Ireland, and Scotland* (Boston: State Street Trust, 1920), I: 25, 27, 36.

30. Appleton, "Report of the Annual Meeting," *OTNE* 11 (April 1921): 163; Henry F. May, *The End of American Innocence: A Study of the First Years of Our Own Time, 1912–1917* (New York: Alfred A. Knopf, 1959), 35–37.

31. Thomas P. Robinson, "The Historic Winslow House at Marshfield, Massachusetts, and Its Restoration," *OTNE* 11 (January 1921): 107; Writers' Project, *Massachusetts*, 625; Deetz, *In Small Things*, 94–95; Glassberg, *American Historical Pageantry*; Bruce C. Daniels, "Did the Puritans Have Fun?" *Journal of American Studies* 25 (April 1991): 8.

32. Appleton, "Annual Report," *OTNE* 11 (April 1921): 183; Walton Advertising, *Towns of New England*, I: 27; Dixon Wecter, *The Hero in America: A Chronicle of Hero Worship* (Ann Arbor: Univ. of Michigan Press, 1966), 46, 49; Baritz, *Good Life*, 56–104; Fass, *Damned and Beautiful*; Stanley Cobben, *Rebellion against Victorianism: The Impetus for Cultural Change in 1920s America* (New York and Oxford: Oxford Univ. Press, 1991).

33. Appleton to Paul Hamlen, n.d. [1916], Trustees file; Appleton, "Annual Report," *Bull.* 7 (May 1916): 32, and *OTNE* 11 (July 1920): 41.

34. Harris Walter Reynolds, "Saving Old Landmarks"; Appleton to Mrs. E. M. Roberts, 20 May 1913, Roberts file, SPNEA; Writers' Project, *Massachusetts*, 402.

35. Appleton, "Annual Report," *OTNE* 12 (April 1922): 179–80; Firey, *Land Use*, 152.

36. Appleton, "Annual Report," *OTNE* 11 (April 1921): 178, and 13 (April

1923): 191; Appleton to Channing Cox, 26 May 1922, and his reply, 29 May 1922, Province House file, SPNEA; Cummings, "Massachusetts and Its First Period Houses," in *Architecture*, ed. Cummings, 121. See also *OTNE* 62 (April-June 1972).

37. New England Tercentenary Club, "Honoring Our Ancestors in Permanent Materials," broadside [1920], SPNEA.

38. Bolton, Note-Book, 1 August 1916, Bolton Papers; Appleton to Seymour, 28 May 1914, Seymour file; Kelly, "The Moulthrop House," *OTNE* 12 (April 1922): 152.

39. Appleton, "Annual Report," *Bull.* 5 (April 1914): 7–8; Writer's Project, *Massachusetts*, 245–46; Appleton, "Annual Report," *Bull.* 6 (April 1915): 14–15; Appleton to Nutting, 23 November 1914, Nutting file; Mass. Comm., *Pathways*, 79–80. It was actually built in the early eighteenth century (Abbott Cummings to author, 14 February 1992).

40. Appleton, "Annual Report," *Bull.* 10 (October 1919): 17.

41. Appleton, "Annual Report," *Bull.* 5 (April 1914): 16–17; Ted Robert Gurr, *Why Men Rebel* (Princeton: Princeton Univ. Press, 1970).

42. Appleton, "Annual Report," *Bull.* 5 (April 1914): 16; Appleton to Millar, 16 April 1918, Millar file.

43. Appleton, "West Roxbury Meeting House," *Bull.* 2 (February 1912): 7–8; Appleton, "Annual Report," *Bull.* 3 (July 1912): 19, and 6 (April 1915): 13; Appleton to Millar, 16 April 1918, Millar file; Cram, *Ministry of Art*, 47; Writer's Project, *Massachusetts*, 170.

44. Appleton, "Annual Report," *OTNE* 11 (July 1920): 30.

45. Appleton, "The Benaiah Titcomb House," *Bull.* 2 (August 1911): 17; Appleton, "Destruction and Preservation," 136. The house was probably built after 1700 (Cummings, "Summary Abstracts," in *Architecture*, 167).

46. Appleton, "Annual Report," *OTNE* 15 (July 1924): 37; Writers' Project, *Rhode Island*, 211–17; Isham and Brown, *Early Rhode Island Houses*, 57.

47. Millar to Appleton, 16 October 1919, Millar file; Hardy, " 'Parks for the People,' " 5–24; Lyndon, *City Observed*, 75; Jacobs, *Death and Life*, 296–97.

48. Robinson to Appleton, 6 March 1915, and Appleton's reply, 15 March 1915, Robinson file, SPNEA; Appleton to Wallace L. Gifford, 15 March 1915, Gifford file; David I. Macleod, *Building Character in the American Boy: The Boy Scouts, YMCA, and Their Forerunners, 1870–1920* (Madison: Univ. of Wisconsin Press, 1983).

49. Appleton, "Annual Report," *OTNE* 13 (April 1923): 187–89, and 15 (July 1924): 30, 35; quoted in Mass. Comm., *Pathways*, 148–50; Writers' Project, *Massachusetts*, 490. Parker Tavern was built in the early eighteenth century (Abbott Cummings to author, 14 February 1992). See also, Charles B. Hosmer, Jr., "The Colonial Revival in the Public Eye," in *Colonial Revival*, ed. Axelrod, 52–70; Schuyler, *New Urban Landscape*.

50. "Notes and Gleanings," *OTNE* 11 (October 1920): 93; Appleton, "Annual Report," *Bull.* 10 (October 1919): 13–14, and *OTNE* 11 (April 1921): 179; Mass. Comm., *Pathways*, 16. The year in which the Balch house was constructed is yet uncertain, as is its attribution to an "Old Planter" (Cummings, *Framed Houses*, 160–61).

51. Appleton, "The Parker-Inches-Emory House," *Bull.* 4 (August 1913); Firey, *Land Use*, 106.

52. Appleton, "Destruction and Preservation," 172; Cram, *My Life*, 219–20; Sullivan, *Boston*, 86; W. Lloyd Warner, *The Social Life of a Modern Community* (New Haven: Yale Univ. Press, 1941), 107.

53. Elizabeth W. Schermerhorn to the editor, *Boston Herald*, 16 September 1923.

54. Harriet Sisson Gillespie, "Reclaiming Colonial Landmarks," *House Beautiful* 58 (September 1925): 239, 273; Firey, *Land Use*, 111, 119; Lyndon, *City Observed*, 110; Holleran, " 'Changeful Times,' " 284.

55. Appleton to Millar, 23 January 1917, Millar file; Appleton to Walter Gilman Page, 25 March 1919, Hancock house file. SPNEA's initial committee on the project was weighted toward architects with Dean, Chandler, and Herbert Browne.

56. Appleton to Page, 21 March 1919, Hancock house file; Lyndon, *City Observed*, 105; Chamberlain, *Beacon Hill*, 279, 283.

57. Appleton to Millar, 15 March 1920, Millar file; "Would Save Hancock Site: Society for the Preservation of New England Antiquities Non-Committal on Demolishing Present Buildings or Erecting War Memorial," *Boston Evening Transcript*, 19 April 1924; Millar, "Notes on the Hancock House, Boston," *OTNE* 17 (January 1927): 121.

7.   Establishing a Scientific Method in Preservation

1. SPAB, Principles of 1877, broadside rept. 1906, SPAB file; Tschudi-Madsen, *Restoration*, Chapter 5.

2. Hans Huth, "The Evolution of Preservationism in Europe," *JASAH* 1 (October 1941): 5–10; Sir John Summerson, "Viollet-le-Duc and the Rational Point of View," in *Eugene Emmanuel Viollet-le-Duc, 1814–1879* (London: Academy Editions, 1980), 7–13; Sir Nikolaus Pevsner, "Ruskin and Viollet-le-Duc," in ibid, 48–53; Daniel J. Sherman, *Worthy Monuments: Art Museums and the Politics of Culture in Nineteenth-Century France* (Cambridge: Harvard Univ. Press, 1989).

3. Appleton, Diary, 18, 24, 26 March 1909; Follett, "Norman Isham," 145; Jacques Dupont, "Viollet-le-Duc and Restoration in France," in *Historic Preservation Today* (Charlottesville: Univ. Press of Virginia, 1966), 3–22; Henry-Russell Hitchcock, *Architecture: Nineteenth and Twentieth Centuries* 4th ed. (New York: Penguin Books, 1977), 279. Later critics have charged that his work appears "almost comically Victorian" (Fitch, *Historic Preservation*, 189).

4. Lindgren, *Preserving the Old Dominion*.

5. Murtagh, *Keeping Time*, 34, 80–82; Morton, "What Do We Preserve?" in *American Mosaic*, ed. Stipe and Lee, 153; Powys, *Repair*.

6. James Deetz, *Invitation to Archaeology* (Garden City, N.Y.: Natural History Press, 1967); Deetz, *In Small Things*; Gordon R. Willey and Jeremy A. Sabloff, *A History of American Archaeology* (San Francisco: W. H. Freeman, 1974).

7. Isham and Brown, *Early Rhode Island Houses*, 6; Porter, *Rambles*, vii; Dow quoted in "First Annual Report," *Bull.* 2 (August 1911): 20.

8. Appleton to Dean, 8 April 1914, Dean file; Hosmer, *Presence*, 205; Writers' Project, *Massachusetts*, 475.

9. Biographical sketch, n.d., Millar file; Millar, *Colonial and Georgian Houses*, iii.

10. Millar to Appleton, 19 February 1916, Millar file; Millar, *Colonial and Georgian Houses*; Schlereth, *Victorian America*, 127–30.

11. Appleton to Mrs. M. W. Thornburgh, 29 October 1921, Thornburgh file. See, for example, Henry C. Mercer, "Ancient Carpenters' Tools," *OTNE* 15 (April 1925): 164–97; Kammen, *Mystic Chords*, 341, 421.

12. [Abbott Cummings], untitled memorial, n.d., Appleton file; George M. Curtis to Appleton, 19 November 1912, Curtis file.

13. "Ancient Buildings of London," *OTNE* 15 (October 1924): 93; Percy W. Lovell, "The London Survey Committee: How It Came to Be Founded, Its Purposes and Achievements," *OTNE* 19 (July 1928): 44–48; Powys, *Repair*, 11; Hosmer, *Presence*, 257.

14. Appleton to Mrs. J. Taylor Ellyson, 13 June 1923, APVA file, SPNEA.

15. SPAB quoted in Jane Fawcett, "A Restoration Tragedy: Cathedrals in the Eighteenth and Nineteenth Centuries," in *Future of the Past*, ed. Fawcett, 96–97; Chandler, *Colonial House*, 161.

16. Bolton, Note-Book, 12 March 1914, 9 May 1918, Bolton Papers; Cram, *Ministry of Art*, 47.

17. Millar to Appleton, 21 January 1915, Millar file; Millar, *Colonial and Georgian Houses*, iv.

18. Appleton to Millar, 23 January 1915, Millar file. Millar did write on the Capen house in *Architectural Record* ("A Seventeenth Century New England House," *A.R.* 38 [September 1915]: 349–61), as well as in *Old-Time New England*. At the time of publication in *OTNE*, Dow served as its editor. Millar's critical mood mellowed, but he noted that Dow had replaced so much of the original structure that the house looked as if it was "fresh from the hands of the builder" (Millar, "A Seventeenth Century New England House," *OTNE* 11 [July 1920]: 3–9). See also Cummings, *Framed House*, 123, 136.

19. Appleton, "Preserving the Antiquities of New England," ms., n.d. [1931], Appleton file.

20. Appleton, "The Swett-Ilsley House," *Advertiser*, 9 June 1915, Properties Dept., SPNEA; Appleton, "Destruction and Preservation," 165; Appleton, "Annual Report," *Bull.* 7 (May 1916): 12–13, and 9 (November 1918): 7.

21. Abbott Cummings, "Evaluation Report," 11 March 1981, C-F-A house file, Stewardship Dept.; Mass. Comm., *Pathways*, 39; Bunting and Nylander, *Survey*, 74–75.

22. Dow, "Museums and Preservation," 19; Appleton, "Society for the Protection of Ancient Buildings," *Bull.* 5 (December 1914): 18–19; Appleton to John Swarbrick, 7 August 1925, AMS file.

23. Appleton, "Annual Report," *OTNE* 11 (April 1921): 166; Cummings, "Massachusetts and Its First Period Houses," in *Architecture*, ed. Cummings, 113–21; Lowenthal, "Age and Artifact," in *Interpretation*, ed. Meinig, 103–28.

24. Horace Wells Sellers, "Protection of Historic Buildings," *Journal of the Society of the American Institute of Architects* 8 (February 1920): 62; Murray P. Corse to Appleton, 13 May 1919, Browne house H&B file; Constance M. Greiff, *Independence: The Creation of a National Park* (Philadelphia: Univ. of Pennsylvania Press, 1987), 37.

25. Dean, "The Restoration of Olde New England Houses," ms., n.d. [1917], Dean file; Appleton, "Annual Report," *Bull.* 10 (October 1919): 10, and *OTNE* 28 (July 1937): 24.

26. Appleton to Swarbrick, 7 August 1925, AMS file; Powys, *Repair*, 193.

27. Appleton to Swarbrick, 7 August 1925, AMS file; Dean, "The Restoration of Olde New England Houses," ms., n.d. [1917], Dean file; Chandler, *Colonial House*, 162.

28. Emmerton, *Chronicles*, 37.

29. Appleton to Millar, 5 January 1917, Millar file; Appleton, "Destruction and Preservation," 146; Mass. Comm., *Pathways*, 155–56.

30. Powys, *Repair*, 192–93; Appleton to Mrs. Thomas Bennett, 2 May 1917, Boardman file; Appleton, "First Report to the Subscribers Towards the Fund to Purchase the 'Scotch'-Boardman House," n.d., ibid; Appleton to Swarbrick, 7 August 1925, AMS file; Appleton, "The Collection of Photographs," *Bull.* 5 (April 1914): 23.

31. Appleton, "Destruction and Preservation," 177–78; Appleton to Mrs. Richard W. Meade, 20 September 1924, Meade file; Appleton to Isham, 8 February 1918, and his reply, 7 March 1918, Isham file; Kelly, *Connecticut's Old Houses*, 33; Orvell, *Real Thing*.

32. Nutting, *Biography*, 151; Nutting, *Virginia Beautiful* (Garden City, N.Y.: Garden City Publishing, 1935), 54; Nutting, *Period Furniture*, 6; Dulaney, "Wallace Nutting," 51, 53; Erving, *Random Notes*, 48; Appleton to Nutting, 24 November 1917, Nutting file. By 1926 Nutting advised his customers that he burned his name into every piece he produced.

33. Appleton, "Annual Report," *Bull.* 9 (November 1918): 31; Writers' Project, *Massachusetts*, 300; Appleton to Mrs. Richard W. Meade, 20 September 1924, Meade file; Appleton to the President of the Portsmouth Historical Society, 14 September 1929, and Appleton to James Sawyer, 14 September 1929, Jackson house H&B file; Candee, *Building Portsmouth*, 33–36.

34. Appleton, "Annual Report," *Bull.* 10 (October 1919): 6; Appleton to Bush, 17 February, 21 April 1914, Lee house file; Appleton to Henry D. Sharpe, 16 April 1920, Appleton file; Appleton to Seymour, 30 April 1914, Lee house file; Appleton to Isham, 27 September 1916, Boardman file.

35. Isham, *Early Rhode Island Houses*, 89; Appleton to Millar, 6 May 1916, Millar file; Appleton to John Shaw, n.d., Boardman file. SPNEA later added electricity and some plumbing to the house (Cummings, "The 'Scotch'-Boardman House," *OTNE* 43 [January-March 1953]: 58).

36. Appleton, "Annual Report," *Bull.* 10 (October 1919): 5; Powys, *Repair*, 194–99.

37. Appleton to Mrs. Henry Tudor, 10 June 1924, Shirley-Eustis house file; Appleton, "Annual Report," *OTNE* 11 (July 1920): 22–23; Isham, "Report on the Old Brick Market or Old City Hall, Newport, Rhode Island," *Bull.* 6 (January 1916): 11. As road construction escalated years later, Appleton took on the road lobby more directly ("What Price the Beauty of New England's Landscape?" *OTNE* 35 [January 1945]: 52–54).

38. Dean, "The Restoration of Olde New England Houses," ms., n.d. [1917], Dean file.

39. Appleton to Seymour, 28 May 1914, and 2 November 1914, Seymour file; Writers' Project, *Connecticut*, 164.

40. Dean, "The Restoration of Olde New England Houses," ms., n.d. [1917], Dean file; Seymour to Appleton, 17 November 1913, and 29 May 1914, Seymour to Bush, 20 October 1914, Appleton to Seymour, 2 November 1914, Seymour file; Kelly "Restoration of Henry Whitfield House," *OTNE* 29 (January 1939): 74–89; Kelly, *Henry Whitfield House*.

41. Appleton to Heloise Meyer, 17 January 1917, Meyer file.

42. Appleton to Isham, 4 October 1917, and Isham's reply, 5 October 1917, Isham file.

43. Chandler to Appleton, 8 October 1917, Chandler file; Appleton to Mercer, 19 June 1922, Mercer file.

44. Isham to Appleton, 22 May 1918, and Appleton to Edward L. Parker, 18 December 1918, Browne house H&B file; Appleton, "Annual Report," *OTNE* 11 (July 1920): 33.

45. Appleton to Winthrop Coffin, 13 May 1919, Browne house Scrapbook; Appleton to Corse, 16 May 1919, Browne house H&B file; Appleton to Millar, 9 May, 8 October 1919, Millar file; *Points of Interest in Boston and Environs* (Boston: The Banks and Trust Companies of Boston, 1937), 85; Writers' Project, *Massachusetts*, 378; Cummings, "Summary Abstracts," in *Architecture*, ed. Cummings, 188–89; Catharine W. Pierce, "The Brownes of Watertown and the Date of the Abraham Browne House," *OTNE* 30 (October 1939): 67–72; "Evaluation Report," November 1980, Browne house Binder, Stewardship Dept.

46. Murtagh, *Keeping Time*, 78–82.

47. Appleton, "Annual Report," *OTNE* 24 (July 1933): 30–31.

48. Appleton to Mrs. C. A. Gosney, 6 July 1939, N.C. Preservation Society file; Kammen, *Mystic Chords*, 369.

49. "Holland Article on Preservation Causes Comment: Group Formed in 1910 Is Placed Ahead of A.P.V.A.," uniden. newspaper, n.d., Organizations file, APVA; Holland to Mrs. J. Taylor Ellyson, 16 November 1933, ibid.; Hosmer, *Preservation*, 551–56; Harlan D. Unrau and G. Frank Williss, "To Preserve the Nation's Past: The Growth of Historic Preservation in the National Park Service during the 1930s," *Public Historian* 9 (Spring 1987): 19–49.

50. Holland quoted in "President Roosevelt Leader in Movement to Halt Destruction of Nation's Landmarks," uniden. newspaper, n.d. [May 1933], Organizations file, APVA; Kay and Chase-Harrell, *Preserving New England*, 50; Hosmer, *Preservation*, 548–62; Hal Rothman, *Preserving Different Pasts: The American National Monuments* (Urbana: Univ. of Illinois Press, 1989).

51. Trout, *Boston*, 349; "Frank Chouteau Brown, 1876–1947," *OTNE* 38 (October 1948): 69.

8.   Presenting History Through Material Culture

1. Dow, "Notes and Gleanings," *OTNE* 12 (July 1921): 45–46; Nutting, *Biography*, 124–25.

2. Isham, "Report on the Old Brick Market or City Hall," *Bull.* 6 (January 1916): 11; Isham and Brown, *Early Rhode Island Houses*, 15; Appleton to Nutting, 25 September 1915, Nutting file; Leon and Rosenzweig, *History Museums*; Henry Glassie, "Meaningful Things and Appropriate Myths: The Artifact's Place in American Studies," in *Material Life*, ed. St. George, 63–92.

3. Dow quoted in Stillinger, *Antiquers*, 151; Dow, "Museums and Preservation," 18; Alexander, "Period Rooms," 264–67; Hosmer, *Presence*, 213–18; Dianne H. Pilgrim, "Inherited from the Past: The American Period Room," *American Art Journal* 10 (May 1978): 4–23; Farnam, "George Francis Dow," 77–90.

4. W. I. Hamilton, " 'America First' Campaign in Massachusetts," *Education* 37 (June 1917): 624; Mabel Hill and Philip Davis, *Civics for New Americans*

(Boston: Houghton Mifflin, 1915), 25; Green and Donahue, *Boston's Workers*, 67–69.

5. Dow, "Museums and Preservation," 19; Robinson to Appleton, 31 December 1914, Robinson file.

6. Erving, *Random Notes*, 45; Harvey Green, "The Ironies of Style: Complexities and Contradictions in American Decorative Arts, 1850-1900," *Nineteenth Century* 8 (1982): 17–34; Stillinger, *Antiquers*, 105–6.

7. Erving, "The Connecticut Chest," *OTNE* 12 (July 1921): 15–18; Erving, *Random Notes*, 59.

8. Ibid., 10, 25, 27, 30; Shi, *Simple Life*, 189.

9. Nutting, *Massachusetts Beautiful*, 282; Nutting, *Period Furniture*, 5–6; Dulaney, "Wallace Nutting," 47–60.

10. Appleton to Nutting, 25 September 1915, Nutting file; Nutting, *Biography*, 124–25; Nutting to Appleton, 17 July 1919, Nutting file; Appleton, "Annual Report," *OTNE* 11 (April 1921): 175.

11. "The Shirley-Eustis House Association," *Bull.* 3 (February 1913): 24; Appleton to Rev. Glenn Tillery Morse, 8 April 1921, Fowler house A&M file; Appleton, "Report," *OTNE* 32 (July 1941): 14; Coleman, *Historic House Museums*, Appendix A.

12. Appleton, Diary, 12 March 1909; Appleton, *Bull.* 1 (May 1910): 6–7; Harry Vinton Long, "Report of the Director of the Museum," *OTNE* 11 (October 1920): 85; Alexander, "Period Rooms," 270; "Museum Report," *Bull.* 10 (October 1919): 26–27; Kammen, *Mystic Chords*, 148; Harris, "The Gilded Age Revisited," 545–66.

13. "Museum Report," *Bull.* 10 (October 1919): 26; Appleton to Judge Samuel H. Fisher, 29 January 1926, SPNEA; Hosmer, *Presence*, 211; Kent, *What I Am Pleased*, 160–61; Stillinger, *Antiquers*, 162–64; Tomkins, *Merchants and Masterpieces*, 195–98.

14. Appleton, "Annual Report," *Bull.* 5 (April 1914): 20; Appleton to Warren King Moorehead, 19 May 1922, Moorehead file, SPNEA.

15. Appleton, "Annual Report," *Bull.* 5 (April 1914): 21; Appleton to Walter Prichard Eaton, 16 April 1920, Eaton file, SPNEA; Appleton to Ida Farr Miller, 3 March 1919, Miller file; Harry Vinton Long, "Report," *OTNE* 11 (October 1920): 84; Ellie Reichlin, "Picturing the Past," *Antiques* 129 (March 1986): 606–11.

16. Prouty, Address on the Possibilities of Museums, 12 March 1913, ms., Annual Meeting file, SPNEA; Charles D. Childs, "Report on the Museum," *OTNE* 27 (April 1937): 155–56.

17. Harry Vinton Long, "Report," *OTNE* 11 (October 1920): 85; Appleton to Gertrude M. Graves, 4 April 1917, Otis house H&B file, emphasis added; Appleton to Millar, 25 November 1922, Millar file.

18. Appleton to Millar, 23 December 1921, Millar file; Appleton, "Annual Report," *Bull.* 7 (May 1916): 32; Appleton to Preston Pond, 30 September 1920, Pond file; Appleton, "Annual Report," *OTNE* 11 (April 1921): 188.

19. Appleton to Millar, 23 January 1917, Millar file; Appleton to Mrs. Edward P. Hodges, 6 January 1919, Otis house H&B file; Appleton to Bolton, 30 June 1921, Bolton file.

20. Ibid.; Green, "Looking Backward," 1–16.

21. Bolton to Appleton, 20 July 1921, Bolton file; Appleton, "Annual Report," *OTNE* 15 (July 1924): 20; Appleton, "The Otis House and Proposed

Fireproof Museum," *OTNE* 17 (October 1926): 90–96; "The Loan Exhibition at the Harrison Gray Otis House," *OTNE* 22 (April 1932): 151–61; Appleton, "Annual Report," *OTNE* 32 (July 1941): 15; Marling, *George Washington*.

22. Philip Hayden, "Beauport, Gloucester, Massachusetts," *Antiques* 129 (March 1986): 622.

23. Appleton to Millar, 3 June 1918, Millar file; Appleton to Nutting, 9 August 1918, and Nutting's reply, 10 August 1918, Nutting file; Writers' Project, *New Hampshire*, 231–32. Museums from Denver and Minneapolis also raided New England homes (Downing, "Historic Preservation," 12).

24. Appleton to Kent, 16 July 1919, Kent file; Tomkins, *Merchants and Masterpieces*, 115–19, 195; Appleton, "Destruction and Preservation," 170–71; Appleton, "Annual Report," *Bull.* 10 (October 1919): 16–17.

25. Hosmer, "Broadening View," 123–24; Tomkins, *Merchants and Masterpieces*, 198–99; "Wentworth-Gardner House," in *"A Noble and Dignified Stream,"* ed. Giffen and Murphy, 213–16; Appleton to Sack, 1 October 1919, Sack file, SPNEA; Appleton, "Annual Report," *Bull.* 10 (October 1919): 16–17, *OTNE* 28 (July 1937): 24, and 28 (April 1938): 152; Kammen, *Mystic Chords*, 326; Hosmer, *Preservation*, 163.

26. "The Colonial Department" quoted in Whitehill, *Museum of Fine Arts*, 394; Aldrich, *Old Money*, 63; Jaher, *Urban Establishment*, 111; Richard Candee to author, 12 June 1992.

27. Appleton, "Annual Report," *OTNE* 11 (July 1920): 33.

28. Writers' Project, *Massachusetts*, 165; Whitehill, *Museum of Fine Arts*, 395, 423–26.

29. Appleton to Heloise Meyer, 12 September 1919, Browne house H&B file; Wendell D. Garrett, "A Century of Aspiration," in *The Arts in America: The Nineteenth Century*, ed. Garrett (New York: Charles Scribner's Sons, 1969), 33; Bolton, Note-Book, 25 April 1916, Bolton Papers.

30. Nikolaus Bolting, "The Law's Delays," in *Future of the Past*, ed. Fawcett, 19–20.

31. Appleton to Swarbrick, 6 January 1926, and his reply, 26 January 1926, AMS file; Calder Loth, ed., *The Virginia Landmarks Register* 3d ed. (Charlottesville: Univ. Press of Virginia), 359.

32. Swarbrick to Appleton, 24 February 1926, and Appleton's reply, 10 April 1926, AMS file.

33. Appleton to Swarbrick, 6 February, 4 August 1926, AMS file; quoted in "Preserving Historic Buildings Intact," *OTNE* 21 (October 1930): 85, 86; Writers' Project, *Massachusetts*, 417; Cummings, "Summary Abstracts," in *Architecture*, ed. Cummings, 150.

34. Morris quoted in Pevsner, "Scrape and Anti-Scrape," in *Future of the Past*, ed. Fawcett, 50; Horne, *Great Museum*; Douglas A. Allan, "Folk Museums at Home and Abroad," *Proceedings of the Scottish Anthropological and Folklore Society* 5 (1956): 93–100.

35. Mary Bronson Hartt, "The Skansen Idea," *The Century* 83 (April 1912): 916–20; Rydell, *All the World's a Fair*.

36. Appleton to Seymour, 2 November 1914, Seymour file; Isham, *In Praise of Antiquaries*, 21; Sandvig quoted in Appleton, "Destruction and Preservation," 177.

37. Appleton, "An Outdoor Museum," *Bull.* 10 (October 1919): 24; Appleton, "Notes," *Bull.* 4 (August 1913): 31–32; D. W. Meinig, "The Beholding Eye:

Ten Versions of the Same Scene," in *Interpretation*, ed. Meinig, 33–48; David Lowenthal, "Age and Artifact," in ibid., 103–28; Horne, *Great Museum*, 29–30, 57.

38. Wood, "Village and Community," 333–46; Wood and Steinitz, "A World We Have Gained," 105–20; Wood, "Three Faces," 3–14; Wood, "New England Village," 54–63; Wood, " 'Build Your Own World,' " 32–50; Bowden, "Invention of American Tradition," 3–26; Steinitz, "Rethinking," 26.

39. Ford quoted in Greenleaf, *From These Beginnings*, 88, 96; Appleton, "Annual Report," *OTNE* 12 (April 1922): 175–76, and 15 (July 1924): 26-28; Lucia Ames Mead, "How the Wayside Inn Came Back," *OTNE* 22 (July 1931): 44; Henry Ford to Bolton, n.d. [1924], Bolton Family Papers III-32, AAS; Robin Winks, "Conservation in America: National Character as Revealed by Preservation," in *Future of the Past*, ed. Fawcett, 142.

40. Samuel Crowther, "Henry Ford: Why I Bought Wayside Inn," *Country Life* 47 (April 1925): 45; Greenleaf, *From These Beginnings*, 105–7.

41. Cornelius Vanderbilt, Jr., *The Living Past of America* (New York: Crown Publishers, 1955), 157–61; Lowenthal, *Past Is a Foreign Country*, 285, 328n.

42. Robert A. M. Stern, *Pride of Place: Building the American Dream* (Boston: Houghton Mifflin, 1986), 22–28.

43. Appleton to Swarbrick, 20 February, 4 August 1926, AMS file; L. M. Angus-Butterworth, "The Early History of the Ancient Monuments Society," (offprint without attribution), 70; Allan, "Folk Museums," 102.

44. Dow, "Notes and Gleanings," *OTNE* 21 (October 1930): 93.

45. Ibid.; Dow, *Domestic Life*, i, 22–23.

46. Dow, "Notes and Gleanings," *OTNE* 21 (October 1930): 93; Allan, "Folk Museums," 102–11.

47. Appleton to Nathaniel Perkins, 14 December 1926, Perkins file; Hosmer, *Preservation*, 167–68; Dow, "The Colonial Village Built at Salem, Massachusetts, in the Spring of 1930," *OTNE* 22 (July 1931): 2–14.

48. Ibid.; Coolidge, 16 October 1930, in *Calvin Coolidge Says* (Plymouth, VT; Coolidge Memorial Foundation, 1972); Writers' Project, *Massachusetts*, 352; Massachusetts Bay Tercentenary, *Guide to Salem, 1630* (Salem: Park Commissioners, 1930).

49. [A. B. Wells,] *Old Quinabaug Village* (Sturbridge, Mass., 1941), 2–4; Penny Holewa, Old Sturbridge Village, to author, 15 June 1993; Writers' Project, *Massachusetts*, 475; Richard Sorrell, "Franco-Americans in New England," *Journal of Ethnic Studies* 5 (Spring 1977): 90–94.

50. Appleton, "Report," *OTNE* 28 (July 1937): 30, and 38 (October 1947): 50.

Epilogue

1. Stilgoe, *Borderland*; Binford, *First Suburbs*; Wood, " 'Build Your Own World,' " 32–50.

2. Cummings, "Charles Bulfinch and Boston's Vanishing West End," *OTNE* 52 (October-December 1961): 31–32; Campbell, *Cityscapes*, 13. Herbert J. Gans concluded that "the West End was not really a slum," but was demolished because the community "constituted a distinct and independent working-class subculture that bore little resemblance to the middle class" (Gans, *The Urban Villagers:*

Group and Class in the Life of Italian-Americans [New York: Free Press of Glencoe, 1962], x).

3. Trout, *Boston*, 14–15; Kennedy, *Planning the City*, 137; Jacobs, *Death and Life*, 9.

4. Holleran, " 'Changeful Times,' " 323; Mass. Hist. Comm., *Cultural Resources*, 46–47.

5. Sidney R. Bland, " 'Miss Sue' of Charleston: Saving a Neighborhood, Influencing a Nation," in *Architecture*, ed. Berkeley, 63–73.

6. See Robert R. Garvey, Jr., "Europe Protects Its Monuments," in United States Conference of Mayors, *With Heritage So Rich* (1966; rept., Washington, D.C.: Preservation Press, 1983), 178–80.

7. Robert Hewison, *The Heritage Industry: Britain in a Climate of Decline* (London: Meuthen, 1987); Umberto Eco, *Travels in Hyperreality* (New York and London: Harcourt Brace Jovanovich, 1986), 3–58.

8. Curley, "Valedictory Address," in *Boston*, ed. Lankevich, 126; Appleton, Diary, 4 November 1936.

9. Abbott Lowell Cummings, "Evaluation Report," 11 March 1981, C-F-A house Binder, Stewardship Dept.; Cummings, "Evaluation Report," November 1980, Browne house Binder, ibid. For a counter proposal, see Mark P. Leone and Barbara J. Little, "Artifacts as Expressions of Society and Culture: Subversive Genealogy and the Value of History," in *History from Things: Essays on Material Culture*, ed. Steven Lubar and W. David Kingery (Washington and London: Smithsonian Inst. Press, 1993), 178–79.

10. Jane C. Nylander quoted in Gillette, "Appleton's Legacy," 37; Kay and Chase-Harrell, *Preserving New England*, 111–19; Downing, "Historic Preservation," 16–27.

11. Stone to Appleton, 26 April 1910, Appleton Scrapbook; Hosmer, *Presence*, 240; McCarthy, *Women's Culture*, 111–45; William J. Murtagh, "Professionalism," in *Preservation: Toward an Ethic in the 1980s* (Washington, D.C.: Preservation Press, 1980), 154–57.

12. Murphy, "The Politics of Preservation," in *"A Noble and Dignified Stream,"* ed. Giffen and Murphy, 193–204; West, "Historic House Museum Movement."

13. Franck, "A Feminist Approach," in *Architecture*, ed. Berkeley, 201–16; Michael Grossberg, "Institutionalizing Masculinity: The Law as a Masculine Profession," in *Meanings for Manhood*, ed. Carnes, 133–51; Carroll Van West and Mary Hoffschwelle, " 'Slumbering on Its Old Foundations': Interpretation at Colonial Williamsburg," *South Atlantic Quarterly* 83 (Spring 1984): 157–75; Wallace, "Reflections," in *Presenting the Past*, ed. Benson, 165–99.

14. "Reclaiming Women's History Through Historic Preservation: The First National Conference" was held in Bryn Mawr, PA, in June 1994. See also Dubrow, "Preserving Her Heritage," Chap. 5: "Claiming Public Space for Women's History in the City: A Proposal for Preservation, Public Art, and Public Historical Interpretation in Boston."

15. Edward A. Chappell, "Social Responsibility and the American History Museum," *WP* 24 (Winter 1989): 247–65; Robert Paynter, "Afro-Americans in the Massachusetts Historical Landscape," in *Politics of the Past*, ed. Gathercole and Lowenthal, 49–62; Antoinette J. Lee, "Discovering Old Cultures in the New World: The Role of Ethnicity," in *American Mosaic*, ed. Stipe and Lee, 180–205.

16. Appleton, "Annual Report," *OTNE* 29 (April 1939): 144; Green, "Pop-

ular Science," 21; Marsh, "Suburban Men," in *Meanings for Manhood*, ed. Carnes, 111–27. "Victoria Mansion" became a museum owned by a women's society.

17. See, for example, Peter Benes, ed., *Early American Probate Inventories*, Vol. XII in The Dublin Seminar for New England Folklife (Boston: Boston Univ., 1987).

18. Steinitz, "Rethinking," 16–26.

19. Bowden, "Invented Tradition and Academic Convention," 189, and "Culture and Place," fig. 18, 20; Cummings, "Study Houses," 613; Garvan, *Architecture*, 7; Richard M. Candee, "A Documentary History of Plymouth Colony Architecture, 1620–1700," *OTNE* 59 (January-March 1969): 59; Mass. Hist. Comm., *Cultural Resources*.

20. Kelly, *Connecticut's Old Houses*, 8–10, and *Early Domestic Architecture*, 2; Chandler, *Colonial House*, 1; Garvan, *Architecture*, 103–4. Cummings found records for 144 framed houses erected before 1725 in Massachusetts. Well over half had been one-room or a half-house plan, and all but a handful were later enlarged. Even after the hall-parlor plan had been established, and well into the eighteenth century, New Englanders continued to build one-room houses (Cummings, *Framed Houses*, 23–24).

21. Cummings, "Study Houses," 612. What is also missing are "upland" houses with their low, linear plan (St. George, " 'Set Thine House in Order,' " in *New England Begins*, ed. Fairbanks and Trent, II: 166–67).

22. Cummings, "Study House," 614–15.

23. Cummings, *Framed Houses*, 204; Cummings, "Scotch-Boardman House," *OTNE* 43 (Winter & Spring 1953): 57–73, 91–102; Beverley Da Costa, *Historic Houses of America* (New York: American Heritage, 1971), 132.

24. Alice G. B. Lockwood, "Problems and Responsibilities of Restoration," *OTNE* 28 (October 1937): 49; Fitch, *Historic Preservation*, 84.

25. Ada Louise Huxtable, *Will They Ever Finish Bruckner Boulevard?* (New York: Collier Books, 1970), 210–60; Mike Wallace, "Mickey Mouse History: Portraying the Past at Disney World," *Radical History Review* 32 (1985): 33–57; Wallace, "The Politics of Public History," in *Past Meets Present: Essays about Historic Interpretation and Public Audiences*, ed. Jo Blatti (Washington, D.C.: Smithsonian Inst. Press, 1987), 37–53.

26. Huxtable, "The Future Grows Old," in *Goodbye History, Hello Hamburger* (Washington, D.C.: Preservation Press, 1986), 165.

27. Mass. Hist. Comm., *Cultural Resources*, 53; "Recommendation for De-Accessioning Samuel Fowler House," n.d., Stewardship Dept.

28. Nylander quoted in Gillette, "Appleton's Legacy," 37.

29. Appleton, "Report," *OTNE* 29 (April 1939): 153; St. George, " 'Set Thine House in Order,' " in *New England Begins*, ed. Fairbanks and Trent, II: 168, 186.

SELECT BIBLIOGRAPHY

Abrams, Richard M. *Conservatism in a Progressive Era: Massachusetts Politics, 1900–1912*. Cambridge: Harvard Univ. Press, 1964.

Aldrich, Nelson W., Jr. *Old Money: The Mythology of America's Upper Class*. New York: Alfred A. Knopf, 1988.

Edward P. Alexander. "Artistic and Historical Period Rooms." *Curator* 7 (1964): 263–81.

———. "Sixty Years of Historic Preservation: The Society for the Preservation of New England Antiquities." *Old-Time New England* 61 (1970-71): 14–19.

Allen, David Grayson. *In English Ways: The Movement of Societies and the Transferal of English Local Law and Custom to Massachusetts Bay in the Seventeenth Century*. Chapel Hill: Univ. of North Carolina Press, 1981.

Appleton, William Sumner. "Destruction and Preservation of Old Buildings in New England." *Art and Archaeology* 8 (May-June 1919): 131–83.

Ashbee, C[harles] R. *A Report to the Council of the National Trust for Places of Historic Interest and Natural Beauty, on His Visit to the United States on the Council's Behalf*. London: Essex House Press, 1901.

Axelrod, Alan, ed. *The Colonial Revival in America*. New York and London: W. W. Norton, 1985.

Baltzell, E. Digby. *The Protestant Establishment: Aristocracy & Caste in America*. New York: Random House, 1964.

———. *Puritan Boston and Quaker Philadelphia: Two Protestant Ethics and the Spirit of Class Authority and Leadership*. Boston: Beacon Press, 1979.

Baritz, Loren. *The Good Life: The Meaning of Success for the American Middle Class*. New York: Alfred A. Knopf, 1989.

Barton, Cynthia H. *History's Daughter: The Life of Clara Endicott Sears, Founder of the Fruitlands Museums*. Harvard, Mass.: Fruitlands Museums, 1988.

Beatty, Jack. *The Rascal King: The Life and Times of James Michael Curley, 1874–1958*. New York: Addison-Wesley, 1992.

Beebe, Lucius. *Boston and the Boston Legend*. New York and London: D. Appleton-Century, 1935.

Bellah, Robert N. *The Broken Covenant: American Civil Religion in Time of Trial*. New York: Seabury Press, 1975.

Bender, Thomas. *Toward an Urban Vision: Ideas and Institutions in Nineteenth Century America*. Baltimore and London: Johns Hopkins Univ. Press, 1975.

Benes, Peter, ed. *House and Home*. Vol. XIII in The Dublin Seminar for New England Folklife. Boston: Boston Univ., 1988.

Berkeley, Ellen Perry, ed. *Architecture: A Place for Women*. Washington and London: Smithsonian Inst. Press, 1989.

Binford, Henry C. *The First Suburbs: Residential Communities on the Boston Periphery, 1815–1860*. Chicago and London: Univ. of Chicago Press, 1985.

Bledstein, Burton J. *The Culture of Professionalism: The Middle Class and the Development of Higher Education in America.* New York and London: W. W. Norton, 1976.

Blodgett, Geoffrey. *The Gentle Reformers: Massachusetts Democrats in the Cleveland Era.* Cambridge: Harvard Univ. Press, 1966.

————. "The Mugwump Reputation, 1870 to the Present." *Journal of American History* 66 (March 1980): 867–87.

Bodnar, John E. *Remaking America: Public Memory, Commemoration, and Patriotism in the Twentieth Century.* Princeton: Princeton Univ. Press, 1992.

Bolton, Charles Knowles. *Brookline: The History of a Favored Town.* Brookline: C. A. W. Spencer, 1897.

————. *Christ Church, 1723.* Boston: Christ Church, 1913.

————. *Portraits of the Founders.* Boston: Athenaeum, 1919.

————. *The Private Soldier under Washington.* New York: Charles Scribner, 1902.

————. *The Real Founders of New England: Stories of Their Life Along the Coast, 1602–1628.* New York: F. W. Faxon, 1929.

————. *Scotch Irish Pioneers in Ulster and America.* Boston: Bacon and Brown, 1910.

————. "What the Small Town May Do for Itself." *New England Magazine* (March 1896): 94–96.

Boris, Eileen. *Art and Labor: Ruskin, Morris, and the Craftsman Ideal in America.* Philadelphia: Temple Univ. Press, 1986.

Boston Committee on Americanism. *A Little Book for Immigrants in Boston.* Boston: City Printing Department, 1921.

Boston Museum of Fine Arts. *Back Bay Boston: The City as a Work of Art.* Boston: Museum of Fine Arts, 1969.

"Boston-1915." *What Boston-1915 Is.* Boston: Chapple Press, 1910.

Boston Society of Architects. *Report Made to the Boston Society of Architects by Its Committee on Municipal Improvements.* Boston, 1907.

Boyer, Paul. *Urban Masses and Moral Order in America, 1820–1920.* Cambridge, Mass.: Harvard Univ. Press, 1978.

Bowden, Martyn J. "The Invention of American Tradition." *Journal of Historical Geography* 18 (January 1992): 3–26.

————. "Culture and Place: English Sub-Cultural Regions in New England in the Seventeenth Century." *Connecticut History* 35 (Spring 1994): 68–146.

Bronner, Simon J., ed. *Consuming Visions: Accumulation and Display of Goods in America, 1880–1920.* New York and London: W. W. Norton, 1989.

Buell, Lawrence. *New England Literary Culture: From Revolution Through Renaissance.* Cambridge and New York: Cambridge Univ. Press, 1986.

Bunting, Bainbridge, and Nylander, Robert H. *Survey of Architectural History in Cambridge: Old Cambridge.* Cambridge, Mass.: Cambridge Historical Commission, 1973.

Bush, Celeste E. *The Old Lee House, East Lyme, Connecticut.* East Lyme: East Lyme Historical Society, 1917.

Bushee, Frederick A. *Ethnic Factors in the Population of Boston.* 1903. Reprint. New York: Arno Press, 1970.

Campbell, Robert. *Cityscapes of Boston: An American City through Time.* Boston and London: Houghton Mifflin, 1992.

Candee, Richard M. *Building Portsmouth: The Neighborhoods & Architecture of New Hampshire's Oldest City.* Portsmouth: Portsmouth Associates, 1992.

Carnes, Mark C., and Griffen, Clyde, eds. *Meanings for Manhood: Constructions of Masculinity in Victorian America.* Chicago and London: Univ. of Chicago Press, 1990.

Carter, Thomas, and Herman, Bernard L., eds. *Perspectives in Vernacular Architecture, III.* Columbia: Univ. of Missouri Press, 1989.

Chamberlain, Allen. *Beacon Hill: Its Ancient Pastures and Early Mansions.* Boston: Houghton Mifflin, 1925.

Chandler, Joseph Everett. *An Architectural Monograph on Colonial Cottages.* New York: White Pine Series, 1915.

———. *The Colonial House.* rev. ed. New York: Robert A. McBride, 1924.

———. "Notes on the Paul Revere House." *Walpole Society Note Book* (1944).

Cheape, Charles W. *Moving the Masses: Urban Public Transit in New York, Boston, and Philadelphia, 1880–1912.* Cambridge and London: Harvard Univ. Press, 1980.

"Civic Conference," *What Boston-1915 Is.* Boston, 1910.

Clark, Clifford Edward, Jr. *The American Family Home, 1800–1960.* Chapel Hill and London: Univ. of North Carolina Press, 1986.

Coleman, Laurence Vail. *Historic House Museums.* Washington, D.C.: American Association of Museums, 1933.

Cram, Ralph Adams. "Architecture." In *Fifty Years of Boston: A Memorial Volume.* Compiled by the Subcommittee on Memorial History of the Boston Tercentenary Committee. Boston: n.p., 1932.

———. *Convictions and Controversies.* 1935. Reprint. Freeport, N.Y.: Books for Libraries Press, 1970.

———. *The Ministry of Art.* 1914. Reprint. Freeport, N.Y.: Books for Libraries Press, 1967.

———. *My Life in Architecture.* Boston: Little, Brown, 1936.

———. *The Nemesis of Mediocrity.* Boston: Marshall Jones, 1917.

Crunden, Robert M. *Ministers of Reform: The Progressives' Achievement in American Civilization, 1889–1920.* New York: Basic Books, 1982.

Cummings, Abbott Lowell, ed. *Architecture in Colonial Massachusetts: A Conference Held by the Colonial Society of Massachusetts, September 19 and 20, 1974.* Boston: Colonial Society of Massachusetts, 1979.

———. *The Framed Houses of Massachusetts Bay, 1625–1725.* Cambridge, Mass. and London: Harvard Univ. Press, 1979.

———. "The Study Houses," *Antiques* 129 (March 1986): 612–17.

Curley, James Michael. *I'd Do It Again: A Record of All My Uproarious Years.* Englewood Cliffs, N.J.: Prentice-Hall, 1957.

Cutler, John Henry. *"Honey Fitz": Three Steps to the White House; the Life and Times of John F. ("Honey Fitz") Fitzgerald.* Indianapolis: Bobbs-Merrill, 1962.

Deetz, James. *In Small Things Forgotten: The Archaeology of Early American Life.* Garden City, N.Y.: Anchor Press, 1977.

———. "A Sense of Another World: History Museums and Cultural Change." *Museum News* 58 (May / June 1980): 40–45.

DeMarco, William M. *Ethnics and Enclaves: Boston's Italian North End.* Ann Arbor, Mich.: UMI Research Press, 1981.

Dow, George Francis. *Arts and Crafts in New England, 1704–1775*. Topsfield, Mass.: Wayside Press, 1927.

———. *Domestic Life in New England in the Seventeenth Century*. Topsfield, Mass.: Perkins Press, 1925.

———. *Every Day Life in the Massachusetts Bay Colony*. Boston: Society for the Preservation of New England Antiquities, 1935.

———. "Museums and the Preservation of Early Houses." *Bulletin of the Metropolitan Museum of Art* 17 (November 1922): 16–20.

———. "The Work of the Society for the Preservation of New England Antiquities." *The House Beautiful* 58 (November 1925): 556–62.

Downing, Antoinette F. "Historic Preservation in Rhode Island." *Rhode Island History* 35 (February 1976): 3–28.

Drake, Samuel Adams. *Old Landmarks and Historic Personages of Boston*. New & rev. ed. 1900. Reprint. Detroit: Singing Tree Press, 1970.

———. *Our Colonial Homes*. Boston: Lee and Shepard, 1893.

Dubrow, Gail Lee. "Preserving Her Heritage: American Landmarks of Women's History." Ph.D. thesis, Univ. of California at Los Angeles, 1991.

Dulaney, William L. "Wallace Nutting: Collector and Entrepreneur." *Winterthur Portfolio* 13 (1979): 47–60.

Eaton, Allen H. *Handicrafts of New England*. New York: Harper & Brothers, 1949.

Emmerton, Caroline. *The Chronicles of Three Old Houses*. Boston: Thomas Todd, 1935.

Erving, Henry Wood. *Random Notes on Colonial Furniture*. Hartford, Conn.: privately pub., 1931.

Fairbanks, Jonathan L., and Trent, Robert F., eds. *New England Begins: The Seventeenth Century*. 3 vol. Boston: Museum of Fine Arts, 1982.

Farnam, Anne. "George Francis Dow: A Career of Bringing the 'picturesque traditions of sleeping generations' to Life in the Early Twentieth Century." *Essex Institute Historical Collections* 121 (April 1985): 77–90.

Farrell, Betty G. *Elite Families: Class and Power in Nineteenth-Century Boston*. Albany: SUNY Press, 1993.

Fass, Paula S. *The Damned and the Beautiful: American Youth in the 1920's*. New York and Oxford: Oxford Univ. Press, 1977.

Fawcett, Jane, ed. *The Future of the Past: Attitudes to Conservation, 1174–1974*. New York: Watson-Guptill, 1976.

Federal Writers' Project. *Connecticut: A Guide to Its Roads, Lore, and People*. Boston: Houghton Mifflin, 1938.

———. *Massachusetts: A Guide to Its Places and People*. Boston: Houghton Mifflin, 1937.

———. *New Hampshire: A Guide to the Granite State*. Boston: Houghton Mifflin, 1938.

———. *Rhode Island: A Guide to the Smallest State*. Boston: Houghton Mifflin, 1937.

Firey, Walter I. *Land Use in Central Boston*. Cambridge: Harvard Univ. Press, 1947.

Fitch, James Marston. *Historic Preservation: Curatorial Management of the Built World*. Charlottesville and London: Univ. Press of Virginia, 1990.

Flower, B[enjamin] O. *Civilization's Inferno; or Studies in the Social Cellar*. Boston: Arena Publishing, 1893.

Follett, Jean A. "Norman Isham & Scientific Restoration in the Early Twentieth Century." In *The Role of the Architect in Historic Preservation: Past, Present, and Future*. Washington, D.C.: American Institute of Architects, 1990.

Formisano, Ronald P., and Burns, Constance K., eds. *Boston 1700–1980: The Evolution of Urban Politics*. Westport, Conn. and London: Greenwood Press, 1984.

French, George, ed. *New England: What It Is and What It Is to Be*. Boston: Chamber of Commerce, 1911.

Garvan, Anthony N. B. *Architecture and Town Planning in Colonial Connecticut*. New Haven: Yale Univ. Press, 1951.

Gathercole, Peter, and Lowenthal, David, eds. *The Politics of the Past*. London and Boston: Unwin Hyman, 1990.

Geertz, Clifford. *The Interpretation of Cultures: Selected Essays*. New York: Basic Books, 1973.

Giffen, Sarah L., and Murphy, Kevin D., eds. *"A Noble and Dignified Stream": The Piscataqua Region in the Colonial Revival, 1860–1930*. York, ME: Old York Historical Society, 1992.

Gillette, Jane Brown. "Appleton's Legacy." *Historic Preservation* 46 (July / August 1994): 32–39 ff.

Glassberg, David. *American Historical Pageantry: The Uses of Tradition in the Early Twentieth Century*. Chapel Hill: Univ. of North Carolina Press, 1990.

Gowans, Alan. *Images of American Living: Four Centuries of Architecture and Furniture as Cultural Expression*. New York and London: Harper & Row, 1964.

Green, Harvey. *Fit for America: Health, Fitness, Sport and American Society*. Baltimore and London: Johns Hopkins Univ. Press, 1986.

———. "Looking Backward to the Future: The Colonial Revival and American Culture." In *Creating a Dignified Past: Museums and the Colonial Revival*. Edited by Geoffrey L. Rossano. Totowa, N.J.: Rowman & Littlefield, 1991.

———. "Popular Science and Political Thought Converge: Colonial Survival Becomes Colonial Revival, 1830–1910." *Journal of American Culture* 6 (Winter 1983): 3–24.

Green, James R., and Donahue, Hugh Carter. *Boston's Workers: A Labor History*. Boston: Boston Public Library, 1979.

Green, Theodore. *America's Heroes: The Changing Models of Success in American Magazines*. New York: Oxford Univ. Press, 1970.

Greenleaf, William. *From These Beginnings: The Early Philanthropies of Henry and Edsel Ford, 1911–1936*. Detroit: Wayne State Univ. Press, 1964.

Hall, Peter Dobkin. *Inventing the Nonprofit Sector and Other Essay on Philanthropy, Voluntarism, and Nonprofit Organizations*. Baltimore and London: Johns Hopkins Univ. Press, 1992.

Hardy, Stephen H. " 'Parks for the People': Reforming the Boston Park System, 1870–1915." *Journal of Sport History* 7 (Winter 1980): 5–24.

Harris, Neil. "The Gilded Age Revisited: Boston and the Museum Movement." *American Quarterly* 14 (Winter 1962): 545–66.

Hartmann, Edward G. *The Movement to Americanize the Immigrant*. New York: Columbia Univ. Press, 1948.

Hartt, Mary B. "The Skansen Idea." *The Century* 83 (April 1912): 916–20.

Hawkes, Nathaniel Mortimer. *Hearths and Homes of Old Lynn*. Lynn, Mass.: Thos. P. Nichols & Sons, 1907.

Hewison, Robert. *The Heritage Industry: Britain in a Climate of Decline*. London: Meuthen, 1987.

Higham, John. *Strangers in the Land: Patterns of American Nativism, 1860–1925*. New York: Atheneum, 1963.

Hobsbawm, Eric, and Ranger, Terence, eds. *The Invention of Tradition*. Cambridge: Cambridge Univ. Press, 1983.

Holleran, Michael. " 'Changeful Times': Preservation, Planning, and Permanence in the Urban Environment, Boston, 1870–1930." Ph.D. thesis, Massachusetts Institute of Technology, 1991.

Horne, Donald. *The Great Museum: The Re-Presentation of History*. London and Sydney: Pluto Press, 1984.

Hosmer, Charles B., Jr. "The Broadening View of the Historical Preservation Movement." In *Material Culture and the Study of American Life*. Edited by Ian M. G. Quimby. New York and London: W. W. Norton, 1978.

———. "George Francis Dow." In *Keepers of the Past*. Edited by Clifford L. Lord. Chapel Hill: Univ. of North Carolina Press, 1965.

———. *Presence of the Past: A History of the Preservation Movement in the United States before Williamsburg*. New York: G. P. Putnam's Sons, 1965.

———. *Preservation Comes of Age: From Williamsburg to the National Trust, 1926–1949*. Charlottesville: Univ. Press of Virginia, 1981.

Howe, Barbara J. "Women in Historic Preservation: The Legacy of Ann Pamela Cunningham." *The Public Historian* 12 (Winter 1990): 31–61.

Isham, Norman M., and Brown, Albert F. *Early Connecticut Houses: An Historical and Architectural Study*. 1900. Reprint. New York: Dover Publications, 1965.

———. *Early Rhode Island Houses: An Historical and Architectural Study*. Providence: Preston & Rounds, 1895.

Isham, Norman M. *A Glossary of Colonial Architectural Terms*. Boston: Walpole Society, 1939.

———. *In Praise of Antiquaries*. Boston: Walpole Society, 1931.

Jackson, Kenneth T. *Crabgrass Frontier: The Suburbanization of the United States*. New York and Oxford: Oxford Univ. Press, 1985.

Jaher, Frederic Cople. "Businessman and Gentleman: Nathan and Thomas Gold Appleton—An Exploration in Intergenerational History." *Explorations in Entrepreneurial History* 4 (Fall 1966): 17–39.

———. *The Urban Establishment: Upper Strata in Boston, New York, Charleston, Chicago, and Los Angeles*. Urbana: Univ. of Illinois Press, 1982.

James, Henry. *The American Scene*. Edited by W. H. Auden. New York: Charles Scribner's Sons, 1946.

Kammen, Michael. *Mystic Chords of Memory: The Transformation of Tradition in American Culture*. New York: Alfred A. Knopf, 1991.

———. *Selvages & Biases: The Fabric of History in American Culture*. Ithaca and London: Cornell Univ. Press, 1987.

Kay, Jane Holtz. *Lost Boston*. Boston: Houghton Mifflin, 1980.

———, and Chase-Harrell, Pauline. *Preserving New England*. New York: Pantheon Books, 1986.

Kellogg, Paul U. "Boston's Level Best: The '1915' Movement and the Work of Civic Organizing for Which It Stands." *Survey* 22 (5 June 1909): 382–96.

Kelly, J. Frederick. *Connecticut's Old Houses: A Handbook and Guide*. 1935. Reprint. Stonington: Pequot Press, 1963.

———. *Early Domestic Architecture of Connecticut*. 1924. Reprint. New York: Dover Publications, 1952.

———. *The Whitfield House 1639: The Journal of the Restoration of the Old Stone House, Guilford*. Edited by Evangeline Walker Andrews. Guilford, Conn.: Henry Whitfield State Historical Museum, 1939.

Kennedy, Albert J., and Woods, Robert A. *The Zone of Emergence*. Abridged and edited by Sam Bass Warner, Jr. Cambridge: Harvard Univ. Press, 1962.

Kennedy, Lawrence W. *Planning the City upon a Hill: Boston since 1630*. Amherst: Univ. of Massachusetts Press, 1992.

Kent, Henry Watson. *What I Am Pleased to Call My Education*. Edited by Lois Leighton Comings. New York: Grolier Club, 1949.

Kloppenberg, James T. *Uncertain Victory: Social Democracy and Progressivism in European and American Thought*. New York and Oxford: Oxford Univ. Press, 1986.

Krieger, Alex, and Green, Lisa J. *Past Futures: Two Centuries of Imagining Boston*. Cambridge: Harvard Univ. Press, 1985.

Lankevich, George J., ed. *Boston: A Chronological & Documentary History, 1602–1970*. Dobbs Ferry, N.Y.: Oceana Publications, 1974.

Lears, T. J. Jackson. *No Place of Grace: Antimodernism and the Transformation of American Culture, 1880–1920*. New York: Pantheon Books, 1981.

Leon, Warren, and Rosenzweig, Roy, eds. *History Museums in the United States: A Critical Assessment*. Urbana: Univ. of Illinois Press, 1989.

Levine, Lawrence W. *Highbrow / Lowbrow: The Emergence of Cultural Hierarchy in America*. Cambridge, Mass. and London: Harvard Univ. Press, 1988.

Lindgren, James M. " 'A Constant Incentive to Patriotic Citizenship': Historic Preservation in Progressive-Era Massachusetts." *New England Quarterly* 64 (December 1991): 594–608.

———. " 'For the Sake of Our Future': The Association for the Preservation of Virginia Antiquities and the Regeneration of Traditionalism." *Virginia Magazine of History and Biography* 97 (January 1989): 47–74.

———. "From Personalism to Professionalism to Feminism: Reconstructing Female Identities in the Preservation Movement." *APVA Newsletter* 13 (Summer 1994): 7–11.

———. "*Pater Patriae*: George Washington as Symbol and Artifact." *American Quarterly* 41 (December 1989): 705–13.

———. *Preserving the Old Dominion: Historic Preservation and Virginia Traditionalism*. Charlottesville and London: Univ. Press of Virginia, 1993.

———. " 'Virginia Needs Living Heroes': Historic Preservation in the Progressive Era." *The Public Historian* 13 (Winter 1991): 9–24.

———. " 'Whatever Is Un-Virginian Is Wrong': The APVA's Sense of the Old Dominion." *Virginia Cavalcade* 38 (Winter 1989): 112–123.

Linenthal, Edward T. *Sacred Ground: Americans and Their Battlefields*. Urbana: Univ. of Illinois Press, 1991.

Little, Bertram K. "William Sumner Appleton." In *Keepers of the Past*. Edited by Clifford L. Lord. Chapel Hill: Univ. of North Carolina Press, 1965.

Lowenthal, David. *The Past Is a Foreign Country*. Cambridge and New York: Cambridge Univ. Press, 1985.

Lyndon, Donlyn. *The City Observed, Boston: A Guide to the Architecture of the Hub*. New York: Vintage Books, 1982.

Mann, Arthur. *Yankee Reformers in the Urban Age: Social Reform in Boston, 1880–1900*. New York: Harper & Row, 1954.

Marc, Olivier. *Psychology of the House*. London: Thames and Hudson, 1977.

Marling, Karal Ann. *George Washington Slept Here: Colonial Revivals and American Culture, 1876–1986*. Cambridge and London: Harvard Univ. Press, 1988.

Massachusetts Bay Colony Tercentenary Commission. *Pathways of the Puritans*. Framingham, Mass.: Old America, 1930.

Massachusetts Constitutional Convention. *Debates in the Massachusetts Constitutional Convention, 1917–1918*. Boston: Wright & Potter, 1920.

Massachusetts General Court. *Report of Hearings before the Committee on Cities, March 8, 1907 on the Bill, Senate 189, to Preserve the Old State House as an Historic and Patriotic Memorial, and to Prohibit Its Use for Any Other Purpose*. Boston: Rockwell & Churchill Press, 1907.

Massachusetts Historical Commission. *Cultural Resources in Massachusetts: A Model for Management*. Preservation Planning Series. Washington, D.C.: Government Printing Office, 1980.

McCarthy, Kathleen D. *Women's Culture: American Philanthropy and Art, 1830–1930*. Chicago and London: Univ. of Chicago Press, 1991.

McCormick, Richard L. "Public Life in Industrial America, 1877–1917." In *The New American History*. Edited by Eric Foner. Philadelphia: Temple Univ. Press, 1990.

Meinig, D. W., ed. *The Interpretation of Ordinary Landscapes*. New York and Oxford: Oxford Univ. Press, 1979.

Millar, Donald. *Colonial Furniture, Measured Drawings*. New York: Architectural Book Publishing, 1925.

———. *Measured Drawings of Some Colonial and Georgian Houses*. New York: Architectural Book Publishing, 1916.

———. "A Seventeenth Century New England House." *Architectural Record* 38 (September 1915): 349–61.

Miller, Page Putnam, ed. *Reclaiming the Past: Landmarks of Women's History*. Bloomington and Indianapolis: Indiana Univ. Press, 1992.

Morison, Samuel Eliot, ed. *The Development of Harvard University: Since the Inauguration of President Eliot, 1869-1929*. Cambridge: Harvard Univ. Press, 1930.

———. *The Intellectual Life of Colonial New England*. 2d ed. Ithaca: Cornell Univ. Press, 1956.

———. *One Boy's Boston, 1887–1901*. Boston: Houghton Mifflin, 1962.

Mumford, Lewis. *The Culture of Cities*. New York: Harcourt, Brace, 1938.

———. *Sticks and Stones*. 2d rev. ed. New York: Dover Publications, 1955.

Murtagh, William J. *Keeping Time: The History and Theory of Preservation in America*. Pittstown, N.J.: Main Street Press, 1988.

Noble, Allen G. *Wood, Brick, and Stone: The North American Settlement Landscape*. 2 vols. Amherst, Mass.: Univ. of Massachusetts Press, 1984.

Norton, Charles Eliot. "Address." In *Commemorative Exercises of the First Parish Church*. Hingham, Mass.: First Parish Church, 1881.

———. "Intellectual Life of America." *New Princeton Review* 6 (November 1888): 312–24.

———. "It's Dogged as Does It." *Handicraft* 1 (December 1902): 225–26.

————. "The Lack of Old Homes in America." *Scribner's Magazine* 5 (May 1889): 636–40.

————. "Reminiscences of Old Cambridge." *Cambridge Historical Society* (1905): 11–23.

————. "Some Aspects of Civilization in America." *Forum* 20 (February 1896): 641–51.

————. "Waste." *Nation* (8 March 1866): 302–3.

————. "The Work of the American Institute of Archaeology." *American Journal of Archaeology* 4 (January-March 1900): 1–16.

Nutting, Wallace. *Massachusetts Beautiful*. Framingham, Mass.: Old America, 1923.

————. *Period Furniture*. Framingham, Mass.: [Old America], [1926].

[Nutting, Wallace]. *Wallace Nutting's Biography*. Framingham, Mass.: Old America, 1936.

Nylander, Jane C. *Our Own Snug Fireside: Images of the New England Home, 1760–1860*. New York: Alfred A. Knopf, 1993.

O'Neill, William L. *The Progressive Years: America Comes of Age*. New York: Harper & Row, 1975.

Orvell, Miles. *The Real Thing: Imitation and Authenticity in American Culture, 1880–1940*. Chapel Hill and London: Univ. of North Carolina Press, 1989.

Painter, Nell Irvin. *Standing at Armageddon, 1877–1919*. New York and London: W. W. Norton, 1987.

Peel, Mark. "On the Margins: Lodgers and Boarders in Boston, 1860–1900." *Journal of American History* 72 (March 1986): 813–34.

Persons, Stow. *The Decline of American Gentility*. New York: Columbia Univ. Press, 1973.

Porter, Rev. Edward G. *Rambles in Old Boston, New England*. Boston: Cupples and Hurd, 1887.

Powys, A[lbert] R. *Repair of Ancient Buildings*. New York: E. P. Dutton, 1929.

Quantrill, Malcolm. *The Environmental Memory: Man and Architecture in the Landscape of Ideas*. New York: Schocken Books, 1987.

Rhoads, William B. "The Colonial Revival and American Nationalism." *Journal of the Society of Architectural Historians* 35 (December 1976): 239–54.

————. "The Colonial Revival and the Americanization of Immigrants." In *The Colonial Revival in America*. Edited by Alan Axelrod. New York and London: W. W. Norton, 1985.

Rodgers, Daniel T. "In Search of Progressivism." *Reviews in American History* 10 (December 1982): 113–32.

————. *The Work Ethic in Industrial America, 1850–1920*. Chicago and London: Univ. Press of Chicago, 1978.

Rosen, Christine Meisner. *The Limits of Power: Great Fires and the Process of City Growth in America*. Cambridge and New York: Cambridge Univ. Press, 1986.

Rosenzweig, Roy. *Eight Hours For What We Will: Workers and Leisure in an Industrial City, 1870–1920*. Cambridge and New York: Cambridge Univ. Press, 1983.

Ross, Denman Waldo. *On Drawing and Painting*. Boston: Houghton Mifflin, 1912.

————. *A Theory of Pure Design: Harmony, Balance, Rhythm*. Boston: Houghton Mifflin, 1907.

Rydell, Robert W. *All the World's a Fair: Visions of Empire at American Inter-*

national Expositions, 1876–1916. Chicago and London: Univ. of Chicago Press, 1984.

St. George, Robert Blair, ed. *Material Life in America, 1600–1860.* Boston: Northeastern Univ. Press, 1988.

Sartorio, Enrico C. *Social and Religious Life of Italians in America.* Boston: Christopher Publishing, 1918.

Schlereth, Thomas J. *Victorian America: Transformations in Everyday Life, 1876–1915.* New York: HarperCollins, 1991.

Schuyler, David. *The New Urban Landscape: The Redefinition of City Form in Nineteenth-Century America.* Baltimore and London: Johns Hopkins Univ. Press, 1986.

Sears, Clara Endicott, comp., *Bronson Alcott's Fruitlands.* Boston: Houghton Mifflin, 1915.

———. *Gleanings from Old Shaker Journals.* Boston: Houghton Mifflin, 1916.

Shackleton, Robert. *The Book of Boston.* Philadelphia: Penn Publishing, 1916.

Shi, David E. *The Simple Life: Plain Living and High Thinking in American Culture.* New York and Oxford: Oxford Univ. Press, 1985.

Shurtleff, Arthur A. "The Practice of Replanning." *Charities and the Commons* 19 (1 February 1908): 1529–32.

Social Register, Boston 1917. New York: Social Register Association, 1916.

Society for the Preservation of New England Antiquities. *Bulletin of the Society for the Preservation of New England Antiquities.* (1910–1919).

———. *Old-Time New England: A Quarterly Magazine Devoted to the Ancient Buildings, Household Furnishings, Domestic Arts, Manners and Customs, and Minor Antiquities of the New England People.* (1920–1981).

Solomon, Barbara M. *Ancestors and Immigrants: A Changing New England Tradition.* Cambridge: Harvard Univ. Press, 1956.

Sproat, John G. *"The Best Men": Liberal Reformers in the Gilded Age.* New York: Oxford Univ. Press, 1968.

Stansky, Peter. *Redesigning the World: William Morris, the 1880s, and the Arts and Crafts.* Princeton: Princeton Univ. Press, 1985.

Steinitz, Michael. "Rethinking Geographical Approaches to the Common House: The Evidence from Eighteenth-Century Massachusetts," in *Perspectives in Vernacular Architecture, III.* Edited by Thomas Carter and Bernard Herman. Columbia: Univ. of Missouri Press, 1989.

Stilgoe, John. R. *Borderland: Origins of the American Suburb, 1820–1939.* New Haven and London: Yale Univ. Press, 1988.

———. *Common Landscape of America, 1540 to 1845.* New Haven and London: Yale Univ. Press, 1982.

Stillinger, Elizabeth. *The Antiquers.* New York: Alfred A. Knopf, 1980.

Stipe, Robert E., and Lee, Antoinette J., eds. *The American Mosaic: Preserving a Nation's Heritage.* Washington, D.C.: US / ICOMOS, 1987.

Stocking, George W., Jr., ed., *Objects and Others: Essays on Museums and Material Culture.* Vol. III in History of Anthropology. Madison: Univ. of Wisconsin Press, 1985.

Story, Ronald. *The Forging of an Aristocracy: Harvard & the Boston Upper Class, 1800–1870.* Middletown, Conn.: Wesleyan Univ. Press, 1980.

Sullivan, Thomas R. *Boston, New and Old.* Boston: Houghton Mifflin, 1912.

Tager, Jack, and Ifkovic, John W., eds. *Massachusetts in the Gilded Age.* Amherst: Univ. of Massachusetts Press, 1985.

Tharp, Louise. *The Appletons of Beacon Hill.* Boston: Little, Brown, 1973.

Thernstrom, Stephan. *The Other Bostonians: Poverty and Progress in the American Metropolis, 1880–1970.* Cambridge: Harvard Univ. Press, 1973.

Thompson, E. P. *William Morris: Romantic to Revolutionary.* New York: Pantheon Books, 1977.

Thornton, Tamara Plakins. *Cultivating Gentlemen: The Meaning of Country Life among the Boston Elite, 1785–1860.* New Haven and London: Yale Univ. Press, 1989.

Tomkins, Calvin. *Merchants and Masterpieces: The Story of the Metropolitan Museum of Art.* New York: E. P. Dutton, 1970.

Tomsich, John. *A Genteel Endeavor: American Culture and Politics in the Gilded Age.* Stanford: Stanford Univ. Press, 1971.

Trachtenberg, Alan. *The Incorporation of America: Culture and Society in the Gilded Age.* New York: Hill and Wang, 1982.

Trout, Charles H. *Boston, the Great Depression, and the New Deal.* New York: Oxford Univ. Press, 1977.

Tschudi-Madsen, Stephan. *Restoration and Anti-Restoration: A Study in English Restoration Philosophy.* 2d ed. Oslo: Universitetsforlaget, 1976.

United States Conference of Mayors. *With Heritage So Rich.* 1966. Reprint. Washington, D.C.: Preservation Press, 1983.

Vanderbilt, Kermit. *Charles Eliot Norton.* Cambridge: Harvard Univ. Press, 1959.

Wallace, Anthony F. C. "Revitalization Movements." *American Anthropologist* 58 (April 1956): 264–81.

Wallace, Michael. "Reflections on the History of Historic Preservation." In *Presenting the Past: Essays on History and the Public.* Edited by Susan Porter Benson et al. Philadelphia: Temple Univ. Press, 1986.

———. "Visiting the Past: History Museums in the United States." In *Presenting the Past: Essays on History and the Public.* Edited by Susan Porter Benson et al. Philadelphia: Temple Univ. Press, 1986.

Walton Advertising Co., comp. *Towns of New England and Old England.* 2 vols. Boston: State Street Trust, 1920.

Warner, Sam Bass, Jr. *Streetcar Suburbs: The Process of Growth in Boston, 1870–1900.* 2d ed. Cambridge: Harvard Univ. Press, 1978.

Warner, W. Lloyd. *The Living and the Dead: A Study of the Symbolic Life of Americans.* Vol. V in The Yankee City Series. New Haven: Yale Univ. Press, 1959.

Wendell, Barrett. *Barrett Wendell and His Letters.* Edited by M. A. DeWolfe Howe. Boston: Atlantic Monthly, 1924.

West, Patricia. "The Historic House Museum Movement in America: Louisa May Alcott's Orchard House as a Case Study." Ph.D thesis, State Univ. of New York at Binghamton, 1992.

Whitefield, Edwin. *The Homes of Our Forefathers: Being a Selection of the Oldest and Most Interesting Buildings, Historical Houses, and Noted Places in Massachusetts.* 3d ed. Boston: A. Williams, 1880.

Whitehill, Walter Muir. *Boston: A Topographical History.* 2d enl. ed. Cambridge: Harvard Univ. Press, 1968.

———. *Museum of Fine Arts: A Centennial History.* Cambridge: Harvard Univ. Press, 1970.

Wiebe, Robert H. *Businessmen and Reform: A Study of the Progressive Movement.* Chicago: Quadrangle Books, 1962.

———. *The Search for Order, 1877–1920.* New York: Hill & Wang, 1967.

Wilson, Richard Guy. "American Arts and Crafts Architecture: Radical Though Dedicated to the Cause Conservative." In Wendy Kaplan, *"The Art that Is Life": The Arts & Crafts Movement in America, 1875–1920.* Boston: Museum of Fine Arts, 1987.

———. "Ralph Adams Cram: Dreamer of the Medieval." In *Medievalism in American Culture.* Edited by Bernard Rosenthal and Paul E. Szarmach. Binghamton, N.Y.: Medieval & Renaissance Texts & Studies, 1989.

Wolfe, Albert B. *The Lodging House Problem in Boston.* Boston and New York: Houghton Mifflin, 1906.

Wood, Joseph S. " 'Build, Therefore, Your Own World': The New England Village as Settlement Ideal." *Annals of the Association of American Geographers* 81 (March 1991): 32–50.

———. "The New England Village as an American Vernacular Form." In *Perspectives in Vernacular Architecture, II.* Edited by Camille Wells. Columbia: Univ. of Missouri Press, 1986.

———. "The Three Faces of the New England Village." *North American Culture* 3 (1987): 3–14.

———. "Village and Community in Early Colonial New England." *Journal of Historical Geography* 8 (October 1982): 333–46.

———, and Steinitz, M. "A World We Have Gained: House, Common, and Village in New England." *Journal of Historical Geography* 18 (January 1992): 105–20.

Woods, Robert A., ed. *Americans in Process: A Settlement Study by Residents and Associates of the South End House.* Boston: Houghton Mifflin, 1902.

———. "Notes on the Italians in Boston." *Charities* 12 (7 May 1904): 451–52.

Wright, Gwendolyn. *Building the Dream: A Social History of Housing in America.* Cambridge and London: MIT Press, 1981.

———. *Moralism and the Model Home: Domestic Architecture and Cultural Conflict in Chicago, 1873–1913.* Chicago and London: Univ. of Chicago Press, 1980.

INDEX

Abraham Browne House, Watertown,
  Mass.: acquisition and interpretation
  of, 91–92, 185; *illus.* 148, 149;
  restoration of, 141, 146, 147–50, 180,
  182; use of, 94, 146, 150, 177. *See also*
  SPNEA
Adams, Charles Francis, 112, 167
Adams, John, 36, 106, 124
Aesthetics. *See* Architectural symbolism
African-Americans, 31; and antiquities, 93,
  127, 132; in New England history, 12,
  43, 117, 179
Agecroft Hall, Lancashire, 165
Aldrich, Thomas Bailey, 27, 33; home of,
  94, 120
Aldrich, William T., 62
American Anthropological Association,
  72–73
American Antiquarian Society (AAS), 16,
  60
American Folklore Society, 72
American Institute of Architects, 140–41,
  151, 165. *See also* Boston Society of
  Architects
Americanization campaign. *See* Civil
  religion; Immigrants; Progressivism
American Revolution, and historic sites,
  34, 37–39, 43, 47–49, 63–64, 107,
  111–13, 124, 129, 132–33, 196n. 52.
  See also Civil religion; Historical
  interpretation
American Scenic Historic Preservation
  Society (ASHPS), 117; work of, 52, 97,
  98, 175
Ancestor worship, 101, 112, 123; and
  nativism, 5, 156–57. *See also* Ancestral
  and patriotic societies; Hereditary
  homes; Nativism
Ancestral and patriotic societies, 10, 132;
  Colonial Dames, 54, 60, 65, 86, 88,
  100, 101, 104, 123; Daughters of the
  American Revolution (DAR), 44, 49,
  60, 65, 144, 177; Daughters of the
  Revolution (DR), 99; failings in
  preservation, 55–56, 97–98, 98–99,
  106; 110; Joint Committee on
  Cooperation in Patriotic Work, 47, 57;

Sons of the Revolution (SR), 23, 25,
  37, 43, 44, 47, 56, 57, 66, 124, 172
Ancient Monuments Society, 141, 165,
  168. *See also* Great Britain,
  preservation movement of
Anglo-Saxonism: decline of, 18, 31, 73,
  81, 92, 126, 127–28; and preservation,
  5, 40, 69–70, 92, 122–23, 126, 128,
  140, 171; promotion of, 3, 19, 40, 65,
  80, 81–82, 93–94, 122–23, 140, 156–
  57. *See also* Immigrants; Nativism
Antiindustrialism: and antiques, 156–57;
  and Skansen, 165–66; and Society for
  the Protection of Ancient Buildings, 53,
  84; and SPNEA, 69–70, 72–73, 89–90,
  140–41, 154, 157, 181–82. *See also*
  Antimodernism; Industrialism
Antimodernism, 27, 53, 121, 131; and
  Barrett Wendell, 18–19, 92; and
  country life, 21, 27, 28, 80, 81–82,
  119–20, 165–67, 172–73, 179; and J.
  Frederick Kelly, 88–90, 119, 144; and
  Joseph Chandler, 74, 119, 138, 140;
  and neurasthenia, 23, 63, 107; and
  preservation, 72, 77–78, 130, 139,
  140–41, 152, 165–70; and Ralph
  Cram, 29, 64–65, 80, 119, 127, 138;
  and Wallace Nutting, 107–8, 157, 181–
  82; and William Sumner Appleton, 74,
  87, 91, 119, 127, 139, 143–45, 147–
  50, 154, 165–67, 175, 180, 181–82,
  184. *See also* Antiindustrialism
Antisemitism, 35, 86, 126, 147
Appleton, Edith Stuart, 17
Appleton, Nathan, 8, 15, 28
Appleton-Parker Houses, 39–40 Beacon
  Street, Boston: and Appleton family,
  15, 17–18, 131; *illus.* 16
Appleton, Samuel, 15
Appleton-Taylor-Mansfield House, Saugus,
  Mass., 84, 108
Appleton, Thomas Gold, 7, 16–17, 23
Appleton, William Sumner, Jr.:
  background of, 11, 15–49; birthplace
  of, 15; and "Boston-1915," 44–45, 56;
  and civil religion, 36, 47–48, 112, 122–
  24, 132–33; European travels of, 18,